D1685899

0 4 DEC 2019

BRISTOL CITY LIBRARIES
WITHDRAWN AND OFFERED FOR SALE
SOLD AS SEEN

BSAL

Please return/renew this item by the last date shown
on this label, or on your self-service receipt.

To renew this item, visit **www.librarieswest.org.uk**
or contact your library

Your borrower number and PIN are required.

4 4 0022602 4

'Philip Almond's new book offers a lively, inclusive and readable historical survey of the arguments about God – ancient and modern, Christian and non-Christian – which any fair-minded reader will find helpful and engaging. Believer and non-believer alike will find here a succinct and useful guide to the crucial questions that as human beings we all continue to struggle with.'

RICHARD HARRIES (Baron Harries of Pentregarth), formerly Professor of Divinity, Gresham College, London, and Bishop of Oxford (1987–2006), author of *The Beauty and the Horror: Searching for God in a Suffering World*

'Without going deep into philosophical arguments for the existence of God, Philip Almond offers rather an engaging and deeply informed *historical* tour through the understandings of God that have emerged in the Middle East and Europe over the past three thousand years. Some of what has been thought and written about God is strange and quirky, and some of it offensive. But Almond never mocks. He always digs down to the fundamental human issues at stake, reminding us that "The story of God is the story of a search for ultimate meaning." Though the biography of God is ongoing, and philosophy too must play a part, this fine book is still a remarkable achievement.'

NICHOLAS WOLTERSTORFF, Noah Porter Professor Emeritus of Philosophical Theology, Yale University, author of *Divine Discourse: Philosophical Reflections on the Claim that God Speaks*

GOD

A New Biography

PHILIP C. ALMOND

I.B. TAURIS
LONDON · NEW YORK

Published in 2018 by
I.B.Tauris & Co. Ltd
London ◆ New York
www.ibtauris.com

Copyright © 2018 Philip C. Almond

The right of Philip C. Almond to be identified as the author
of this work has been asserted by the author in accordance
with the Copyright, Designs and Patents Act 1988.

All rights reserved. Except for brief quotations in a review, this book, or any part
thereof, may not be reproduced, stored in or introduced into a retrieval system, or
transmitted, in any form or by any means, electronic, mechanical, photocopying,
recording or otherwise, without the prior written permission of the publisher.

Every attempt has been made to gain permission for the use of the images
in this book. Any omissions will be rectified in future editions.

References to websites were correct at the time of writing.

ISBN: 978 1 78453 765 4
eISBN: 978 1 78672 388 8
ePDF: 978 1 78673 388 7

A full CIP record for this book is available from the British Library
A full CIP record is available from the Library of Congress
Library of Congress Catalog Card Number: available

Typeset by Tetragon, London
Printed and bound in Sweden by ScandBook AB

To Pat

Contents

List of Plates

collection / the Stapleton Collection / Bridgeman Images (STC67487).

11. *Job and His Alleged Comforters.* Tallandier / Bridgeman Images (TAD1749466).

12. *The Birth of Christ* by Hans Leonard Schaufelein (c.1480–c.1539). Hamburger Kunsthalle, Hamburg, Germany / Bridgeman Images (XKH234220).

13. *Calvary*, central panel from the St Zeno altarpiece (1456–60) by Andrea Mantegna (1431–1506). Louvre, Paris, France / Bridgeman Images (XIR45968).

14. *Mohammed (c.570–c.632) and the Archangel Gabriel*, from the *Siyer-i Nebi.* Turkish School (sixteenth century). Topkapi Palace Museum, Istanbul, Turkey / Bildarchiv Steffens / Bridgeman Images (STF251912).

15. *The Holy Trinity*, central panel of the high altarpiece of the church of the Holy Trinity in Mosóc (today Mošovce, Slovakia) (1471) by Master GH (fl. 1471). Hungarian National Gallery, Budapest, Hungary / Bridgeman Images (BAL49164).

16. *The Council of Nicaea*, from the calendar showing the month of October, icon, Novgorod Region, Russia (mid-eighteenth century). De Agostini Picture Library / Bridgeman Images (DGA536735).

17. *Annunciation* (1489), by Sandro Botticelli (1444/5–1510). Galleria degli Uffizi, Florence, Italy / Bridgeman Images (XAL227150).

18. Fol.48r *Pentecost*, from *Heures a l'usage de Rome.* French School (sixteenth century). Musée National de la Renaissance, Écouen, France / Bridgeman Images (XIR162151).

19. *Plato's Cave.* Flemish School (sixteenth century). Musée de la Chartreuse, Douai, France / Bridgeman Images (XIR179312).

20. *The Song of Songs*, from the Queen Mary Psalter (late 1920s) by Dorothy Mahoney (1902–84). Private collection / © Liss Fine Art / Bridgeman Images (LIS423383).

21. *The Ecstasy of St Teresa*, attributed to Jean Baptiste de Champaigne (1631–81). Musée des Beaux-Arts, Tourcoing, France / Bridgeman Images (XIR173412).

Acknowledgements

This book was written in the Institute for Advanced Studies in the Humanities at the University of Queensland in Australia. For the past decade this institute and its predecessor, the Centre for the History of European Discourses, have provided a congenial, stimulating and – more often than one might hope to expect – exciting context in which to work. For this I am indebted in particular to my friends and colleagues Professor Peter Harrison, the director of the institute, Emeritus Professor Peter Cryle, Emeritus Professor Ian Hunter and Professor Fred D'Agostino, the president of the Academic Board of the University of Queensland, who have given of their time to talk with me on many occasions. I am grateful also to the many postdoctoral fellows of the institute, all of whose dedication to their work has provided so much encouragement to my own.

A wide-ranging book such as this is inevitably indebted to those scholars who have previously done the hard yards in this intellectual domain. Without their often groundbreaking work, this book would not have been possible. In particular, I want to acknowledge the works of Alan G. Padgett, Larry Hurtado, Andrew Louth, Joseph A. Buijs, Arthur Green, John Hick, Geoffrey Rowell, Steven Nadler, Robert C. Whittemore and Jack Miles. I am especially indebted to Karen Armstrong, whose book *A History of God* (1993) was one 'to boldly go' where no tome had gone before and gave me the confidence to have a go myself.

I take the opportunity once again to thank Alex Wright, my editor at I.B.Tauris, for his support and encouragement. He it was who suggested this work to an initially very wary writer. I thank him too for the friendship we have forged over the decade we have worked on projects together for I.B.Tauris.

I am grateful too to my partner Patricia Lee, who has listened day by day to the text as it progressed, and offered much helpful advice. This book is dedicated to her in gratitude for her love and affection over many years.

Prologue

Then the Lord sent a plague on the people, because they made a calf – the one that Aaron made.

Exodus 32.35[1]

'After the fourth day the rats started to emerge in groups to die. They came up from basements and cubby-holes, cellars and drains, in long swaying lines; they staggered in the light, collapsed and died, right next to people.'[2] Then, Albert Camus's *The Plague* (1947) tells us, it spread to the people of the North African town of Oran. Like the rats, they too started to die in ever-increasing numbers.

The Jesuit priest Father Paneloux saw the plague as a punishment delivered by God on the wicked people of the town. 'The just have no need to fear,' he preached,

> but the unjust should tremble. In the vast granary of the universe, the implacable flail will thresh the human corn until the chaff is divided from the grain [...] No earthly power – not even, note this well, vain human science – can shield you from this hand as it reaches out to you. Beaten on the bloody threshing floor of pain, you will be cast out with the chaff.[3]

By contrast, the atheist Doctor Rieux could not accept a God who stood by while innocent children died in agony. 'Do you believe in God, doctor?' he was asked by his friend Tarrou. 'No,' he replied, 'but what does that mean? I am in darkness, trying to see the light.'[4] Against the passive faith of Paneloux and in the face of an indifferent God, Rieux proposed an active humanism that refused to give way to the pestilence: 'perhaps it is better for God that we should not believe in

Him and struggle with all our strength against death, without raising our eyes to heaven and to His silence.'[5]

The dispute between Father Paneloux and Doctor Rieux is about a question of fact: does God exist or not? But it is much more than that. For Rieux, it is not simply a question about what is or is not the case. It is also a question about what kind of God it is that allows such suffering in the world and yet remains so apparently unconcerned about it.

But the dispute between them is also about more than whether God exists and what kind of God he might be. In the face of the plague, the question of God cannot be reduced to a philosophical puzzle and an intellectual riddle. For it is also a question of how we should think about the world, of how we should feel about it, of how we should comport ourselves towards it and of how we should act within it. The question of God shapes our understanding, engages our emotions and guides our wills. Thus, the question of the existence of God is about the intelligibility of the universe, the nature of human existence and the meaning of our lives. It is, in short, a matter of ultimate meaning, ultimate concern and deep importance. Thus is the story of God at the same time a history of how we have construed the meaning of life.

This question of God's existence or non-existence is nonetheless a very modern one, one that it has only been intellectually possible to ask for the past several centuries. Only in the modern world has the existence of God become a matter of serious intellectual doubt and the option not to believe a genuine one. For the much better part of the last two millennia, it has not been a question of *whether* God existed but rather, granted that he undoubtedly did, of what kind of person or being he was, what his attributes were, what he had done or not done and what he could do or not do.

In the modern world, we know what kind of being God is. But whether he exists or not is unknown. By contrast, in the pre-modern world, it was known that God existed. But his nature was ultimately beyond our comprehension. God *was* a being greater than which we cannot conceive. But he was, at the same time, always a being greater than we could conceive. The inexpressible God transcended all attempted expressions of him. Language was stretched beyond its normal limits in attempts to talk about God. Thus is the story of God the story of attempts to comprehend a being who, it was believed, was ultimately beyond our comprehension.

It was this very incomprehensibility that meant that the story of God was one of a series of conflicts and compromises, of paradoxes both resolved and unresolved. The nature of God was always over the horizon of the sea of faith, ever eluding certainty. In part, this was a matter of ambivalence about God's personal attributes. Where was the balance to be found between his love, mercy and compassion on the one hand and his wrath, vengeance and justice on the other? In part too, it was a matter of disquiet over the connection between his personal and impersonal attributes. How was the God who was unable to suffer to be aligned with the God who, Christians believed, suffered on the cross? How was the God who was unchanging to be squared with one who regularly changed his mind? It was also a question about the relationship between God and the world. How was a transcendent God who created the world out of nothing to be aligned with a God who emanated the world out of himself? How could an infinite God become a finite man in Jesus Christ? Did or could God intervene in the world when he wished to?

To a significant extent, these conflicts and compromises were the consequence of God's living, as it were, in a number of distinct linguistic 'universes' with apparently little overlapping territory. God was the God of the Bible *and* the God of the philosophers. He was the God of the prophets *and* the God of the mystics. He was both the God of revelation and the God of reason. He was the God of knowledge but he was also the God of faith. He was the transcendent God of the monotheists, the transcendent and immanent God of the panentheists *and* the immanent God of the pantheists. He was the God of the Old Testament, the New Testament *and* the Qur'ān.[6] He had loyalties to Jerusalem but also to Mecca and Athens. The story of God is thus the story of the attempts to unite or divide these 'Gods', passionately to argue for their fundamental unity or vehemently to proclaim their essential differences.

This book explores the story of God from that moment in the sixth century BCE when the God of only one nation became the only God of all nations. God's life since then and up to now has been a complex and complicated one. But I have tried to demonstrate how and why it is so intricate while telling the story simply, sympathetically and intelligibly. From a subject area so vast, I have had to choose key moments and major players. These latter were often ones who exemplified the nature of the divine, analysed his persona, pondered his character or detailed his activities. They were often also the ones who established the conflicts, thrashed out the compromises, embraced or rejected the paradoxes, justified or denounced God's actions or even questioned his being and his goodness.

Underlying this book is the recognition that the rivers of Judaism, Christianity and Islam flow, albeit in complicated ways, from two sources – Athens and Jerusalem. They are complicated because neither 'reason' nor 'revelation' was historically stable. What counted as Jerusalem was as much in a process of continual change and constant refinement as what counted as Athens. This book is, at the end of the day, perhaps more sympathetic to the philosophers of Athens than to the prophets of Jerusalem or Mecca. But I have tried nevertheless to do intellectual justice to both the God of reason *and* the God of revelation. Even among those who incline to the Athenian tradition, 'revelation' serves as an important reminder of the limitations of reason – a view ever present in Western thought about God since the time of Thomas Aquinas (c.1225–74).

For some, this biography of God will be a work of historical fiction, for others a work of non-fictional history. I have tried to write it as the history of an idea for both kinds of reader. Whether this book is read as imagining a life or reflecting one, the idea of God is one that, for good or ill, whether embraced or rejected, still matters profoundly. For now, as in the past, it goes both to the depths of ourselves and to the truth of things.

The Transcendent God

> In the year that King Uzziah died, I saw the Lord sitting on a throne, high and lofty; and the hem of his robe filled the temple. Seraphs were in attendance above him; each had six wings; with two they covered their faces, and with two they covered their feet, and with two they flew. And one called to another and said: 'Holy, holy, holy is the Lord of hosts; the whole earth is full of his glory.'
>
> Isaiah 6.1–3

The holiness of God

Uzziah, king of the land of Judah, died in 739 BCE. It was in that year that, while he was worshipping in the Temple in Jerusalem, the closest place between heaven and earth, Isaiah had a vision of God the King in his heavenly court. God was seated in the throne room in heaven, surrounded by his heavenly attendants. His clothing reached down from heaven, the hem of it filling the Temple.

This was a heavenly kingdom populated by many angels and other heavenly courtiers. The winged seraphim hovered over God. They needed only two wings for flight. With another two wings, they covered their 'feet' (genitals). With the remainder, they covered their faces. The heavenly beings, like everyone else, were forbidden to see the face of God. Whoever saw it had to die. The seraphim exemplified in heaven the worship due to God by those on earth. God was pre-eminently holy, exalted above all creatures. He was both holy in contrast to the profaneness and impurity of his creatures and wholly and overwhelmingly other. His gloriousness not only pervaded heaven but reached to the ends of the earth.

The pillars of the Temple shook at the voices of the seraphim. Isaiah had seen the King, the Lord of hosts; he had heard the seraphim and he was terrified. In the face of the holiness of God, he became conscious of his and his community's impurity, sin and guilt. 'Woe is me! I am lost, for I am a man of unclean lips, and I live among a people of unclean lips.' But God was also gracious and forgiving:

> Then one of the seraphs flew to me, holding a live coal that had been taken from the altar with a pair of tongs [see Plate 1]. The seraph touched my mouth with it and said: 'Now that this has touched your lips, your guilt has departed and your sin is blotted out.' (Isa. 6.5–7)

Now worthy to stand before God, Isaiah had become someone ready to be recruited into God's service and to carry out his will. God asked his heavenly council for advice: 'Whom shall I send, and who will go for us?' The newly purified Isaiah grabbed the opportunity: 'Here am I; send me!' (6.8). And with that, God commissioned Isaiah as a prophet to speak to the people on his behalf and with his authority. The news that Isaiah was to proclaim was not good, for God intended to destroy the kingdom of Judah, and that the people of Judah should not listen to his prophet nor turn back to God. Isaiah recognised that he was to be a prophet of doom. 'How long, O Lord?' he asked. 'Until cities lie waste without inhabitant,' declared God, 'and houses without people, and the land is utterly desolate' (6.11).[1]

In the eloquent words of the German theologian Rudolf Otto (1869–1937), Isaiah experienced the Holy as a *mysterium tremendum et fascinans*, a mysterious, wholly other being who was both awesome and terrifying yet captivating and fascinating – a being of justice and wrath, yet also one of love and compassion. It is a characterisation of God that resonates throughout the religions of the world, not least throughout Judaism, Christianity and Islam.[2] God is a being with personal attributes like ours, and yet is always transcending them, on occasion to such an extent that he is no longer recognisably like us at all. He is *other* than all things, not least because all things other than him ultimately depend on him. He is, first and foremost, the creator.

The creation of the gods and the god of creation

If God created the world, then who created God? Much philosophical and theological ink would later be spilt in trying to show that the question could not be answered because it was one that it made no sense to ask. But the ancient Babylonians did ask it. And their answer is contained in a text from around 1150 BCE known as the *Enuma Elish*. According to this, there was in the beginning nothing but primordial, watery chaos and darkness. Out of the mixing of the waters there emerged the begetter gods Apsu and Mummu-Tiamat, the divine parents of all the gods to come.[3]

Unlike in the *Enuma Elish*, there was in the account of creation in the Bible no hint of God being a created entity. On the contrary, he it was who did the creating. However, as in the *Enuma Elish*, there was a primordial watery chaos – but alongside God. Then, 'the earth was a formless void and darkness covered the face of the deep, while a wind from God swept over the face of the waters' (Gen. 1.2). It is out of this formless and undifferentiated chaos that God created the heavens and the earth. After that, God created the particular 'creatures' in the ascending hierarchy with which we are all familiar.

According to the first account of creation in the Bible (Gen. 1.1–2.3), written around the fifth–sixth century BCE, on the first day was the separation of light and dark, named day and night. The next day God created a dome in the heavens to separate the waters of chaos from what was inside. On the third day God gathered together the remaining waters (the seas) and the dry land (the earth) and made the vegetation. On the fourth he fashioned the sun, the moon and the stars. These were finite heavenly objects and not eternal living beings worthy of any worship. They were followed on the fifth day by the fish of the sea and the birds of the air. On the sixth day God made the terrestrial animals and, as his final and finest act of creation, humankind: 'So God created humankind in his image, in the image of God he created them; male and female he created them' (1.27). God looked upon everything that he had made and was pleased with his work: 'it was very good' (1.31), or, as we might say, fit for its intended purpose. This was the world with which we are all familiar – no gods, goddesses, mythical beings or monsters, just the everyday world.

And having done the work of creation over six days, the next day God rested.

When was the creation of the world? The founder of the Christian view of time was Theophilus of Antioch (late second century CE). Poring over the biblical records, together with Greek and Roman histories, he concluded that the creation of the world had occurred 5,698 years earlier (5529 BCE).[4] His purpose was twofold. First, it was to demonstrate that the world had not always existed but had come into existence at a certain time. This was an important argument to make against those Greek philosophers who believed it to be eternal. Second, it was to demonstrate that the biblical accounts were the most reliable source for such a chronology, not least because they pre-dated the 'profane' accounts.

But there was a further, profound implication to this. Within the Platonic philosophical tradition, time was cyclic. As Henri-Charles Puech summarises it,

> both the entire cosmic process and the time of our world of gen-
> eration and decay develop in a circle or according to an indefinite
> succession of cycles, in the course of which the same reality is made,
> unmade, and remade [...] The same sum of being is preserved;
> nothing is created and nothing lost.[5]

By contrast, Christianity adopted from the Hebrew tradition a linear understanding of time. Thus, within the Jewish, Christian and Islamic traditions, history began at the time of creation and would end in a final divine judgement. The time between was linear and each event was unique and unrepeatable. History itself, and the course of events within it, now had an intrinsic meaning. More particularly, history was now purposeful and in the hands of God – not an eternal cycle empty of meaning. God was a God who, although outside history, acted within it.

The Christian tradition, like that of Judaism, claimed not only that it knew when the world had begun, but that the world would end as a result of God's intervention. Surprisingly, the creation story in Genesis provided the key for one of the most common calculations of when this end would occur. God had created the world in six days; the Bible indicated clearly the relationship of God to our time: 'with the Lord one day is like a thousand years, and a thousand years are like one day' (2 Pet. 3.8, also Ps. 90.4). Thus, the earth would last 6,000 years from its creation to its end. As Lactantius (*c*.240–*c*.320 CE), tutor to the son of the Emperor Constantine, explained it:

> Plato and many others of the philosophers [...] said that many thousands of ages had passed since this beautiful arrangement of the world was completed [...] Therefore let the philosophers, who enumerate thousands of years from the beginning of the world, know that the six thousandth year is not yet completed, and that when this number is completed the consummation must take place [...] Therefore, since all the works of God were completed in six days, the world must continue in its present state through six ages, that is, six thousand years. For the great day of God is limited by a circle of a thousand years.[6]

In the *Enuma Elish* there was, in the beginning, only the watery chaos out of which the gods arose. In the book of Genesis there were two primary 'objects', namely, God and the primal chaos. Yet Genesis also suggested that God created not so much by the physical manipulation of pre-existent primal waters as by his spoken word: God spoke and it came to be. It was this metaphor of creation through the divine word and not from pre-existent 'stuff' that came to dominate the story of God as creator within the Jewish and Christian traditions. It was to eventuate in the doctrine of *creatio ex nihilo* – that God created the world out of nothing. In the words of the first canon of the Fourth Lateran Council of the Western Church in 1215:

> We firmly believe and openly confess that there is only one true God [...] Creator of all things invisible and visible, spiritual and corporeal, who from the beginning of time and by His omnipotent power made *from nothing* creatures both spiritual and corporeal.[7]

That said, early Christianity was divided on whether God had created the world out of nothing, worked with pre-existent material or even created it out of himself. The Alexandrian Christian theologian Justin Martyr (*c.*100–*c.*165 CE), for example, followed the classical tradition and opted for the second of these possibilities. Justin was concerned to demonstrate the compatibility of Christianity with Greek philosophy, and especially with the Middle Platonism of his time that endorsed a creation out of pre-existent matter.[8] He did so by arguing that Plato had taken his ideas from Moses and the prophets. Thus, Justin declared, 'it was from our teachers [the prophets] that Plato borrowed his statement that God, having altered matter which was shapeless, made the world.'[9]

By the late second century CE, however, rather than aligning the Christian tradition with Middle Platonism, most Christian thinkers were asserting the distinctiveness of Christianity by arguing for creation out of nothing. This became the standard Christian view from that time on. Thus, Clement of Alexandria (*c.*150–*c.*215 CE) became the first Christian theologian to assert *creatio ex nihilo*: 'For God alone made it [...] By his sheer act of will, he creates; and after he has merely willed, it follows that things come into being.'[10] Theophilus of Antioch criticised Plato for regarding matter as uncreated because it diminished the 'sovereignty' (*monarchia* or 'sole first principleship') of God. 'The power of God is manifested in this,' he wrote, 'that out of things that are not He makes whatever He pleases.'[11] The Latin theologian Tertullian (*c.*160–*c.*220 CE), of all the early Christian theologians the one most opposed to Greek philosophy, devoted a complete work refuting the opinions of Hermogenes (late second century CE) on the creation of the world out of pre-existent matter. Similarly, late in the second century CE, Irenaeus, bishop of Lyons, reaffirmed what was by that time becoming a fixed principle within Western Christianity:

> While men, indeed, cannot make anything out of nothing, but only out of matter already existing, yet God is in this point pre-eminently superior to men, that He Himself called into being the substance of His creation, when previously it had no existence.[12]

This doctrine of *creatio ex nihilo* entailed that, prior to the creation of the world, there was *only* God. Granting the impropriety of the question 'who created God?' it entailed also that God was eternal. Within the Bible, this meant that there was no time when he was not and no time when he would not be. That is to say, God had always existed and would always exist. One of the key passages in the Old Testament to establish God's eternity was Psalm 90.2: 'Before the mountains were brought forth, or ever you had formed the earth and the world, from everlasting to everlasting you are God.' God's eternity is here understood as 'of everlasting duration'. We find the same understanding in the book of Isaiah. When the people complain that God had not heard them, the prophet Isaiah responded: 'Have you not known? Have you not heard? The Lord is the everlasting God, the Creator of the ends of the earth' (Isa. 40.28). In short, God is limitless in time (everlasting) and in space (ends of the earth). The same notion is found in the New Testament: the eternal God is he 'who is and who was and who is to come' (Rev. 1.4). As Oscar Cullmann sums it up, in New Testament Christianity, eternity is understood only as 'endlessly extended time'.[13]

But early Christianity went down a different path to that of the Bible. It adopted a Platonic rather than a biblical understanding of the divine eternity. Thus, it read 'eternity' not as *endless duration* but as *timelessness*. That is, God did not exist in time so much as outside and beyond time. It was the Middle Platonist Plutarch (*c.*45–120 CE) who was the first to associate God with timelessness. God (ὁ θεός), he declared,

> exists for no fixed time, but for the everlasting ages which are immov-
> able, timeless, and undeviating, in which there is no earlier nor later,
> no future nor past, no older nor younger; but He, being One, has
> with only one 'Now' completely filled 'For ever'.[14]

But it was the Platonised Origen of Alexandria (*c.*185–*c.*254 CE) who was the first Christian theologian to identify God's eternity as timeless in contrast to the temporal order of creation. The statements we make about God, he explained in his major theological work *On First Principles*, 'must be understood as transcending all time and all ages and all eternity [...] The rest of things, however [...] must be measured by ages and periods of time'.[15] The same point was made by Origen's contemporary, the Neoplatonist Plotinus (*c.*205–70 CE).[16] Ultimate reality, declared Plotinus, is that which simply is: 'That which neither has been nor will be, but simply possesses being; that which enjoys stable existence as neither in process of change nor having ever changed – that is Eternity'.[17]

For Plotinus then, eternity as timelessness was defined in terms of changelessness or immutability. Influenced by Neoplatonism, Augustine (354–430 CE) similarly distinguished time from eternity in terms of change and movement as compared to immutability and immobility. Thus, in *The City of God*, he wrote: 'eternity and time are rightly distinguished by this, that time does not exist without some movement and transition, while in eternity there is no change'.[18] Thus, God's timelessness was a consequence of God's immutability. Time came into existence at the time of the creation, along with everything else. God remained, however, outside time. Thus, the question 'What did God do before the creation of the world?' made no sense. Augustine resisted the facetious answer: 'He was preparing hell for those who pry into God's mysteries.' Rather, he declared: 'in the excellency of an ever-present eternity, Thou precedest all times past, and survivest

all future times [...] Thy years stand at once since they do stand [...]
Thy to-day is eternity.'[19]

In the image of God

Humankind, as the pinnacle of creation, was the only creature made in
the image of God. But what is it in us that 'images' the divine and what
clue might this give us to the nature of God? The simplest explanation
is to be found in the context in Genesis in which the phrase occurs.
Immediately after having created man, God gave him dominion over
all living things. He appointed man as his ruler over the created order.
In the *Enuma Elish*, it was the god Marduk who created man out of
the blood of the god Kingu. 'Blood I will mass,' declared Marduk, 'and
cause bones to be. I will establish a savage, "man" shall be his name [...]
He shall be charged with the service of the gods / That they might be
at ease!'[20] Unlike the *Enuma Elish*, humankind in the book of Genesis
stands between God and the animals and is God's viceroy on earth. But
if man shares with the animals their corporeality (although unlike them
he stands upright) and their sexuality, what does he share with God?

The simplest answer was that the human body was the image of
God in man (see Plate 2). This was the suggestion in the second creation
account in the book of Genesis (Gen. 2.4–4.26), written around the
seventh century BCE. The God of the first creation account in Genesis
1–2.3 created the universe in a measured, stately, organised and systematic way. The God of the second account was much less organised,
much more experimental, and quite literally down to earth. In this story,
God 'formed man from the dust of the ground, and breathed into his
nostrils the breath of life' (2.7). Like any other gardener, God 'planted
a garden in Eden' (2.8). Having first created the animals, which turned
out to be unsatisfactory companions for Adam, he finally created a
woman from Adam's rib. After Adam and Eve had eaten the forbidden
fruit, they heard God 'walking in the garden at the time of the evening
breeze' (3.8). Soon afterwards, God drove both Adam and Eve out of
the garden for disobeying his orders (see Plate 3).

This was the very human God who appeared to Abraham as one of 'three men standing near him' (Gen. 18.2), to whom Abraham offered water for their feet, rest under a tree and a meal of veal, curds and milk (see Plate 7). This was the same God with whom Abraham's son Jacob wrestled before he later realised that he had 'seen God face to face, and yet my life is preserved' (Gen. 32.30). This was the God of Michelangelo (1475–1564) in the Sistine Chapel in Rome – an elderly, white-bearded man with arm outstretched to give life to the man he has created from dust in his own image (see Plate 4). This was a God whose body was decisively human and decidedly male.

By the time of Michelangelo, the depiction of God as a 'flesh and blood' man had become a commonplace in late medieval Christian art. Both Judaism and Islam forbade pictorial representations of God. But the Christian doctrine of the Trinity made theologically possible depictions of God the Father. God the Son was theologically begotten of the Father. So a very human divine Son could artistically 'beget' a very 'human' divine father. *The Holy Trinity* (1427–8) by the Italian painter Tommaso Masaccio (1401–28) in the church of Santa Maria Novella in Florence was an early and very influential example of what was to become a standardised form of representing the Trinity. Here was a very 'naturalistic' God the Father (with his left foot just showing), elderly and bearded, both awesome and benign, supporting his crucified Son with his hands, the Holy Spirit as a dove hovering between them (see Plate 5).

If the Old Testament God who appeared to Abraham was more or less the height of a man, elsewhere in the Old Testament he had a human body in a definitely gigantic form. Thus, for example, when Moses first encountered God, he was not allowed to see God's face. God told him that, while his glory passed by, he would cover him with his hand. If his hand was the size of Moses, that would make God around 20 metres tall. Similarly, the God whom Isaiah confronted in the Temple was so big that just the hem of his garment filled it (Isa. 6.1). Elsewhere, God had a gigantic body but now transformed to be as large as the heavens, on top of the earth above the firmament (see

Plate 8). The prophet Ezekiel described a throne in appearance like sapphire, above the dome of the world, upon which there sat 'something that seemed like a human form'; that which was above what appeared like the loins gleamed like amber, while below was something that looked like fire (Ezekiel 1.26–8).[21]

That the image of God in man was connected to bodiliness or corporeality continued into the early Christian tradition. Its most notable exponent was the fourth-century Syrian theologian Audius, who took 'in the image of God' in its most literal sense. 'Since scripture has said that God made man from the earth,' declared Audius, 'see how it has said with perfect truth that the entire earthy part is "man". Therefore it said earlier [in Genesis] that the earthy part of man will itself be in the image of God.'[22] That God *literally* had a body was, by the time of Theodoret (*c*.393–*c*.458 CE), labelled a heresy. He thought Audius's account absurd. That God was described in human terms, he wrote, was only for simple minds. God is said in Scripture to have only parts of the human body 'since by these means the providence of God is made more easily intelligible to minds incapable of perceiving any immaterial ideas.'[23]

The rejection of the corporeality of God within early Christianity was part of its efforts to differentiate itself from paganism and *its* 'bodily' representations of the gods. It was also part of its critique of the Judaism of the time, which was dominated by a literal reading of the texts that implied that God had a body.[24] That the corporeality of God could be labelled a heresy was the consequence of Christianity having absorbed the Platonic doctrine of the incorporeality of the divine as early as the middle of the second century. It was to become a central feature of the theology of the Platonic Christianity of Origen. He began his *On First Principles* with a polemic against those who maintained 'that even according to our Scriptures God is a body, since they find it written in the book of Moses'.[25] On the contrary, declared Origen, God must not be thought to be a body, or even to exist in a body, but 'to be a simple intellectual existence [*intellectualis natura simplex*] [...] and the mind and fount from which originates all intellectual existence or mind.'[26]

For his part, Origen had two sets of opponents in his sights. The first of these were those Christians, influenced by the Stoics, who accepted the corporeality of God. The second were those Christian Gnostics who, persuaded of the incorporeality of the deity, rejected the God of the Old Testament because of his bodily nature. Against both of these, Origen utilised an interpretative theory first applied to the Bible by the Jewish philosophers Aristoboulos (*c.*160 BCE) and Philo (*c.*20 BCE–*c.*50 CE) to harmonise Greek philosophy and the Bible. This was to the effect that the Bible could be read both literally and spiritually. Thus, according to Origen, the Christian Gnostics had failed to read the Scriptures *literally* and the Christian Stoics had failed to read it *spiritually*. In contrast, Origen suggested that the Scriptures could be read in three ways: the simple could read it literally, the more advanced according to its 'soul' and the most advanced according to its 'spirit'. For 'just as man consists of body, soul and spirit, so in the same way does the scripture.'[27]

In essence, this meant that behind the literal truth of the Bible lay deeper truths about God. The corporeal God of the Bible was in essence the incorporeal God of the philosophers. From this time on, God was both the God of the Bible and the God of the philosophers, a God who was both personal and impersonal. But also, as a being who was essentially incorporeal, he was a God who was *qualitatively* other than the universe that he had created – a being who was purely spiritual and not material. In short, God was *essentially* 'spirit'. Cyril of Alexandria (d.444 CE) told us loudly and clearly what he really thought: 'to believe that the deity is of human form […] is completely stupid […] God is incorporeal. The Savior himself will teach us this, saying, "God is spirit."'[28]

There is one profound conclusion to be drawn from this discussion. Within Judaism, Christianity and Islam, God is generally referred to by the masculine personal pronoun. Nevertheless and simply put, by virtue of his non-corporeality, God is without sex – neither male nor female. No body, no sex! The consequence of this is that any references to the sex or gender of the divine are metaphorical only. In principle, although custom and tradition are on the side of the masculine pronoun for the personal God, 'he' or 'she' is equally appropriate (or equally inappropriate), while the pronoun 'it' is most apt for the impersonal divine.[29]

In contrast to the wholly spiritual God, humankind was something of a hybrid. While Christianity was defining God as an essentially incorporeal being, it was absorbing Greek philosophical definitions of the nature of man. The Hebrew understanding of man as a psycho-physical unity was being replaced by a conception of man as essentially body *and* soul, matter *and* spirit. Thus, around 180 CE, in a work entitled *De resurrectione mortuorum* (On the resurrection of the dead), Athenagoras (second century CE) declared that 'the whole nature of men in general is composed of an immortal soul and a body which was fitted to it in the creation'.[30] So the choice for the image of God in man now became a choice between body/matter and soul/spirit. The latter was chosen. The image of the incorporeal God in man now became focused on the incorporeal soul. Thus, Ambrose the bishop of Milan (*c*.339–97) concluded: 'Our soul, therefore, is made to the image of God. In this is man's entire essence, because without it [the soul] man is nothing but earth and into earth he shall return.'[31]

Granted that the soul was that which was in the image of God, was one part of the soul more God-like than another? In the history of Christianity, almost every personal attribute of the human was identified with the image of God. Thus, the best in us was projected onto God. But along with his dominion over the animals, two attributes predominated. The first of these was man's reason. Thus, for example, the Alexandrian theologian Athanasius (*c*.296–373 CE) identified the image with man's rational nature. God made men after his own image, he wrote,

> giving them a portion even of the power of His own Word; so that having as it were a kind of reflexion of the Word, and being made rational, they might be able to abide ever in blessedness, living the true life which belongs to the saints in paradise.[32]

The other explanation that was especially favoured was that the image of God in man was that which reflected the divine Trinity. As there were three persons in one God, so there were three attributes in one reason – memory, will and understanding. Augustine was to synthesise all of these themes and his account was to become the dominant one. Thus, he declared:

> spiritual believers in the Catholic teaching do not believe that God is limited by a bodily shape. When man is said to have been made to the image of God, these words refer to the interior man, where reason and intellect reside [...] Man is said to have been made to the image of God, not on account of his body, but on account of that power by which he surpasses the cattle. For all the other animals are subject to man, not by reason of the body, but by reason of the intellect which we have and which they do not have.[33]

God the destroyer

Augustine may have determined that God was immutable. But the God of the Bible was anything but. According to the biblical account, it was 1,656 years after the creation of Adam that God realised that the world had not gone the way he had hoped. The wickedness of humankind was so great that God 'was sorry that he had made humankind on the earth, and it grieved him to the heart' (Gen. 6.6). The biblical story of God is the story of his disappointments with men and women. So God decided to destroy everything he had created – 'people together with animals and creeping things and birds of the air' (6.7) – regretting that he had ever made them. The only exception was Noah, 'a righteous man', to whom God confided his intentions: 'I have determined to make an end of all flesh, for the earth is filled with violence' (6.13). God instructed Noah to build an ark and to take into it, along with his family, two of every kind of living thing.[34] Noah did as he was ordered and God shut them in the ark. God then allowed the waters of chaos to re-enter the earth and flood it so that every living thing perished in the waters. Only Noah and those in the ark with him were left (see Plate 6).

Eventually the waters subsided and the ark came to rest on the mountains of Ararat. On the instruction of God, Noah and his family finally emerged from the ark, followed by the other creatures. Noah built an altar and sacrificed burnt offerings upon it. When God smelt the odour of the sacrifices, in spite of the evil nature of human beings, he swore to himself, 'I will never again curse the ground because of humankind [...] nor will I ever again destroy every living creature as I have done' (Gen. 8.22).

This was a new creation and God's second attempt to get it right. To inaugurate it, God made a covenant with Noah and his descendants. As a sign of it, he created a rainbow. It would remind him of the agreement he had made not to destroy the earth again. Even so, this was not a God to be crossed. He created life, but the story of Noah was a reminder that he could just as easily take it away. Predictable he wasn't.

According to the Genesis story, Abraham was the tenth generation in a direct line from Noah via Noah's son Shem. Between Noah and Abraham, God spoke to no man. But to Abraham he gave a command and a blessing:

> Go from your country and your kindred and your father's house to the land that I will show you. I will make of you a great nation, and I will bless you, and make your name great, so that you will be a blessing [...] in you all the families of the earth will be blessed. (Gen. 12.1–3)

God began yet again, this time with chosen people – all the descendants of Abraham – and a promised land. The question of whether *all* people are God's chosen or only *some* will resonate throughout the history of the Abrahamic religions (Judaism, Christianity and Islam), with the balance in favour of the select few rather than the vast majority.

With Abraham, however, God demanded that all males be circumcised as a marker of the covenant between God, Abraham and his direct offspring (Gen. 17.10–14). It is a reminder to Abraham and his descendants that God, not Abraham, is in charge of their futures. At that time too, God told Abraham his name: 'El Shaddai' – 'God Almighty'

(17.1). The name suggests power. Thus, when God announced his name, Abraham fell flat on his face. God had chosen Abraham. But El Shaddai was only one of many gods and Abraham had chosen him. That was the deal.

In biblical chronology, it was 2,021 years after the creation that Abraham obeyed God's command and set out with his wife Sarah and his nephew Lot for the land of Canaan. He arrived in Canaan and God appeared to him in a vision, this time to promise him that the land would be given to his descendants. Unfortunately, the Promised Land failed to live up to its promise. A severe famine led Abraham and Sarah to move temporarily to Egypt. Believing that Sarah was so beautiful that the Egyptians would kill him to possess her, Abraham persuaded Sarah to say that she was his sister. As Abraham had feared, on account of her beauty she became one of Pharaoh's concubines. Abraham cared little, so it seemed, for God's plan for him to be the father of all nations. And he was well paid for selling Sarah – 'sheep, oxen, male donkeys, male and female slaves, female donkeys, and camels' (Gen. 12.16). Abraham may have been pleased with the deal, but God wasn't. He had plans for Sarah to be the mother of all nations. So God took back control and 'afflicted Pharaoh and his house with great plagues because of Sarai' (12.17). The Pharaoh, realising that Sarah was Abraham's wife, threw them out of Egypt.

To fulfil his promise to Abraham that he would be the father of a great nation, God gave him a son, Isaac. Having done so, he appeared to renege on his promise. 'Take your son,' God said to Abraham, 'your only son Isaac, whom you love, and go to the land of Moriah, and offer him there as a burnt offering on one of the mountains that I shall show you' (Gen. 22.2). This was a God the exercise of whose arbitrary power went way beyond the ethically acceptable. The Enlightenment philosopher Immanuel Kant (1724–1804) saw it as a key moment in the conflict between the God of the Bible and the God of the philosophers:

> Abraham should have replied to this supposedly divine voice: 'That I ought not kill my good son is quite certain. But that you, this

apparition, are God – of that I am not certain, and never can be, not even if this voice rings down to me from (visible) heaven.'[35]

Abraham, however, unlike Kant, *did* take it as the voice of God and set off with Isaac. When he reached the hilltop, he built an altar, bound his son Isaac and laid him on it. Just as he was about to kill his son with a knife, he heard a voice from heaven staying his hand: 'Do not lay your hand on the boy or do anything to him; for now I know that you fear God, since you have not withheld your son, your only son from me' (Gen. 22.12; see Plate 9). And yet again, God bestowed his blessing upon Abraham and his descendants. God now knew that Abraham's obedience had no limits. He was willing to murder his only son for him. And Abraham now knew that, even though God stopped him at the very last moment from murdering Isaac, there were no limits to what God might demand.[36] The question of whether the demands of God can *legitimately* transcend the ethical or whether God is bound by the moral law resonates throughout the three religions of Abraham to the present.[37]

God the lawmaker

In biblical chronology, it is 2,666 years since the creation of the world, and the descendants of Abraham – the people of Israel – have been in Egypt for 430 years. God's promise of a Promised Land is not yet fulfilled and not looking all that likely. The Israelites are now Pharaoh's slaves. Moses, an Israelite, raised as an Egyptian, has murdered an Egyptian overseer and fled to Midian. There, on Mount Horeb, God appears to him 'in a flame of fire out of a bush' (Exod. 3.2). He tells Moses that he is the God of Abraham, of his son Isaac, and of his grandson Jacob. He was known to them as 'El Shaddai'. But now he has another name – Yahweh (יַהְוֶה) (6.3).

Yahweh was a God for the oppressed but not for the oppressors: 'I have observed the misery of my people who are in Egypt [...] So come, I will send you to Pharaoh to bring my people, the Israelites, out

of Egypt' (Exod. 3.12). God sent Moses to Egypt. Upon a recalcitrant
and resistant Pharaoh, God sent plagues – of frogs, gnats, flies, disease,
boils, thunder and hail, locusts, darkness. And in each case it was not
Pharaoh himself but God who hardened Pharaoh's heart not to let
the people go. Finally, God killed all the firstborn in Egypt, although
he passed over the houses of the Israelites.[38]

With that, Pharaoh sent Moses and the Israelites on their way. But
God hardened the heart of Pharaoh yet again and he set off in pursuit
of the Israelites. The Egyptians were destroyed by God as the waters
of the sea that had miraculously opened for the Israelites to cross
rolled back over the Egyptians: 'the entire army of Pharaoh that had
followed them [the Israelites] into the sea; not one of them remained
[…] And Israel saw the Egyptians dead upon the sea shore' (3.28–30).
The Israelites celebrated the awesome power of their warrior God:

> The Lord is a warrior; the Lord [Yahweh] is his name. […] Who
> is like you, O Lord, among the gods? Who is like you, majestic in
> holiness, awesome in splendour, doing wonders? You stretched out
> your right hand, the earth swallowed them. (15.3–12)

The warrior God who murdered the firstborn of Egypt and drowned
the army of Pharaoh was now to become a lawgiver. In a demonstration
of his transcendent power, God descended upon Mount Sinai 'in fire;
the smoke went up like the smoke of a kiln, while the whole mountain
shook violently' (19.18). Moses alone went up to the summit and
received Ten Commandments from God (see Plate 10):

> Then God spoke all these words: I am the Lord [Yahweh] your
> God, who brought you out of the land of Egypt, out of the land of
> slavery; you shall have no other gods before me. You shall not make
> for yourself an idol […] You shall not make wrongful use of the name
> of the Lord your God […] Remember the Sabbath day and keep
> it holy […] Honor your father and your mother […] You shall not
> murder. You shall not commit adultery. You shall not steal. You shall
> not bear false witness against your neighbour. You shall not covet

your neighbour's house; you shall not covet your neighbour's wife,
or male or female slave, or ox, or donkey, or anything that belongs
to your neighbour. (20.3–17)

Here, we are at the origins of the tradition in Judaism, Christianity
and Islam that sees God as the source of the moral law. But what this
actually means has been a matter of contention within all three traditions. It was a dilemma that these religions inherited from the Platonic
tradition. In Plato's dialogue *Euthyphro*, Socrates asked Plato, 'Is what
is holy holy because the gods approve it, or do they approve it because
it is holy?'[39] Transposed from piety to ethics, the question became: 'Is
what is morally good commanded by God because it is morally good,
or is it morally good because it is commanded by God?' The notion
of the absolute sovereignty of God appears to endorse the latter. For
were God *obliged* to act according to a moral law independent of him,
God would be dependent on something else and his sovereignty
correspondingly decreased. On the face of it, the Exodus story of
the delivery of the Commandments by God to Moses endorses the
so-called 'divine command theory' of ethics – that is to say, the good
is simply that which is commanded by God.

That the good was identical with what God commanded was a
theory that provided a way around those incidents in the Bible in
which God appeared to breach his own Commandments and to act
wickedly. And it provided (as it still does) a mandate for believers, in
the name of God's commands, similarly to breach morality. As we have
seen, in Genesis 22.2 God ordered Abraham to murder his son. In
Exodus 11.2 God gave the Israelites permission to plunder the goods
of the Egyptians. In Hosea 1.2 God commanded the prophet Hosea
to have sex with an adulteress.

Augustine dealt with the problem (or at least tried to) in his *The
City of God*. An exception to any commandment, argued Augustine,
was 'by a special commission granted for a time to some individual'.
Thus, in obeying God, far from doing wrong, Abraham 'was not merely
deemed guiltless of cruelty, but was even applauded for his piety,
because he was ready to slay his son in obedience to God'.[40] A similar

position was adopted by the fourteenth-century Franciscan Andrew of Neufchâteau. On the basis of a divine command theory of ethics, he concluded, Abraham 'wished to kill his son so that he would be obedient to God commanding this, and he would not have sinned in doing this if God should not have withdrawn his command'.[41] On this account, God can do no wrong; nor, a little frighteningly, can those who obey him.

Divine doom and prophetic gloom

As part of their covenant with God, the Israelites had to promise that Yahweh would be their only God and that they would obey the Commandments. It was an agreement that was to be more honoured in the breach than in the observance. The history of Israel was to be one of its breaking of these treaties with God, nowhere more so than when it finally entered the Promised Land 2,706 years (in biblical chronology) after the creation of the world. The story of God would then become that of his sending his prophets to warn Israel of the catastrophe that was to come were it not to return to his ways and of the predicted and inevitable punishment of Israel for its failure to do so. Thus, the story of God in the books of Joshua, Judges, 1–2 Samuel and 1–2 Kings in the Old Testament is the story of his visiting punishment upon the people of Israel as a consequence of their sins.

The prophets, therefore, spoke on God's behalf, against an Israel that, far from being the oppressed, had become the oppressor. The message of the prophet Amos (mid-eighth century BCE) was typical:

Hear this word that the Lord has spoken against you, O people of Israel, against the whole family that I brought up out of the Land of Egypt: You only have I known of all the families of the earth; therefore I will punish you for all your iniquities. (Amos 3.1–2)

Thus, that they were God's chosen people brought special responsibilities rather than special privileges. They were not indemnified against punishment. And just to remind them that they might not have been as special as they thought they were, and maybe not special at all: 'Are you not like the Ethiopians to me, O people of Israel? says the Lord. Did I not bring Israel up from the land of Egypt, and the Philistines from Caphtor and the Arameans from Kir? (9.7). In short, Israel faced God's judgement. No amount of pleading on the grounds of its special status could save it.

Above all, it was the failure of Israel to live up to its ethical obligations that had doomed it. The rich and the powerful oppressed the poor and the weak. Israel's failure was the pursuit of ritualistic religion at the expense of social justice:

> I hate, I despise your festivals, and I take no delight in your solemn assemblies. Even though you offer me your burnt offerings, and grain offerings, I will not accept them. [...] But let justice roll down like waters, and righteousness like an ever-flowing stream. (Amos 5.21–4)

God remained the destroyer. However, his destruction of Israel was not arbitrary but based on his justice. Israel had breached its ethical contract with God. With Amos we learn for the first time that the God of the prophets, far from being a capricious despot, was a God who demanded ethically high standards from his people. As the prophet Micah, a contemporary of Amos, summed it up: 'what does the Lord require of you but to do justice, and to love kindness, and to walk humbly with your God?' (Mic. 6.8).

That said, while God demanded ethical behaviour of others, it was not something that he himself always exemplified. Simply put, God did not measure up to the standards that he demanded of others. All of which brings us back to Isaiah and his pronouncing doom upon the people of Judah at the behest of a God who had already determined that Judah should not listen to his prophet nor turn back to God. God intended to destroy not only the ruling oppressors but also those whom they oppressed. They would all be equally punished, because they were all equally guilty: 'That is why the Lord did not have pity

on their young people, or compassion on their orphans and widows'
(Isa. 9.17). As Andrew Davies neatly puts it:

> if Yahweh truly intends to destroy the poor, then it turns out that
> the condemnation that Isaiah heaps upon the civic leaders is only
> for doing something that God has declared he intends to do himself
> (but wouldn't need to do if they hadn't done it themselves!).[42]

Moreover, not only are the innocent punished along with the guilty,
but the punishments of the guilty appear disproportionate to their
sins. The punishments to be meted out to the women who indulged in
cosmetics, jewellery and *haute couture* (Isa. 3.24–4.1) – stench instead
of perfume, rope instead of a sash, baldness instead of coiffured hair,
rape – are extreme by anyone's understanding. '[N]ot so much an eye for
an eye as an eye for an eyelash,' as John Barton sardonically comments.[43]

In the book of Job (400–300 BCE), however, there was no prior
wickedness to account for God's punishment. Job was 'blameless and
upright, one who feared God and turned away from evil' (Job 1.1).
And yet a series of inexplicable disasters befell him. His livestock was
stolen or destroyed and his servants died, along with his sons and
daughters. He was then inflicted with loathsome sores all over his
body (see Plate 11). To Job's complaint that he had done nothing to
deserve this kind of treatment, God responded by reminding him that
his ways could not be understood by such as him. Finally, Job realised
that the world was not a place in which the righteous were rewarded
and the wicked punished: on the contrary, bad things happened to
good people, and vice versa. The series of questions that God eventually
asked Job pointed only to the unfathomableness of God's creation and
the incomprehensibility of his ways (38–41). The natural order and
the moral order were equally unintelligible to men. All Job could do,
for good or ill, was to subject himself in faith to the inscrutable will
of God. We can perceive but 'the outskirts of his ways; and how small
a whisper do we hear of him!' (26.14).

Yet, as we recall, if the God that confronted Isaiah in the temple
in Jerusalem was awesome and terrifying, he was also gracious and

comforting. Beyond the catastrophes, hope remained. Thus, in Isaiah 40, a compassionate God emerged: 'Comfort, O comfort ye my people, says your God. Speak tenderly to Jerusalem, and cry to her that she has served her term, that her penalty is paid' (Isa. 40.1–2) – this while the Jews were in exile in Babylon during the second half of the sixth century BCE.[44] And this, from around the same time:

> For a brief moment I abandoned you, but with great compassion I will gather you. In overflowing wrath for a moment I hid my face from you, but with everlasting love I will have compassion on you, says the Lord, your Redeemer. (54.8)

While the writers of the Psalms can praise God, call upon God's pity, give thanks for God's deliverance, call for God's vengeance against enemies or even rage at God himself, the overall tone is one of quiet trust in God, especially in times of peace. Thus, from the peaceful period after the Babylonian exile, there arose the most well-known Psalm in English literature, particularly in its translation in the 1611 King James Bible:

> The Lord is my shepherd, I shall not want. He maketh me to lie down in green pastures: he leadeth me beside the still waters. He restoreth my soul: he leadeth me in the paths of righteousness for his name's sake. Yea, though I walk through the valley of the shadow of death, I will fear no evil: for thou *art* with me; thy rod and thy staff they comfort me. Thou preparest a table before me in the presence of mine enemies: thou anointest my head with oil; my cup runneth over. Surely goodness and mercy shall follow me all the days of my life: and I will dwell in the house of the Lord for ever. (Ps. 23)

Thus, the personal transcendent God of the Old Testament was both wrathful and compassionate, merciful and punitive, forgiving and judgemental, and he was all of these in ways quite incomprehensible to us.

By the beginning of the Christian era, then, God had become both the origin of the natural order and the source of the moral order, yet transcending both. The sovereignty of God had been asserted, but at the expense of his goodness. Yet, as we will see in Chapter 3, as the God of the Bible entered into dialogue with the God of the philosophers, both in Judaism and Christianity, the 'positive' attributes of God were able to coalesce with the notion of a God who could only do good because he was goodness itself. That solved the problem of his goodness. But it did so at a cost, namely, his sovereignty. For then, apparently, he lacked the power to do anything about evil.

The God of Jesus

Like his Old Testament predecessors, Jesus was a prophet (see Plate 12). The first words that we hear from Jesus in Mark, the earliest Gospel (*c.*50–70 CE), were a pronouncement of doom and a message of hope: 'The time is fulfilled and the Kingdom of God is at hand. Repent and believe in the good news' (Mark 1.15; my translation). Jesus undoubtedly thought of himself as a prophet, and perhaps as the Messiah, the one who was to come to liberate Israel. He was perceived as such by those who heard his teaching. When Jesus asked his disciples whom people thought he was, they replied:

> John the Baptist; and others Elijah; and still others one of the prophets. He asked them, 'But who do you say that I am?' Peter answered him, 'You are the Messiah.' And he sternly ordered them not to tell anyone about him. (8.28)

The message of Jesus, like that of the earlier prophets, was one of imminent catastrophe. It was not so much a prediction of the end of the world as of the end of the world as Jesus and his contemporaries knew it – the destruction of Jerusalem, the end of the old Israel and an invitation to be part of a new Israel. The old Israel and its religious system was to be superseded by a new Israel, focused on the God whom Jesus preached. God's new Israel would be for the select few and not for the majority. 'Enter through the narrow gate,' declared Jesus,

for the gate is wide and the road is easy that leads to destruction, and there are many who take it. For the gate is narrow and
the road is hard that leads to life, and there are few who find it.
(Matt. 7.13)

In the Kingdom that was to come, God would distinguish sharply
between the righteous and the wicked. Those who had thought that
they were the chosen people would find out that they were not:

I tell you, many will come from east and west and will eat with
Abraham and Isaac and Jacob in the kingdom of heaven, while the
heirs of the kingdom will be thrown into the outer darkness, where
there will be weeping and gnashing of teeth. (Matt. 8.11–12)

Jesus also drew on the tradition of Jewish wisdom, exemplified in the
figure of King Solomon, which went back to the Old Testament books
of Proverbs and Ecclesiastes. Jesus was not only a prophet but also a
subversive sage. When the Kingdom of God finally came, the righteous and the wicked would be separated. But in the meantime, God
appeared to be impartial at worst, even-handed and generous at best:
God 'makes his sun rise on the evil and on the good, and sends rain
on the righteous and on the unrighteous' (Matt. 5.45). Punishments
for the wicked and rewards for the righteous were not to be expected
from God in the present world.

Yet God did care for his creation and the human beings within
it. 'Look at the birds of the air,' said Jesus, 'they neither sow nor reap
nor gather into barns, and yet your heavenly Father feeds them. Are
you not of more value than they?' (Matt. 6.26). But the God of Jesus
gave no guarantees. 'If any want to become my followers,' said Jesus,

let them deny themselves and take up their cross and follow me.
For those who want to save their life will lose it, and those who lose
their life for my sake will save it. For what will it profit them to gain
the whole world and forfeit their life? Indeed, what can they give in
return for their life? (Mark 8.34–7)

The God of Jesus therefore called for a radically different way of life from those who would be the new Israel. As with the God of the prophets of the Old Testament, the God of Jesus was on the side of the poor, the oppressed and the despised. The allegiance of these would no longer be to the religious system of the old Israel but to the teaching of Jesus. The Commandments of the Mosaic Law were reduced to two guiding principles. When Jesus was asked by one of the scribes which commandment was the greatest of all, he replied:

> The first is, 'Hear, O Israel: the Lord our God is one; you shall love the Lord your God with all your heart, and with all your soul, and with all your mind, and with all your strength.' The second is this, 'You shall love your neighbour as yourself.' There is no other commandment greater than these. (Mark 12.29–31)

Elsewhere, Jesus summed up the law and the prophets in one commandment: 'In everything do to others as you would have them do to you' (Matt. 7.12). This was a commandment that entailed love for all regardless:

> You have heard that it was said, 'You shall love your neighbour and hate your enemy.' But I say to you, Love your enemies and pray for those who persecute you, so that you may be children of your Father in heaven. (Matt. 5.43–5)

Rejecting violent resistance to the occupying Roman power, Jesus's Sermon on the Mount showed how God's new Israel needed to comport itself in the coming Kingdom of God:

> Blessed are the poor in spirit. For theirs is the kingdom of heaven. Blessed are those who mourn, for they will be comforted. Blessed are the meek, for they will inherit the earth. Blessed are those who hunger and thirst for righteousness, for they will be filled. Blessed are the merciful, for they will receive mercy. Blessed are the pure in heart, for they will see God. Blessed are the peacemakers, for

they will be called children of God. Blessed are those who are persecuted for righteousness' sake, for theirs is the kingdom of heaven. Blessed are you when people revile you and persecute you and utter all kinds of evil against you falsely on my account. Rejoice and be glad, for your reward is great in heaven, for in the same way they persecuted the prophets who were before you. (Matt. 5.3–12)

The God whom Jesus called upon his followers to love was a personal one, one whom Jesus, along with some of his contemporaries, referred to respectfully as 'Father' in the prayer that he gave to his disciples. It was a prayer for the Kingdom to come, for God's will to be followed on earth as in heaven, for the provision of daily food, of the hope for God's forgiveness and the will to forgive others, for deliverance from the time of testing as the Kingdom rapidly approached and from the temptations of 'the evil one' (Satan) (Matt. 6.9–13).[45]

In the end, Jesus himself took on the suffering that he expected God was soon to inflict on Israel. He was the Messiah whom Israel had been expecting to inaugurate the rule of God as King. But in turning the idea of the expected military Messiah upside down, in the tradition of the suffering servant of Isaiah 40–55, Jesus 'gave his life as a ransom for many' (Mark 10.45). The God of Jesus was one who, at the end of the day if not at the end of the world, demanded of Jesus his life (see Plate 13).

Behind this God of mercy and compassion there nonetheless remained a God of justice and wrath. Jesus was offering Israel its last chance and God would be merciless to those who failed to heed his message. Better to suffer a little now than much worse later:

If your hand causes you to stumble, cut it off; it is better for you to enter life maimed than to have two hands and to go to hell, to the unquenchable fire. And if your foot causes you to stumble, cut it off; it is better for you to enter life lame than to have two feet and to be thrown into hell. And if your eye causes you to stumble, tear it out; it is better for you to enter the kingdom of God with one eye than

to have two eyes and to be thrown into hell, where their worm never
dies, and the fire is never quenched. (Mark 9.43–8)[46]

As with the God of Isaiah, the God of Jesus was merciful and punitive,
forgiving and judging, wrathful and compassionate.

Allah and Muhammad the Prophet

Allah, the God of Muhammad (c.570–632), like the God of Jesus and
the Old Testament prophets before him, had a similarly complex and
ambivalent character. To those who turned to him in repentance, he
was (above all else) compassionate and benevolent. Those who failed
to find the path or, having found it, failed to follow it, would know
his wrath. Thus the opening words of the holy book of Islam – the
Qur'ān:

> In the name of God, the Merciful, the Compassionate. Praise (be) to
> God, Lord of the worlds, the Merciful, the Compassionate, Master
> of the Day of Judgment. You we serve and You we seek for help.
> Guide us to the straight path: the path of those whom You have
> blessed, not (the path) of those on whom (Your) anger falls, nor of
> those who go astray. (Qur'ān 1.1–2)[47]

Muhammad saw himself as the last in a line of prophets (33.40) that
reached back through Jesus to Moses, beyond him to Abraham and
as far back as Noah. And like a number of his prophetic predecessors,
Muhammad's mission began with a vision of God:

> One harsh in power has taught him – One full of strength! He
> stood poised, while He was at the farthest horizon, then he drew
> near and came down. He was two bow lengths tall, or nearly. And
> so He inspired His servant (with) what he inspired. His heart did
> not lie about what it saw. Will you dispute with him about what
> he sees? (53.5–12)[48]

Subsequently we read that God had sent down 'the Book with the truth [the Qur'ān], confirming what was before it, and He sent down the Torah [of Moses] and the Gospel [of Jesus] before (this) as a guidance for the people' (3.3–4; see Plate 14).[49]

What, then, does the Qur'ān teach us about God? Above all, as the opening verses indicate, he was 'Lord of the worlds' or 'Lord of all being'. As such, he was a God of absolute sovereignty:

> God – (there is) no god but Him, the Living, the Everlasting. Slumber does not overtake Him, nor sleep. To Him (belongs) whatever is in the heavens and whatever is on the earth [...] His throne comprehends the heavens and the earth. Watching over both of them does not weary Him. He is the Most High, the Almighty. (2.255)

He was sovereign not least because he was the creator and maintainer of the heavens and the earth and everything in them. Of everything, he created two kinds, including human beings. God 'created you from one person, and from him created his wife, and scattered from the two of them many men and women' (4.1). The life and death of each person was determined by God:

> From what did He create him? From a [sperm] drop! He created him, and determined him [male or female], then He made the way easy for him, then He caused him to die and buried him, then, when He pleases, He will raise him (again). (80.19–22)

As with the God of the Old Testament, the sovereignty of Allah was guaranteed at the expense of his goodness. God created everything evil as well as everything good. 'I take refuge,' declared Muhammad, 'with the Lord of the daybreak, from the evil of what He has created, and from the evil of the women who blow on knots [witches], and from the evil of an envier when he envies' (113.1–5). On occasion, God appeared to give human beings a free choice to believe in God or not to believe in God. Thus: 'The truth is from your Lord. Whoever pleases,

let him believe, and whoever pleases, let him disbelieve' (18.29). In this
case, each soul would eventually be rewarded or punished according
to its virtues or vices (40.17). We appear free to choose our ultimate
destiny. Yet, elsewhere, it was God who determined choices and led
astray whomever he wished:

> Surely those who disbelieve – (it is) the same for them whether you
> warn them or do not warn them. They will not believe. God has set
> a seal on their hearts and on their hearing, and on their sight (there
> is) a covering. For them (there is) a great punishment. (2.6–7)

The God of Muhammad, like the God of Abraham, wielded power arbitrarily beyond the ethically acceptable. 'God! Master of the Kingdom,'
declared Muhammad,

> You give the Kingdom to whomever you please and You take away
> the Kingdom from whomever You please. You exalt whomever You
> please and you humble whomever You please. In Your hand is the
> good. Surely you are powerful over everything […] You provide for
> whomever you please without reckoning. (3.26–7)

That said, at the end of the world, God would act as a God of justice.
All the dead would be resurrected to receive God's judgement. God
would then reward or punish each person in the gardens of Paradise
or the fires of hell according to their deeds. Each would be presented
with a record of his deeds – in the right hand for those to be saved, in
the left for those to be damned (69.19–37). The scales of justice would
be set up: 'Whoever's scales are heavy, those – they are the ones who
prosper, but whoever's scales are light, those are the ones who have
lost their (own) selves, because of the evil they have done to Our signs'
(7.8–9). From the fires of hell there would never be an escape. Those
who 'burn in the great Fire' would 'neither die there nor live' (87.13).
For those who were saved, the delights of Paradise awaited – elaborate
feasts, pleasant conversation, the company of wives and children, the
fulfilment of all desires.

Those who died in the cause of Allah did not need to wait for the Last Judgement. They would go straight to heaven (2.154, 3.169). The key to salvation was above all surrender (*islam*) to God, obedience to his commands as revealed in the Qur'ān and allegiance to his messenger Muhammad. Like Yahweh, Allah was a lawmaker. The Qur'ān provided (often varied) guidance to the believing community in matters of marriage and family law, women, inheritance, food and drink, worship and purity, warfare, punishments for adultery and false accusations of adultery, alcohol and theft. In short, it provided the foundation of what was later to be much elaborated in sharia law.

And thus to the infamous incident of the 'Satanic verses'. Within a century of Muhammad's death, the tradition had developed that Muhammad, distressed by the rift between him and the Meccans after he had forbidden their cult of the goddesses, sought a way of softening their attitude towards him. Satan saw his chance and whispered in the Prophet's ear: 'These [goddesses] are the high-flying cranes and their intercession [with Allah] is to be hoped for.' Muhammad, taking these to be the words of God, duly recited it. The Meccans were delighted with this compromise. But Gabriel came to the Prophet and told him that he had recited the words of Satan. He told Muhammad to replace the Satanic passage with a declaration that the goddesses were mere figments of men's imaginations: 'They are only names which you have named, you and your fathers' (53.23).[50] Elsewhere in the Qur'ān, as in early Christianity's critique of the pagan gods, they were relegated to the status of demons (6.100).

At the core of Muhammad's teaching was the absolute power and sovereignty of Allah, in part a declaration of the supremacy of Allah over other gods, in part an assertion of the oneness of God, in part a denial of the existence of any god but God: 'Give warning that (there is) no God but Me, so guard (yourselves) against Me!' (16.2). The oneness of Allah was not only about those gods external to him. It was also about his internal nature. The affirmation of God's *oneness* was explicitly directed against the Christian doctrine of the divinisation of Jesus and the resulting doctrine of the Trinity, which suggested *threeness* in God. 'People of the Book,' Muhammad proclaimed, do not go beyond the limits in your religion, and do not say about God (anything) but the truth. The Messiah, Jesus, son of Mary, was only a messenger of God and his word, which He cast into Mary, and a spirit from Him. So believe in God and his messengers, but do not say, 'Three'. Stop! (It will be) better for you. God is only one God. Glory to Him! (Far be it) that He should have a son! (4.171)

To associate partners with God was the ultimate sin of *shirk*, which led to the injunction to 'kill the idolaters [polytheists]' unless they convert (9.5) or are willing to be humiliated and pay a tax (9.29). According to Muhammad, Christians believed that a man had become God. They were guilty of both idolatry and polytheism. But to Christians, it was the other side of the same coin – not a man becoming God but God becoming a man in Jesus the prophet.

2

The God–Man

And the Word became flesh and lived among us, and we have seen his glory, the glory as of a father's only son, full of grace and truth.

John 1.14

Monotheism

It is perhaps no surprise that at least some early Christians wrestled with the fact that the world, in spite of its being created by God, was a pretty awful place. So awful, indeed, that for a ship owner from Pontus, Marcion (d. *c.*160 CE), it could only be the creation of an evil God. Thus, as Irenaeus pointed out:

> the followers of Marcion do directly blaspheme the Creator [that is the good God], alleging him to be the creator of evils, [but] holding to a more tolerable theory as to his origin, [and] maintaining that there are beings, gods by nature, differing from each other – the one being good, but the other evil.[1]

Moreover, according to Marcion, it was this evil God, the creator/demiurge, who was the God of the Old Testament, and more particularly of the Jews. Thus, it was this God who was the lawmaker and the God of the prophets. Marcion, declared Irenaeus,

> advanced the most daring blasphemy against Him who is proclaimed as God by the law and the prophets, declaring Him to be the author of evils, to take delight in war, to be infirm of purpose, and even to be contrary to Himself.[2]

This was not a case of the God of the Bible versus the God of the philosophers. Rather, it was the God of the Old Testament against that of the New. The Latin theologian Tertullian (*c*.160–*c*.220 CE) summed up these opposing deities as follows: 'one judicial, harsh, mighty in war; the other mild, placid, and simply good and excellent'.[3] In the story of God, Marcion was to become little more than an interesting footnote (although much more than that here). His importance resides in his forcing Christianity into the declaration that there was a continuity between the God of the Old Testament and that of the New Testament. And while Christianity asserted that the New Testament had transcended the Old, it recognised the Old Testament as Christian Scripture and it never again doubted that the Gods of each Testament were one and the same.

Marcion's was a neat solution to the problem of the apparently immoral at worst, amoral at least God of the Old Testament. Christianity decided to live with the problem. That it could not go along with Marcion's solution was the result of its commitment to the monotheism of the Jewish tradition that developed during the Babylonian exile in the sixth century BCE. It was during this period that God announced that he was the only God and that all the other gods *did not exist*. 'I am the Lord, and there is no other,' he said, 'besides me there is no god' (Isa. 45.5). This was monotheism with a vengeance, both literally and metaphorically, as we will see.

It is helpful to distinguish this kind of monotheism from other available versions of the relations between God and the gods. In some forms of 'qualified polytheism', for example, one god rose to the top of the divine pantheon. Thus, within the classical Greek tradition, Zeus became the god of all Greeks, at the top of the divine pile. In the *Iliad*, Zeus, rather like a prime minister with his or her cabinet, zealously guarded his position of primacy over a pantheon inclined to disregard or disregard him:

> Now Dawn the saffron-robed was spreading over the face of all
> the earth, and Zeus that hurleth the thunderbolt made a gathering
> of the gods upon the topmost peak of many-ridged Olympus,

and himself addressed their gathering; and all the gods gave ear: 'Hearken unto me, all ye gods and goddesses, that I may speak what the heart in my breast biddeth me. Let not any goddess nor yet any god essay this thing, to thwart my word, but do ye all alike assent thereto, that with all speed I may bring these deeds to pass. Whomsoever I shall mark minded apart from the gods to go and bear aid either to Trojans or Danaans, smitten in no seemly wise shall he come back to Olympus, or I shall take and hurl him into murky Tartarus, far, far away, where is the deepest gulf beneath the earth, the gates whereof are of iron and the threshold of bronze, as far beneath Hades as heaven is above earth: then shall ye know how far the mightiest am I of all gods.'[4]

Even so, the relationship between the gods within Greek religion was anything but stable. The boundaries between the gods were permeable and those between the gods and the supreme or cosmic God were similarly fluid. Consequently, the supreme God with many subordinates could metamorphose into the one God with many names. This is the kind of 'qualified monotheism' that we find in the Babylonian *Enuma Elish*, which ends with a hymn to the god Marduk and a list of his 50 names.[5]

However, in contrast to 'qualified polytheism' or 'qualified mono-theism', the Jewish monotheism of the Babylonian exile was radically exclusive. As Jan Assmann puts it:

Biblical monotheism is not the latent monotheism of polytheism finally become manifest under the motto 'All gods are one' but rather a totally new form of monotheism that excludes rather than absorbs the other gods under the motto 'No other gods!' or 'No god but God!' This form of monotheism, which may be called 'exclusive', is a matter not of evolution but of revolution.[6]

For the Jews in exile in Babylon, it was no doubt comforting to be told of the power of Yahweh and the non-existence of all other gods. As they wept by the rivers of Babylon and remembered Zion (Ps. 137.1),

God reinforced their sense of being a chosen people. There was only one God and he had chosen them.

This was a key moment in the history of religious exclusivism and intolerance. The nations who had not been chosen were, if only they knew it, worshippers of non-existent gods, of idols – in their blindness bowing down to wood and stone. Implicit within this kind of exclusive monotheism there was the binary of believer and unbeliever, chosen and rejected, friend and foe, the saved and the damned, theist and idolater. So we might say that, within exclusive monotheism, there lay the seeds of intolerance and violence, if not for all of those who, not having heard 'the truth', lived outside it, at least for those who, having heard the message of the one true God, rejected it.

On the other hand, God was the god of all nations even if they did not know it. As well as being exclusive, God was also inclusive. Yahweh was God 'from the rising of the sun and from the west' (Isa. 45.6). When the Jews began to return from exile to Zion (from 539 BCE), the nexus between God and Israel was broken, at least in the sense that God invited others to become members of his chosen people:

> And the foreigners who join themselves to the Lord [...] these I will bring to my holy mountain, and make them joyful in my house of prayer [...] for my house shall be called a house of prayer for all peoples. (Isa. 56.6–7)

From this time, Judaism, and later Christianity and Islam, held open the possibility of conversion from idolatry to the worship of the one true God. The boundaries between the chosen and the rejected, the damned and the saved remained fixed. But, in principle, the invitation to cross the border was made by God to all. From this time on too, the God of 'exclusive monotheism' would be in a complex historical battle with the God of 'inclusive monotheism'. This was a battle that would not only be fought between these religions (Muslims vs Christians vs Jews) but within them: Catholic vs Protestant, Sunni vs Shi'a, Ashkenazi vs Mizrahi, and between conservatives and liberals generally within each of these groups.

Exalted beings

In 53 CE, Paul of Tarsus (d. *c.*65 CE), a Jewish convert to the religion of Jesus, was writing a letter to the Christians in Corinth. He was warning off those Christians who, knowing that there were no gods behind the idols representing them and 'that there is no God but one', saw no problem in eating food offered to idols. Paul argued that, while these beings were not gods, they were spiritual, even demonic, entities. Thus, to eat food offered to them did matter because it was in effect to engage with preternatural powers, powers that he called elsewhere 'weak and beggarly elemental spirits' (Gal. 4.9). But for us, he wrote, 'there is one God, the Father, from whom are all things and for whom we exist, and one Lord, Jesus Christ, through whom are all things, and through whom we exist' (1 Cor. 8.6).[7]

What is remarkable about this last passage is that Jesus, within only 20 years of his death, was by then believed to have pre-existed his life on earth and to have been there at the creation of the world. Even more, he has become, after God, the key player in that creation. He is the mediator between the creator and his creation. He may not yet be completely divine, or, perhaps better, his divine status may not yet have been thoroughly thought through. But, as exalted beings go, it doesn't get much more exalted than this. Remarkably, then, the newly formed group of worshippers of Jesus were on the verge not only of declaring that *this* man was God but that God had become *this* man.

Still, within the context of Graeco-Roman religions, perhaps it was not so remarkable after all. Indeed, it could be argued that, as Christianity moved from the world of Hellenistic Judaism into the Hellenistic culture more generally, it was perhaps inevitable that Jesus would become a God–man. For the borders between the divine and the human in Graeco-Roman religion were anything but fixed. The Graeco-Roman world could happily absorb another divine human hero. However, it would have balked at Christian claims of Jesus's uniqueness. Christianity was making the claim that Jesus was not merely one of many God–men, but the only one. And it was making complicated assertions about the unique status of Jesus within the framework of both the rejection of Graeco-Roman polytheism *and* the assertion of Jewish monotheism.

That said, Jewish monotheism was anything but simple. God did not rule alone in an empty heavenly court. He was accompanied, for example, by the exalted patriarchs and prophets – Adam, Enoch, Abraham, Jacob, Moses, and so on. These were 'historical' figures who, as Larry Hurtado writes, 'are pictured as having a glorious place of heavenly power and honour'.[8] For its part, Christianity was to follow Judaism's lead and populate the heavenly court not only with the patriarchs and prophets whom Jesus released from Hades when he descended there between his death and Resurrection, but also with the Apostles, saints and martyrs of its own making. Similarly, in the Qur'ān, the prophets and martyrs were among the number of exalted humans in Paradise: 'the prophets, and the truthful, and the martyrs, and the righteous' (Qur'ān 4.69).[9]

Post-exilic Judaism also populated the heavenly court with angels, a tradition inherited by both Christianity and Islam. As beings quite distinct from God and created by him, angels did not infringe on Jewish monotheism. But pure monotheism looked a little less pure with the development in Judaism of *personalised* divine attributes, notably the figures of Sophia (Wisdom) and Logos (the Word), in which the divine attributes appeared to have taken on existences independent of God. In effect, Jewish monotheism had moved at least to a 'qualified monotheism', even to a 'qualified polytheism'. The Jewish philosopher Philo, for example, was certainly heading in this direction in his account of the role of 'the Word' in the creation of the world. Thus, in his discussion of creation, Philo declared that the God in whose image man was created was the Logos, 'for no mortal thing could have been formed on the similitude of the supreme Father of the universe, but only after the pattern of the *second deity* [*ton deuteron theon*], who is the Word of the supreme Being.'[10] At the very least, the Logos was functioning for Philo as the mediator between God and man at the creation of the world. The Logos was also the key 'figure' in the hierarchy of powers in the heavenly court: 'the great archangel of many names [...] the authority, and the name of God, and the Word.'[11]

Thus, within the Jewish tradition, God's heavenly court at the beginning of the Christian era included not only exalted humans and purely spiritual beings, but also personified divine attributes. The resources were therefore available for early Christians to stretch a Jewish monotheism, already modified by prophets, angels and personalised divine attributes, and view Jesus as the *exclusive* redeemer of the world and the *unique* mediator of salvation between God and his creation. This was not least because it was believed that he had risen from the dead, had ascended into heaven, had been 'exalted at the right hand of God' (Acts 2.33) and would eventually return in glory at the end of the world. All the various titles that accrued to Jesus in the New Testament – the Logos, the Wisdom of God, the Son of God, the Son of Man, the Lamb, the Servant, the Christ, the second Adam, the Light of the World, the Image of the invisible God, Lord – attested to this unique status. Jesus was conceived as greater than the prophets, beyond the angels and identical with the personified attributes of God. Thus, the Letter to the Hebrews (*c*.80–95 CE) exemplified what, by the end of the first century CE, had become Jesus's divine status:

> Long ago God spoke to our ancestors in many and various ways by the prophets, but in these last days he has spoken to us by a Son, whom he appointed heir of all things, through whom he also created the worlds. He is the reflection of God's glory and the exact imprint of God's very being, and he sustains all things by his powerful word. When he had made purification for sins, he sat down at the right hand of the Majesty on high, having become as much superior to angels as the name he has inherited is more excellent than theirs. (Heb. 1.1–4)

This was a qualified monotheism in which, rather than multiple manifestations of the one God, Jesus had become (almost) the sole and unique divine manifestation.

I say 'almost' above since we are now to see how there is in the New Testament yet another 'manifestation' of God – the Holy Spirit. According to Acts of the Apostles, after Jesus had risen from the dead and before he had been taken up into heaven, he promised his Apostles that, in the near future, they would be 'baptised in a holy spirit' from God (Acts 1.5). Soon after, when the Apostles were gathered together on the day of Pentecost to celebrate God's giving of the Commandments to Moses, there came a sound like the rush of a violent wind. Tongues as if of fire appeared among them, one of which came to rest on each of them. All of them 'were filled with a holy spirit' (2.4) and they began to speak in other tongues (see Plate 18). The crowd from many nations that gathered was amazed since each heard them speaking in their own language. The presence of the spirit of holiness from God was a sign of the imminent Kingdom of God and a mark of belonging to the new Israel. Tongues of fire would become one of the two key symbols of the Holy Spirit. The other was a dove. Thus, when Jesus was baptised by John the Baptist at the beginning of his prophetic activities, he 'saw the heavens torn apart and the spirit like a dove descending into him' (Mark 1.10).

This spirit of holiness was just one of many. The world of early Christianity was filled with spirits. The angels were, of course, spirit beings. There were also the unclean and evil spirits that Jesus and the Apostles exorcised from those possessed. But there were also various 'divine' spirits alongside the spirit of holiness – the spirit of the Lord, the spirit of God, the spirit of Jesus, the spirit of truth or just the spirit. The person filled with 'the holy spirit' or 'the spirit of holiness' from God became holy – set apart by God. When Paul laid his hands on some 12 Christians in Corinth (who had not even heard of a holy spirit), 'the holy spirit came upon them and they spoke in tongues and prophesied' (Acts 18.6). It was being filled with the spirit of holiness from God that enabled the recognition that Jesus was Lord: 'no one can say "Jesus is Lord" except by the Holy Spirit' (1 Cor. 12.3).

The spirit of holiness brought obligations to the new community and to God. When a man named Ananias sold a piece of property, he brought only a part of the profits to the Apostles. Peter asked him why Satan had persuaded him to lie to the holy spirit and to keep back part of the proceeds. 'You did not lie to us,' declared Peter, 'but to God' (Acts 5.4). When Ananias heard that, he fell down and died.

This was a powerful and dangerous spirit. And it so took control of those who were quite *literally* filled by it that they spoke and acted in strange ways, so much so that the people of Lystra thought that, in Paul and Barnabas, 'the gods have come down to us in human form' (Acts 14.11). Paul and Barnabas were mortified to be thought of as gods, tearing their clothes and rushing out into the crowds shouting: 'We are mortals just like you.' But the crowds in Lystra were close: the transcendent God *had* become immanent in those who, filled by a spirit of holiness, were marked out as speaking and acting in the service of God.[12]

Although there were many 'divine' spirits in the New Testament, 'the holy spirit' (τὸ πνεῦμα τὸ ἅγιον) became eventually the 'generic' term in early Christian theology for all of these various 'spiritual' manifestations of the divine. This was no doubt the consequence of 'the holy spirit' being the dominant term in the New Testament. But it was also the consequence of its particular role in early Christian initiation rites. Thus, in the community out of which the Gospel of Matthew arose (75–100 CE), the baptism of converts was 'in the name of the Father and of the Son and of the Holy Spirit' (Matt. 28.19).

Trinitarian puzzles

By the end of the first century, then, the divine had become triadic rather than dyadic or monadic in nature. But the nature of the Father, the Son and the Holy Spirit, their relationship to God and the relation of each to the other within the one God was anything but clear. The next 350 years of Christian thinking about God would be devoted to determining the nature of God, not so much by saying what it was as by deciding what it was not. Throughout this period, God was very much a work in progress, full of false starts and dead ends.

Such uncertainties were exemplified in *The Shepherd of Hermas*, one of the most popular works of early Christianity in the second century. In its account of God, his Son and his Spirit, it made what came later to be believed were three theological 'errors'. The first of these was that the pre-existent Son of God was identical with the Holy Spirit rather than a being distinct from the Spirit. Thus, it declared, before God became man, there was only a Father and a Holy Spirit. The second error was that, when God became man, it was the 'holy pre-existent Spirit that created every creature' that God made to dwell in flesh. The third error was that, rather than being a God who became man, the man Jesus, after living a pure life in accordance with the indwelling Spirit, was adopted as Son of God as a reward for his virtuous life.[13] So it was not at all obvious whether God was one, two or three.

By contrast, Justin Martyr in his *First Apology* (c.155 CE) held to what was to become the orthodox position, namely, that God was not dyadic but triadic in nature, and this *before* he became incarnate in Jesus. However, Justin's error was to subordinate the Son to the Father and the Spirit to the Son. This was understandable, for Justin did so while defending Christians against the charge of atheism – by which was meant not the denial of the existence of the pagan gods but their demonisation. We are not atheists, declared Justin,

> worshipping as we do the Maker of this universe, and declaring [...] that He has no need of streams of blood and libations and incense [...] Our teacher of these things is Jesus Christ [...] we reasonably worship Him, having learned that He is the Son of the true God himself, and holding Him *in the second place*, and the prophetic Spirit *in the third*.[14]

Always anxious to show that Christianity was in alignment with Greek philosophy, Justin referred his readers to Plato's *Timaeus*, where (he argued) Plato gave second place to the Logos and third place to the Spirit of God.[15] Justin was also not all that clear on what happened at the conception of Jesus. In contrast to the identification of the divine Word (Logos) with the pre-existent Jesus, Justin equated it with the Holy Spirit. 'It is wrong, therefore,' he wrote,

> to understand the Spirit and the power of God as anything else than the Word [τον λoγoν], who is also the first-born of God [...] and it

was this which came upon the virgin and overshadowed her, caused her to conceive, not by intercourse but by power.[16]

It was only in the latter half of the second century CE that the term 'trinity' (τριάς) came to be used of God, by a Bishop Theophilus of Antioch in his letter to Autolycus. In this case, however, it was not yet used of the Father, the Son and the Holy Spirit, but 'of God, and His Word and His wisdom', each of which, he suggested, corresponded to the first three days of the week of creation.[17] Earlier in this letter, moreover, it is clear that Theophilus was very much a qualified monotheist who did not restrict manifestations of the divine to merely three. Thus, he wrote,

> if I call Him Word, I name but his sovereignty; if I call Him Mind, I speak but of His wisdom; if I say He is Spirit, I speak of His breath; if I call Him Wisdom, I speak of His offspring; if I call Him Strength, I speak of his sway

and so on.[18] So whether God was one or three or many was all very uncertain.

However, during this same period, there was the first clear declaration in Christianity of both a oneness and a threeness in God. Again, the intention was to demonstrate that Christians were not atheists. Thus, the second-century CE apologist Athenagoras, in his *Plea for the Christians* (c.177 CE), declared that Christians were conducted to a future life by one thing alone:

> that they know God and his Logos, what is the oneness of the Son with the Father, what the communion of the Father with the Son, what is the Spirit, what is *the unity of these three*, the Spirit, the Son, the Father, and *their distinction in unity*.[19]

Granted there was *both* a oneness *and* a threeness, the next step was to denote this 'threeness' as a 'Trinity'. It was the Latin theologian Tertullian who was the first to use the term 'Trinity' (*trinitas*) to denote the Father, the Son and the Holy Spirit. He did so in a work entitled *Against Praxeas* (after 213 CE). Praxeas was a qualified mono-theist, a supporter of 'Patripassianism', who, in order to defend the unity of God, declared that God the Father emptied himself into the man Jesus and suffered on the cross to redeem mankind. He was part of a broader movement called 'Monarchianism' (or 'modalism'), so-called because it asserted the 'monarchy' (or sole government) of God and proclaimed that the Father, Son and Holy Spirit were merely modes or names of the one 'person'. By contrast, declared Tertullian, we believe

> that there is one only God, but under the following dispensation or οἰκονομία [economy], as it is called, that this one only God has also a Son, His Word, who proceeded from Himself [...] who sent also from heaven from the Father, according to His own promise, the Holy Ghost, the Paraclete [Comforter].[20]

Thus, while emphasising the unity of God, Tertullian distributed the unity into a trinity, not of one but of three *persons* – Father, Son and Holy Spirit. In short, the Godhead was one substance (*substantia*) in three grades, aspects or manifestations. God was one in essence but as revealed to humankind he was in three persons (*personae*). The relation between the one and the three was like that between a river and its source, the sun and its light – both identical and different.

In spite of the fact that Tertullian was attempting to argue for the threeness of God over against his oneness, there was nonetheless a whiff of Monarchianism about his solution. He had not located both the unity *and* the Trinity as *both* of the essence of God but only the unity. Tertullian's understanding of God was thus, after all, only a form of 'qualified monotheism' in which the Trinity was *not of the divine essence*. This was the problem that the third-cen-tury Platonist Origen of Alexandria attempted to overcome. On the one hand, he did so by asserting the oneness of the Godhead. Thus, in a discussion of the question of whether God had a body, Origen wrote:

God therefore must not be thought [...] to exist in a body, but to be a simple intellectual existence, admitting in himself of no addition whatever [...] but is Unity [Monad], or if I may so say, Oneness [Henad] throughout.[21]

On the other hand, he just as decisively declared that, *within* the one Godhead, there were individual persons (ὑποστάσεις, *hypostases*) existing independently. Thus, for example, he wrote, 'we worship the Father of the truth and the Son who is the truth; they are two distinct existences [ὑποστάσεις], but one in mental unity, in agreement, and in identity of will.'[22] With Origen, therefore, oneness *and* threeness were now of the divine essence – of how the Godhead was *in itself* and not merely how it revealed itself to humankind.

Thus did paradox become part of the very being of the Christian God. God was both one and three. It was a paradox that Origen himself recognised and endorsed. Thus, in his *Dialogue with Heraclides* (c.244–9 C E), he rhetorically asked:

Is it not true, then, that there was a God, the Son of God and only begotten of God [...] and that we do not hesitate to speak in one sense of two Gods, and in another sense of one God?[23]

Taking a leaf from Philo's book, Origen called the Son of God 'a second God'.[24]

All in all, it was a pretty delicate balancing act between a monotheism and a polytheism that the Cappadocian Father Gregory of Nazianzus (329–89 C E) summed up neatly:

And when I say God, I mean Father, Son, and Holy Ghost; for Godhead is neither diffused beyond These, so as to introduce a mob of gods, nor yet bounded by a smaller compass than These, so as to condemn us for a poverty-stricken conception of Deity, either Judaizing to save the Monarchia, or falling into heathenism by the multitude of our gods. For the evil on either side is the same, though found in contrary directions.[25]

Neither monotheistic nor polytheistic, the oneness and threeness in God was hard to think of. 'No sooner do I conceive of the One,' he declared, 'than I am illuminated by the Splendour of the Three; no sooner do I distinguish Them than I am carried back to the One.'[26]

That each of the three was a distinct *hypostasis* or person entailed also that they had been eternally so and had not been created at some point in time. That is, the Son had not been generated by the Father at the time of his becoming man, nor even at the time of creation. Rather, the Son of God had been eternally generated by the Father. 'I would dare to add,' wrote Origen,

> that as he is a likeness of the Father *there is no time when he did not exist* [...] Let the man who dares to say, 'There was a time when the Son was not,' understand that this is what he will be saying, 'Once wisdom did not exist, and word did not exist, and life did not exist.'[27]

The Holy Spirit was something of a poor relation in all of this. Origen really did not have much of a clue how to deal with 'him'. He was clear that the Holy Spirit inspired the prophets of the Old and the Apostles of the New Testament. He was clear too that the Holy Spirit gave the gift of sanctity more generally. And he also asserted that the Holy Spirit existed independently: 'the Holy Spirit is an intellectual existence with a subsistence and being of its own.'[28] Like his contemporaries, Origen was certain that all things were created through the Son (or the Word). But did this mean that the Holy Spirit was created through the Son? On the one hand, to argue that the Spirit was not created by the Son would be equivalent to making him, as unbegotten, superior to the Son. On the other hand, to see the Spirit as a created being would be to make him merely equivalent to other created things. Origen's solution was to have the Spirit the 'most excellent and the first in order of all that was made by the Father through Christ' and, crucially, to argue that, unlike all other created things, he had been made *eternally* (timelessly) and not at any point *in time*.[29] All that said, by arguing that, within the one Godhead, the Father, the Son and the Holy Spirit existed independently, Origen had embedded both unity and Trinity at the very essence of the divine (see Plate 15). Thinking about God was never meant to be easy. And to many, it appeared that Origen had impugned the unity of God and had erred on the side of polytheism or at least tritheism.

Christological crises

In February 313 CE, about 60 years after the death of Origen, the Edict of Milan (the result of an agreement between the Roman emperors Constantine I and Licinius) established religious toleration for Christianity within the Roman Empire. Unfortunately, Christians took it as a perfect opportunity to be intolerant of each other. The edict amounted, much to Constantine's dismay, to an open invitation for Christians to begin fighting among themselves, literally and metaphorically, over the nature of God, and particularly over the question of the relationship between the Father and the Son. It was a brawl that was to last for the next century and a half. The Greek theologian Bishop Gregory of Nyssa (*c.*330–*c.*395) reflected on the passion engendered among all and sundry by the arguments at the Council of Constantinople in 381 CE. 'The whole city is full of it,' he wrote,

> the squares, the market places, the cross-roads, the alleyways; old-clothes men, money changers, food sellers: they are all busy arguing. If you ask someone to give you change, he philosophizes about the Begotten and the Unbegotten; if you inquire about the price of a loaf, you are told by way of reply that the Father is greater and the Son inferior; if you ask 'Is my bath ready?' the attendant answers that the Son was made out of nothing.[30]

The immediate cause of the crisis about Jesus Christ in the second decade of the fourth century CE was the Alexandrian priest Arius (*c.*250–*c.*336 CE). Arius was at one, so to say, with Origen in his belief in the transcendence of the Father, at least in the sense that the Father was eternally self-existent. 'We acknowledge One God, alone Ingenerate [ἀγγέητον], alone Everlasting [ἀναρχον, without beginning], alone True, alone having Immortality, alone Wise, alone Good [...] unalterable and unchangeable.'[31] He was also in agreement with Origen that the Son was made by the Father and therefore not self-existent. However, in contrast to Origen, he did not believe that the Son had been generated by the Father *eternally*. To Arius, to have been generated eternally was effectively no different from being ungenerated. Consequently, for Arius, if the Father and the Son were both eternal, this would entail 'two self-existent principles' – a clear breach of monotheism. Therefore, even though the Son was born before time, there was *a time when he was not*: 'before he was begotten, or created, or purposed, or established, He was not.'[32] For his opponents, Arius appeared to have radically subordinated the Son to the Father and made of him at worst just another creature *ex nihilo* – albeit one with powers and abilities way beyond those of mortal men, or at best a semi-god – a kind of high-flying angel.

On 20 May 325 CE, the Emperor Constantine entered the palace in Nicaea to open what was to become known as the Council of Nicaea (see Plate 16). He proceeded, Eusebius, the bishop of Caesarea (*c.*260–*c.*234 CE), tells us,

> like some heavenly messenger from God, clothed in raiment which glittered as it were with rays of light, reflecting the glowing radiance of a purple robe, and adorned with the brilliant splendour of gold and precious stones [...] he surpassed all present in height of stature and beauty of form, as well as in majestic dignity of mien, and invincible strength and rigour.[33]

Constantine intended to impress the more than 250 bishops, along with their attendants, from all parts of the Roman Empire who were present. Those who attended the council that had been called by the emperor were undoubtedly impressed, even overawed.

Determined to consolidate his power as emperor, Constantine had had enough of the warfare between the supporters and opponents of Arius that had rapidly spread from Alexandria throughout the empire and was destabilising its unity. The tone of his opening speech was irenic. But the bishops would have heard the clear message that failure to come to an agreement was not an option:

> begin from this moment to discard the causes of that disunion which has existed among you, and remove the perplexities of controversy by embracing the principles of peace [...] and you will confer an exceeding favour on me who am your fellow-servant.[34]

After a month of occasionally heated 'discussion', a statement was agreed to by all but two of the bishops present (and Arius). The so-called 'Nicene Creed' read as follows:

> We believe in one God, the Father almighty, maker of all things, visible and invisible;
>
>   And in one Lord Jesus Christ, the Son of God, begotten from the Father, only-begotten, that is, from the substance of the Father, God from God, light from light, true God from true God, begotten not made, of one substance with the Father, through whom all things came into being, things in heaven and things on earth, Who because of us men and because of our salvation came down and became incarnate, becoming man, suffered and rose again on the third day, ascended to the heavens, and will come to judge the living and the dead;
>
>   And in the Holy Spirit.
>
>   But as for those who say, There was when He was not, and, before being born He was not, and that He came into being out of nothing, or who assert that the Son of God is from a different hypostasis or substance, or is created, or is subject to alteration or change – these the Catholic Church anathematizes.[35]

The last section of the creed made it clear to all, including Arius, that his views were outlawed. But while it was clear to the bishops what it was that they were rejecting, it was less clear what it was that they were endorsing. In particular, the meaning of 'of one substance with the Father' (όμοούσιον τω πατρί) was ambiguous. It was, as it happens, a term imposed upon them by the emperor. On the one hand, the Arians took it as implying a quasi-physical division within God and promptly rejected it. On the other hand, it could be taken minimally as meaning 'of the same nature as the Father' and read as an assertion that the Son was fully divine (against Arius's apparent demotion of him) while still allowing an essential separateness between the Father and the Son. This was probably the reading of the majority at the council who, while endorsing the oneness and threeness of God, preferred the Trinity over the unity. Or, finally, it could be read as a declaration that, since God was both immaterial and indivisible, the three persons in God must be numerically one substance. This was probably the reading taken by some at the council who, while endorsing the oneness and threeness of God, preferred the unity of God over the Trinity. This last was the understanding of the term that came later to be accepted.

Little surprise, therefore, that the unity of the council was more in form than in substance. In its aftermath, as the opponents of Arianism continued to bicker among themselves, Arianism re-emerged. The tensions between the imperial church and the imperial state were exacerbated. The battle raged for 60 more years. Bishop Basil of Caesarea (c.330–79) summed it up: 'To what then shall I liken our present condition?' he asked.

> It may be compared, I think, to some naval battle [...] fought by men who cherish a deadly hate against one another [...] Watchwords are indistinguishable in the confusion, and all distinction between friend and foe is lost [...] Of the combatants some are turning traitor; some are deserting in the very thick of the fight [...] Jealousy of authority and the lust of individual mastery splits the sailors into parties which deal mutual death to one another [...] they do not cease from their struggle each to get the better of the other, while their ship is actually settling down into the deep.[36]

In Basil's time, around the middle of the fourth century CE, there were three main competing theologies (with a variety of positions in between). First, there were the supporters of Nicaea (the Homoousians), represented above all by Athanasius (*c*.296–373). They argued that the Son was *of the same substance* (*homoousios*) as the Father. Second, there were the moderates (the Homoiousians) who argued that the Son was *of a like substance* (*homoiousios*) to the Father. And third, there were the radical Arians (the Anomoeans), who argued that the Son (by virtue of his generated nature) was utterly *unlike* (*anomoios*) the ungenerated Father. Politically, as Athanasius was to realise, the interests of the Homoousians lay in aligning themselves with the Homoiousians against the hard-line Arians. And he recognised that, theologically, there was hardly (in fact *only*) an iota of difference between them. Thus, Athanasius wanted to talk to the Homoiousians, not as (the wonderfully called) 'Ariomaniacs', but 'as brothers with brothers'.[37]

So both strategic nous *and* brotherly love were evident at the Council of Alexandria chaired by Athanasius in 362 CE. Those who emphasised the threeness of God were able to assure their opponents that, when they spoke of three 'persons' (*hypostases*), they did not intend to assert that there were three Principles or three Gods but only the independent existence of each of the three persons within the Godhead. Those who emphasised the oneness of God were able to assure their opponents that, when they spoke of one 'person' (*hypostasis*), they were not wishing to deny that the Father, Son and Holy Spirit existed independently but were merely emphasising the unity of nature between them. Each side was, as a consequence, able to accept that their differences were only ones of emphasis.[38] Both sides happily endorsed Nicaea and anathematised Arius and various other non-Nicaean riff-raff. They were now as close as makes no difference to affirming what was to become the orthodox view of the Trinity: one 'essence' (*ousia*) in three 'persons' (*hypostases*).

Refining the spirit

The focus on the relation between the Father and the Son had been at the expense of the relation of the Holy Spirit to the two other persons

in the Trinity. To its lengthy description of the nature of the Son, the
Nicene Creed of 325 CE had in effect merely added, 'Oh, and by the
way, we also believe in the Holy Spirit.' It was only at the Council of
Alexandria in 362 CE that Athanasius secured the agreement that the
Holy Spirit, along with the Son, was *both* of the essence of the divine
and a separately existing being. That said, while the nature of the
Holy Spirit was now fully on the theological agenda for the first time,
Athanasius had aggravated the issue more than solved it. Disputes
around the Spirit soon appeared.

Thus, it was in 380 CE that the theologian Gregory of Nazianzus
laid out the variety of opinions available. Some, he remarked, thought
of the Holy Spirit merely as an activity, some as a creature, some as
a God. Others, due to the uncertainty within Scripture, remained
uncertain. Then again, even among those who accepted his divinity,
there were those who confirmed him as the least divine within the
Trinity.[39] These so-called 'Pneumatomachi' (Πνευματομάχοι, Spirit-
fighters) led Gregory to an unqualified assertion of the divine nature
of the Holy Spirit: 'Is the Spirit God? Yes, indeed. Then, is he
Consubstantial [of one substance with the Father]? Of course, since
He is God.'[40]

Granted the Holy Spirit was just as fully divine as the Father
and the Son, there remained the question of his origin. It was the
younger brother of Basil of Caesarea and the friend of Gregory of
Nazianzus, Bishop Gregory of Nyssa, who took the biblical notion
that the Spirit 'proceeds' (ἐκπορεύεται) from the Father (John 15.26)
and elaborated it by placing the Son as the intermediary between
the Father and the Spirit. Thus, the Holy Spirit was 'from God and
of the Christ'. As such, the Spirit was to be distinguished from the
Father, who was uncaused, and from the Son, who was the only-be-
gotten. The spirit, he said, was 'proceeding from the Father' and
'receiving from the Son'.[41] Elsewhere, Gregory clarified this further
(if only marginally). The Son, he declared, was *directly* from the
Father, and the Spirit indirectly from the Father *through* the Son.[42]
The distinctions between the procession of the Holy Spirit from
the Father *alone*, from the Father *through* the Son or from both the

Father *and* the Son were clearly (or perhaps not so clearly) fine ones. It may look like a dispute about angels dancing on the head of a pin (which they actually never did since they were incorporeal) – and in one sense it was just that. But it nonetheless had, as we will see, enormous historical importance.

The Council of Constantinople in 381 CE dodged the apparent subordination of the Spirit to both the Son and the Father implied in procession from *both the Father and the Son* and opted for procession out of (ἐκ) the Father *alone*. This has remained the position of the Eastern (Orthodox) Church since that time (although it remains ambivalent about the legitimacy of 'through the Son'). In contrast, the Western (Latin) Church opted for the procession of the Holy Spirit from both the Father *and* the Son (Filioque), primarily as a result of Augustine's acceptance of a double procession. Augustine's clearest statement came in his somewhat tetchy response to the Arian Maximinus:

> You ask me, 'If the Son has the substance of the Father and the Holy Spirit also has the substance of the Father, why is one a son and the other not a son?' Look, here is my answer whether you get it or not. The Son comes from the Father; the Holy Spirit comes from the Father. The former is born; the latter proceeds. Hence, the former is the Son of the Father from whom he is born, but the latter is the Spirit of both because he proceeds from both. When the Son spoke of the Spirit, he said, *He proceeds from the Father* (John 15:26), because the Father is the author of his procession. The Father begot a Son and, by begetting him, gave it to him that the Holy Spirit proceeds from him as well.[43]

Augustine's intent was to emphasise the Spirit's equality with the Father and the Son by representing him as the 'mutual love, wherewith the Father and the Son reciprocally love one another'.[44] At its core, this was yet another variation on the debate about the oneness versus the threeness of God. Both East and West were as one in wanting to emphasise the unity of God. Augustine's account of the double procession appealed to the West since it suggested the idea of the 'co-inherence' (περιχώρησις) of God. The doctrine of co-inherence meant that the action of one person in the Trinity involved the co-operation of all. Thus, the procession of the Father from the Son emphasised that what the Father did the Son co-operated in. The unity of God was thus affirmed. Moreover, granted that the procession of the Spirit could not but have happened *eternally*, the double procession entailed that the Son had *also* been eternally involved in the procession of the Spirit. This provided one more weapon in the armoury against Arian claims that there was a time when the Son was not. But this was not how the East saw it. While the East was equally concerned to combat Arianism, the apparent subordination of the Spirit to the Father *and* the Son appeared not only to destroy the balance of the three persons within the one God but also to suggest that the spirit was not an independently existing person.

All this might not have mattered all that much had not the Third Council of Toledo in 589 CE added 'and the Son' to 'proceeded from the Father' to the version of the Nicene Creed endorsed at the Council of Constantinople in 381 CE. From there, 'and the Son' gradually spread throughout the West. However, it was not until 1014 that the addition of 'and the Son' to 'proceeded from the Father' in the Niceno-Constantinopolitan Creed of 381 CE was endorsed by Pope Benedict VIII (r.1012–24) and became part of the Roman liturgy. The papal endorsement meant that, from then on, the issue of the procession of the Holy Spirit was to become embroiled in the ecclesiastical struggle between the popes in Rome and the patriarchs in Constantinople around the right of the Roman popes to define the faith of the universal church. Forty years later, in 1054, the final separation of the Eastern (or Orthodox) and Western (or Catholic) churches began. The 'Filioque' (and the Son) debate then became a genuinely church-dividing issue, and the question of its omission/ addition to the creed of one became symbolic of the other's more general heretical ways.[45] More crucially, the 'Filioque' drove a wedge between the understanding of the nature of God in Western and Eastern Christianity that had begun 1,600 years ago with Augustine and remains to this day.

Of God and man

In its affirmation of the theology of the Council of Nicaea, the Council of Constantinople in 381 CE had, more or less, solved the problem of Arianism. There was no time when Jesus Christ was not. In its declaration that the Spirit had proceeded from the Father, it thought that it had solved the problem of the Pneumatomachi who denied the divinity of the Holy Spirit. As we have seen, it hadn't – well, not quite, anyway. It also determined that Jesus Christ was both *fully God and fully man*.[46] In so saying, it was reacting against the Christology of Apollinarius (*c.*310–*c.*390), who was interpreted as arguing, on the analogy of man as body and soul, that while the body of Christ was human, his will, his intellect and his animating spirit were divine.[47] 'We confess,' he wrote, 'that the Word himself has become flesh without having assumed a human mind, i.e. a mind changeable and enslaved to filthy thoughts, but existing as a divine mind, immutable and heavenly.'[48] On the face of it, this got around the problem of having a Christ in two minds with two opposing wills and intellects. But to his opponents, it did so at the cost of Christ's being genuinely human. The Christ of Apollinarius and his followers seemed to be some kind of divine–human hybrid. For the enemies of Apollinarius, a genuinely human Christ demanded a genuinely human soul as well as a genuinely physical body. Hence, the Council of Constantinople's declaration that Christ was *both fully God and fully man*.

What Christ's full divinity meant had been sorted out (more or less) at Nicaea. He was of one substance with the Father. But the question of how, during his life on earth, he could be both God and man was to be bitterly contested, not least because it was articulated in such complex and ambiguous terms that not only would the laity 'in the pews' not have had a clue, but most of the priests and bishops would have been struggling to grasp it (so not much change there then, a millennium and a half later).[49] The dispute was driven by two bishops, one of whom, Nestorius of Constantinople (d. *c.*451 CE), always thought that he was the most intelligent man in any room, and the other of whom, Cyril of Alexandria (d.444 CE), was a nasty piece of work about whom it was said at the time of his death, 'His survivors are indeed delighted at his departure. The dead, maybe, are sorry.'[50] This was a dispute that was never going to end happily and it was to occupy the church from 428 CE, when Nestorius became bishop of Constantinople, until the Council of Chalcedon in 451 CE.

Christological combat began when Nestorius attacked the popular title 'Theotokos' (God-bearer) for Mary the mother of Jesus (see Plate 17). To Nestorius, it reeked of Apollinarianism. For the term suggested to him a denial of the full humanity of Christ. The Christ of Nestorius was one who, as fully divine, was unable to suffer because he was just that – divine – and hence could not change or be limited in any way. But for Nestorius a Christ so divine that he could not suffer could not redeem us. For him, redemption was only possible by the actions of a Christ who was (although sinless) fully human, a Christ who thought and felt, was tempted and could suffer – in short, was like us in every way. As Gregory of Nazianzus put it most famously, 'that which He [the Word] has not assumed He has not healed.'[51]

So for Nestorius, the person of Christ contained two natures, the divine and the human, and thus was more like a vessel containing water and oil that remain unmixed than one holding wine and water that become inextricably mixed together. These two natures remained, as it were, side by side throughout the life of Christ. The divine Word and the human Jesus both retained their distinctiveness, although united in Christ: 'Christ is indivisible in that he is Christ,' Nestorius wrote, 'but he is twofold in that he is both God and Man.'[52] This 'two natures' theory enabled Nestorius to account both for those events in Christ's life that manifested his humanity and also for those that demonstrated his divinity. It had the virtue of being a neat, logical solution, both to the Christ of the faith and the Jesus of history.

It was perhaps just a tad *too* neat and *too* logical. For, in spite of his attempt to suggest that the two natures were somehow united in the person of Christ, he seemed to many of his contemporaries to be suggesting that there were two quite distinct 'subjects', each with its own distinct personality, in the earthly Christ. Nestorius had been able to save the humanity of Christ from those who absorbed it into his divinity. But he did so at the expense of Christ being always 'in two minds' because there *were actually* two minds in Christ.

In contrast, Cyril of Alexandria, Nestorius's key opponent, began with the assumption of a single 'subject' and then worked through how the humanity and the divinity related to it. Cyril's most telling analogy was that between the body and the soul in the individual man. These were quite different things, he declared. Yet, 'when they are united, they constitute the single nature of man.'[53] So too, in the single nature of Christ, there was a unity of God and man. Thus, when God became man, the human was not destroyed; nor was the divine diminished. Rather, in the Incarnation, the single divine subject, the Word of God, became 'enfleshed'. This meant that

> two natures come together with one another, without confusion and change, in an indivisible union. The flesh is flesh and not Godhead, even though it became the flesh of God; and similarly, the Word is God and not flesh even if he made the flesh his very own in the economy.[54]

Thus, after the Incarnation, the Word of God lived on earth as the man Jesus. He was both the Son of God and the son of Mary too. The unity between the humanity and divinity in the one nature was such that each participated in the properties of the other (*communicatio idiomatum*). Thus, the God who could not suffer as God was able to suffer, by virtue of the intimate links he had with humanity, which could suffer:

> we say that he both suffered and rose again; not meaning that the Word of God suffered in his own nature [...] for the divinity is impassible [...] But in so far as that which had become his own body suffered, then he himself is said to suffer these things for our sake, because the Impassible One was in the suffering Body.[55]

The conflict between the supporters of 'one nature' and those of 'two natures' needed to be sorted and, to this end, the Council of Chalcedon was convened by the Emperor Marcian in 451 CE. The formal definition of faith that emerged from the council was a complicated compromise. On the positive side, it did produce a definition of the nature of Christ that was to become the standard for the Orthodox, Roman Catholic, Anglican and mainstream Protestant churches up to the present:

> the same perfect in divinity and perfect in humanity, the same truly God and truly man, of a rational soul and a body; consubstantial with the Father as regards his divinity, and the same consubstantial with us as regards his humanity; like us in all respects except for sin; begotten before the ages from the Father as regards his divinity, and in the last days the same for us and for our salvation from Mary, the virgin God-bearer, as regards his humanity.[56]

On the negative side, the Chalcedonian definition not only articulated unity in the understanding of Christ but also perpetuated disunity. It did emphasise Cyril's position on the union between the divine and the human in Christ. But under the influence of the *Tome* of Pope Leo (d.461 CE), it also asserted that Christ was made known *in two natures* (ἐν δύο φύσεσιν), the properties of each of which were preserved within the union.[57] This could be read as no more than an endorsement of Cyril's view that the two natures were not fused or mixed together in their union. But it could also be read, and was, in counterpoint to Cyril's emphasis on the unity in Christ, as an endorsement of the duality of 'subjects' within the God who became man, and thus as an endorsement of Nestorius.

Thus, in attempting to compromise between the 'one nature' (of wine and water mixed) of Apollinarius and the 'two natures' (of oil and water unmixed) of Nestorius, Chalcedon failed to heal the divisions. The agreed formula appeared to argue, along with Cyril, that Christ had 'one nature' (μία φύσις) and, along with Pope Leo, that he was 'in two natures'. But supporters of 'two natures' (dyophysites) peeled off in one direction and read the formula as a crypto-Apollinarian endorsement of 'one nature', while supporters of 'one nature' (miaphysites) peeled off in the other and read it as a crypto-Nestorian endorsement of 'two natures'. That said, the mainstream Western Church stuck by the Chalcedonian compromise of 'oneness' and 'twoness' but read it through the eyes of Pope Leo's *Tome* with the stress on 'twoness'. For its part too, the mainstream Eastern Church stuck with the compromise but read it through the eyes of Cyril with the stress on 'oneness'.[58]

Yet, in spite of all this division and amid all this complexity, perhaps surprisingly to us (and probably also to them), by the middle of the fifth century CE there was a general agreement about the nature of God within Christianity, both Eastern and Western. All were agreed that God was both one and three – a unity in Trinity. There was agreement also that the Holy Spirit processed from God, although whether from the Father alone or from both the Father and the Son remained a crucial division between Eastern and Western churches. Substantial agreement had also been reached that the second person of the Trinity – the Son – was of one substance with the Father and had been *eternally* begotten by him – 'before the ages' as Chalcedon put it. That he was both *fully God* and *fully man*, all were also agreed, although, as we have seen, how this was 'operationalised' in Christ remained highly problematic.

All of this may appear as so much idle philosophising. At times it was just that. It was also deeply politicised, both ecclesiastically and imperially, more relevant to the temporal than the eternal realm. But the stakes were genuinely momentous. This was a debate not only about the nature of ultimate reality but also about human destiny. So there was a determination to articulate as decisively as possible who Christ *was*, even if this could only be ultimately expressed paradoxically, because *who Christ was* was intimately and intricately related to *what he did* through his life, death and Resurrection. This did matter for it was what Christ did that was at the core of the four and a half centuries that it took to think through who he was.

Who Christ was did matter to the early Christian church, quite simply, because Christ, as fully human, represented all humanity. When Adam fell, all men fell because all were present in him. In the same way, when Christ triumphed over sin, evil and death, all men triumphed because all were present in Christ as the second Adam. It

was all 'for us and for our salvation', as Chalcedon put it. In one version of this, Christ triumphed over the Devil, gaining freedom from
death for humanity by paying a ransom to the evil one. Satan had led
man captive, wrote Irenaeus, 'but was justly captured in his turn by
God; but man, who had been led captive, was loosed from the bonds
of condemnation.'[59] In another version, Christ sacrificed himself for
sinful humanity, satisfying the debt that humanity owed to God for sin.
Christ set us free 'who were held captive under sin', declared Gregory
of Nazianzus, 'giving Himself a Ransom for us, the Sacrifice to make
expiation for the world'.[60]

But there was also a third version: God became man so that we
might become divine. In the East, it was most famously expressed by
Athanasius: 'For He was made man that we might be made God.'[61] It
was echoed in the West by Augustine: "To make human beings gods,
He was made man who was God.'[62] Thus, on this account, the gap
between the divine and humanity had been immeasurably lessened,
not only in the Incarnation of God in Christ but, as a result, between
God and us. The possibility of a God, not only transcendent to the
world but immanent within it and within us, both in the things of the
world and in the depths of us, was now in play.

3

The God Within

Nor will his vision of the beautiful take the form of a face, or of
hands, or of anything that is of the flesh. It will be neither words,
nor knowledge, nor a something that exists in something else [...]
but subsisting of itself and by itself in an eternal oneness, while
every lovely thing partakes of it in such sort that, however much
the parts may wax and wane, it will be neither more nor less, but
still the same inviolable whole.

Plato, *Symposium*[1]

An other-worldly realm

In the seventh book of his *Republic*, Plato (427–347 BCE) tells the
allegory of the cave. Socrates asks Glaucon to imagine an underground
cave in which prisoners have been kept since childhood, all chained
such that they are able only to look at the wall in front of them. Behind
the prisoners is a fire, and between the fire and the prisoners a low
wall, behind which, like puppeteers, men can walk, and above which
they can show their puppets. These men carry past the wall all kinds
of things, including human and animal shapes, the shadows of which
are cast by the fire onto the wall of the cave in front of the prisoners.
The prisoners are only able to see the shadows cast onto the wall.
Naturally enough, the prisoners presume the images to be real rather
than merely shadowy images of what is actually real (see Plate 19).

Socrates then asks Glaucon to consider what would happen were
one of the prisoners to be released from his fetters and made to turn
and look towards the fire. Eventually he would come to realise that
the flickering images which he had previously taken as real objects

were only shadows of the real items that were showing above the wall now in front of him. Were the prisoner then to be taken up the slope to the entrance of the cave and thence into the light, he would eventually be able to see from reflections of things in water to the things themselves, thence up to heaven to the objects within it. Finally, 'he would be able to look upon the sun itself and see its true nature, not by reflections in the water or phantasms of it in an alien setting, but in and by itself in its own place.'[2] Then the prisoner would conclude that it is the sun that not only provides the seasons of the year and presides over everything in the visible world but is also the cause of all the things that he has seen.

What are the conclusions that are to be drawn from this story?

First, Plato was suggesting that our everyday world was nothing but a reflection of the real world. Thus, reality was not grounded in the world as we see it but in another, transcendent realm. This was a turning point in the history of Western thought. As Dean Inge puts it, it was in Plato 'that this conception of an unseen eternal world, of which this visible world is but a pale copy, gains a permanent foothold in the West.'[3] Second, this transcendent real world was not a world of things but of 'Ideas' ('Forms'). Ultimate Reality or Absolute Being was, in essence, intellectual or spiritual. As a result, while in our world things were temporary and changeable, in the real world Ideas were eternal and unchangeable. Temporary and changeable though they may be, all things are as they are in our world as a result of their participation in the world of Ideas. Third, since true knowledge could only be of that which was eternal and unchanging, the only true knowledge was knowledge of the realm of Ideas. To apprehend the world of the truly real therefore, the faculty of knowledge 'must be turned around from the world of becoming together with the entire soul [...] until the soul is able to endure the contemplation of essence and the brightest region of being.'[4]

Fourth, these Ideas were themselves eternal and immutable by virtue of their being derived from something beyond them, something that is of its essence eternal and unchangeable – 'the Idea of Ideas' (the sun in the allegory). Fifth, and most importantly, this Idea of Ideas was *Goodness itself*. As the ultimately real, Goodness was the chief object of desire for all of us. And those who attained it 'are not willing to occupy themselves with the affairs of men, but their souls ever after feel the upward urge and the yearning for that sojourn above'.[5] Goodness itself, therefore, was the only ultimately satisfactory object of intellectual contemplation and of desire. So, at the pinnacle of Plato's hierarchy of being, there was Absolute Being and Absolute Goodness, from which all things derived and in which all things, to a greater or lesser extent, shared. Thus, and without putting too fine a highly contentious point on it, Absolute Being that was also Absolute Goodness was Plato's God.

Finally, according to Plato therefore, we can *think* our way from 'this world' to the conclusion that there is 'another world'. Moreover, reason shows that, at the pinnacle of the intelligible realm, there must be a God. This all meant that there was another source of possible knowledge of God apart from God's revelation of himself in, for example, the books of the Bible. In short, by the use of our unaided reason, knowledge of God could be generated, a knowledge which might or might not be in accord with revelation. The God of the philosophers was not necessarily the God of revelation. And, with that, the philosophical quest for God began.

That it was possible for the soul spiritually to ascend to knowledge of the Good was the consequence of the process by which the world came into being. It is in Plato's *Timaeus* that we find his account of the creation:

> Let me tell you then why the creator made this world of generation. He was good, and the good can never have any jealousy of anything. And being free from jealousy, he desired that all things should be as like himself as they could be. This is in the truest sense the origin of creation and of the world [...] God desired that all things should be good and nothing bad, so far as this was attainable.[6]

Here, then, we are told that the other-worldly being – the creator – was good. As a consequence, he could not be jealous of anything that was not himself and there was no reason why there should not be other things than only him. Indeed, his goodness was such that it demanded that he *could not* be alone. His goodness was incomplete unless it was manifested in other things and in as many other things as was possible. Moreover, the creator desired that all things should be as like him as possible. Thus, as a result, goodness 'flowed' through the system. Unlike the God of the Bible, the Platonic creator was not free to choose to create the world: it was a necessity of his nature that he did so. Consequently, the created world was a complete replica of the transcendent world of Ideas, an image of the truly real filled completely with living beings mortal and immortal, a world that was 'the greatest, best, fairest, most perfect'.[7] This was the best of all possible worlds.

Moses and Plato

But how was the God of Plato related to the God of the Bible? The answer for the early Church Father Tertullian was simple: he wasn't. For his part, Tertullian saw all 'pagan' philosophy as nothing but a vain deceit, and he had the authority of Paul not to be taken 'captive through philosophy' (Col. 2.8). Above all, these doctrines of men and of demons were the source of all heresies. 'What indeed has Athens to do with Jerusalem?' he asked. 'Away with all attempts to produce a mottled Christianity of Stoic, Platonic, and dialectical composition!'[8]

Until the time of the Reformation in the sixteenth century, Tertullian's was to be the minority approach. The majority were much more inclined to seek a rapprochement between Moses and Plato. The Jewish philosopher Philo, for example, viewed Plato as essentially Moses speaking Greek. This was a result of his view that the Greek philosophers were directly dependent upon Moses, and that their views had been already anticipated by him. At times, however, Philo suggested that philosophy was God's gift to the Greeks, thus enabling them to discern through reason what the Jews knew from revelation. 'It is the heaven,' he wrote, 'which has showered philosophy upon us [...] and philosophy is the fountain of all blessings, of all things which are really good.'[9] He went on, in a way reminiscent of Plato's prisoner liberated from the cave, to reflect on how the sight moves from contemplation of the sun, the moon, the planets and the stars, of the animals, the fish and the birds of the earth to the Father who created them and who still cares for his creation, 'exerting his providence in behalf of the whole universe and of its parts'.[10] This theory of God's revelation of himself in the Bible and in philosophy enabled Philo to align the truth of the Bible with the truth of philosophy. He did so, as we noted in Chapter 1, by finding two levels of meaning in Scripture – a surface, literal meaning and a deeper, spiritual one. Thus could the inner meaning of Scripture be discerned through philosophy.

For Philo, philosophy was, then, ultimately in the service of Scripture and not the other way around. But this was something of a two-edged sword. Scripture retained its dominance as historically prior, having the virtue of antiquity. And divine revelation was infallible compared to human philosophy, which was prone to error. But Scripture did need philosophy to bring out its deeper meaning and ultimate significance. This implied that the philosophical reading was higher than the literal one. The conflict between God and the Bible had not been resolved so much as moved onto a different ground, namely, to a contest between the literal meaning of Scripture and its spiritual (or mystical or philosophical) significance, between an exoteric and an esoteric reading of the Bible.

Like Philo, Christian apologists were also inclined to find Greek philosophy foreshadowed in Moses. They followed the lead set by Philo, but they did so with a Christocentric variation. In their case it was the divine Word (Logos) later to be fully incarnated in Jesus whose presence could be partially discerned – not only in the Old Testament, but also in Greek philosophy. The Alexandrian theologian Justin Martyr, for example, accepted that whatever the lawgivers or philosophers got right they 'elaborated by finding and contemplating some part of the Word'.[11] Justin, taking his lead from the Stoics, declared that it was the 'seed of reason' (λόγος σπερματικός, *logos spermatikos*) within each man that enabled him to speak truth proportionately to the share he had of this 'spermatic Logos'.

Stoic influences aside, it was Platonism and the God of Plato
that seemed most congenial to an intellectual defence of Christianity.
Augustine, for example, deemed Platonism of all the philosophies the
nearest to Christianity. Thus, in *The City of God*, he wrote:

> Whatever philosophers, therefore, thought concerning the supreme
> God, that He is both the maker of all created things, the light by
> which things are known, and the good in reference to which things
> are to be done; that we have in Him the first principle of nature,
> the truth of doctrine, and the happiness of life – whether these
> philosophers may be more suitably called Platonists, or whether they
> may give some other name to their sect […] we prefer these to all
> other philosophers, and confess that they approach nearest to us.[12]

That Platonism was the 'nearest to us' was the consequence of two
things. First, Augustine had identified the ultimate reality of Plato – the
Idea of the Good – with the God of Christianity. Thus, for example,
in his early work *Concerning the Nature of Good* (after 404 CE), he
declared: 'The highest good, than which there is no higher, is God, and
consequently He is unchangeably good, hence truly eternal and truly
immortal.'[13] And second, because the God who is Goodness itself is
also the creator, 'every nature, so far as it is nature, is good […] all good
things, even those of most recent origin, which are far from the highest
good, can have their existence only from the highest good.'[14] Thus was
Plato's God aligned with the God of Genesis, who 'saw everything that
he had made, and indeed, it was very good' (Gen. 1.31).

If only it were all that simple! For the God of Plato and the God
of the Bible were not so easily to be equated. In the first place, the
God of Plato, the essence of whom was goodness, was a God who
could not but do good. The God of the Bible, by contrast, was a God
who was free to do whatever he liked. In the second place, the God of
Augustine was a God who created the world out of nothing. But the
Platonism of Augustine was mediated through the systematisation of
Platonic philosophy (known as Neoplatonism) by Plotinus. As E. R.
Dodds notes, in Plotinus

converge almost all the main currents of thought that come down from 800 years of Greek speculation; out of it there issues a new current destined to fertilise minds as different as those of Augustine and Boethius, Dante and Meister Eckhart, Coleridge, Bergson and T. S. Eliot.[15]

In the philosophy of Plotinus, the world was not created by God out of nothing at a point in time. Rather, it emanated and emanates out of him and has done so eternally. The many flow forth from the One.

The God who emanates

At the top of the hierarchy of being, for Plotinus, there lay the One who was also the Good. It was the One because it was beyond all multiplicity. As such it was beyond all expression. What it is could only be said by what it was not:

> Generative of all, The Unity is none of all; neither thing nor quantity nor quality nor intellect nor soul; not in motion; not at rest, not in place, not in time; it is the self-defined, unique in form or, better, formless.[16]

Following Plato's lead, Plotinus saw this self-sufficient Absolute as *of necessity* creating other than itself. Thus:

> The One is perfect because it seeks for nothing, and possesses nothing, and has need of nothing; and being perfect, it overflows, and thus its superabundance produces an Other [...] How then should the Most Perfect Being and the First Good remain shut up in itself, as though it were jealous or impotent – itself the potency of all things? [...] Something must therefore be begotten of it.[17]

The first stage of this process of emanation from the One was the realm of Intelligence or *nous*. This was Plato's realm of the Ideas. Intelligence in its turn overflowed into Soul. This was the world of sense perception, of knowledge and of reasoning. From Soul there emanated embodied life, down to pure matter – not, as we would think of it today, as something solid, enduring and extended, but rather as something bereft of any relation to idea, formless and measureless.

The process of emanation from the One was also a process of emanation of the good. The great descending chain of being was also the great descending chain of the Good. At the furthest point of emanation from the One, matter existed not only at the limits of being but at the limits of the Good. And thus matter, construed as the complete absence of good, was evil:

> Given that the Good is not the only existent thing, it is inevitable that, by the outgoing of it [...] there should be produced a Last, something after which nothing more can be produced: this will be evil [...] This Last is Matter, the thing which has no residue of good in it: here is the necessity of Evil.[18]

The One was never diminished as a result of this process. Plotinus invited us to consider a spring that has no source outside itself. It gave itself to all the rivers, 'yet is never exhausted by what they take, but remains always integrally what it was'.[19] Thus, the God of Plotinus was both transcendent to the world and immanent within it, an absolute reality within a world of relativity, both eternal and unchangeable and yet temporal and changeable, both a One and a many. As a consequence, in the Plotinian scheme of things, the world outside us genuinely presented divinity to us. But it was not only a divinity present within things but also one present within us. It was this presence of God both within the world and within us that enabled all of us, in principle, intellectually to apprehend that reality which is God as the source of all things. Thus, as there was a process of emanation from the One, so too there was a process for return to it.

According to Plotinus, souls have forgotten God and become enmeshed in the world, absorbed by selfishness: 'The evil that has overtaken them has its source in self-will [...] their regard for the mundane and their disregard of themselves bring about their utter ignoring of the Divine.'[20] 'We are become dwellers,' he remarked elsewhere, 'in the Place of Unlikeness, where, fallen from all our resemblance to the Divine, we lie in gloom and mud.'[21] The return to God therefore required the overcoming of the consciousness of the world external to us and the development of the consciousness of our selves through moral and intellectual purification.

The path of return to the One was not by the contemplation of the world outside the self and ascending upwards to God, but by contemplation of the self within. As Andrew Louth neatly puts it, 'the higher is not the more remote; the higher is the more inward: one climbs up by climbing in, as it were [...] As the soul ascends to the One, it enters more and more deeply into itself.'[22] The Plotinian path was thus one particular form of the mystical path more generally, where 'mystical path' denotes a set of practical, contemplative and intellectual disciplines that proceed from the assumption that the ultimately real, that which lies at the depths of all things, was finally to be found at the depths of the self.[23] Thus, in the mysticism of Plotinus, the transcendent One was both 'beyond' and 'within'. The soul became its true self as it moved away from the world of sense perception to the inner realm of the Ideas (*nous*), finally passing out of itself into the One 'beyond' the self. In the ecstatic experience of the One, all difference between the soul and the One was swallowed up.

> The man formed by this mingling with the Supreme [...] is become the Unity, nothing within him or without inducing any diversity; no movement now, no passion, no outlooking desire, once this ascent is achieved; reasoning is in abeyance and all Intellection and even, to dare the word, the very self: caught away, filled with God, he has in perfect stillness attained isolation; all the being calmed, he turns neither to this side nor to that, not even inwards to himself; utterly resting he has become very rest. He belongs no longer to the order of the beautiful; he has risen beyond beauty; he has surpassed even the choir of the virtues [...] This is the life of gods and of the god-like and blessed among men, liberation from the alien that besets

us here, a life taking no pleasure in the things of earth, the passing
of solitary to solitary.[24]

And thus back to Augustine, who, in the opening chapter of his
Confessions, reflected this Plotinian desire to return to the source of all
things: 'Thou hast formed us for Thyself, and our hearts are restless
till they find their rest in Thee.'[25] In a similarly Plotinian mode was his
account of the mystical vision he had at Ostia in the company of his
mother, Monica, in which we read how he and his mother ascended
'upwards' and 'inwards' into the depths of the soul. They gradually
passed, he wrote,

> through all corporeal things, and even the heaven itself, whence sun,
> and moon, and stars shine upon the earth; yea, we soared higher
> [...] and we came to our own minds, and went beyond them, that
> we might advance as high as that region of unfailing plenty.[26]

And, for a moment, they tasted the joys of heaven:

> If this could be continued, and other visions of a far different kind
> be withdrawn, and this one ravish, and absorb, and envelope its
> beholder amid these inward joys, so that his life might eternally like
> that one moment of knowledge which we now sighed after, were not
> this, 'Enter thou into the joy of Thy Lord.'[27]

Augustine was thus able to find the God who disclosed himself at the
depths of his soul. In Plotinus, the possibility for the soul to experience
the divine was due to the efforts of the individual (although, even there,
there is a sense at the very summit of a 'breaking in' of the One).[28] In
Augustine, by contrast, it is God's love in his becoming man and the
presence of the Holy Spirit who is love within us that brings this about:

> Too late did I love Thee, O Fairness, so ancient and yet so new!
> Too late did I love Thee! For behold, Thou wert within [me], and
> I without, and there did I seek Thee; I, unlovely, rushed heedlessly

among the things of beauty thou madest. Thou wert with me, but I
was not with Thee [...] Thou calledst, and criedst aloud, and forced
open my deafness. Thou didst gleam and shine, and chase away my
blindness. Thou didst exhale odours, and I drew in my breath and
do pant after Thee. I tasted, and do hunger and thirst. Thou didst
touch me, and I burned for Thy peace.[29]

The possibility of the return to God was not a consequence of God's
having emanated the soul out of himself. For Augustine's God was a
God who had created the world out of nothing. Thus, although the
created world was good, it was not so as a result of the emanation of the
divine into it. That said, there was something unique about humanity
that made it qualitatively different from the rest of the created realm,
namely, that man had been made in the image of God (Gen. 1.27).
Even the Fall of Man due to his disobedience had not completely
destroyed that image: 'the little spark of reason, which was the image
of God in him, has not been quite quenched.'[30] So it is not surprising
that Augustine finds in the memory, will and understanding of reason
the image of the divine Trinity. It is reason that enables the soul to
come to participate in the divine and become what it truly is because
it remembers, understands and loves him by whom it was created,
anticipating in the here and now what it will fully experience in the
hereafter: 'it will be in the hidden place of His presence, filled with
so great fullness of Him, that sin thenceforth will never delight it.'[31]
    Implicit within Augustine's mystical theology were two understand-
ings of the return to God that were interwoven, if not in tension with
each other: on the one hand the path of 'knowing' (or 'unknowing')
and on the other the path of loving union. On the one path, God was
pre-eminently apprehended through the intellect; on the other, God
was apprehended through the affects or the emotions. These were
in turn reflective of that other tension within the Western tradition
between the impersonal absolute of the Platonic tradition and the
personal God of the biblical tradition: between a One whose goodness
was expressed in the eternal outpouring of itself into creation and a
God whose love was expressed in his engagement in human history, not

least in his becoming man in Jesus. This was the tension between a God
who was in essence impassible – free of the sufferings that characterise
human life and feeling (and perhaps indifferent to them) – and one
who was passible – able to have emotions and thus to suffer as we do.

This was a problem with which the Christian tradition had to
wrestle as soon as it had accepted the Platonic tradition of an impassible Deity.[32] It was driven, in part, by the desire to establish that the
God of Christianity was immune from the unworthy emotions of the
pagan gods: well above debauchery, lust, envy and anger. In part, too,
it was motivated by the critique of the pagan philosophers themselves
that the Old Testament God was hardly better than his pagan counterparts. As the Emperor Julian 'the Apostate' (332–63 CE) asked:
'But what is the imitation of God with the Hebrews? Anger and rage
and savage zeal.'[33]

To head off the critique of the philosophers and to avoid a
Marcionite criticism of the Old Testament God as evil, some of the
early Christian theologians read the anger of God as a just and righteous condemnation of sin. Thus, the author of the *Recognitions* (early
third century CE) declared:

> the philosophers say that God is not angry, not knowing what they
> say. For anger is evil when it disturbs the mind so that it loses right
> counsel. But that anger which punishes the wicked does not bring
> disturbance to the mind; but it is one and the same affection […] that
> which assigned rewards to the good and punishment to the evil.[34]

Unlike our anger, God's anger was not one that disturbed his mind.
It was the same with the other 'negative' divine emotions. Thus,
Augustine:

> far be it from us to suspect an impassible God of suffering any
> annoyance. Just as He is jealous without any ill will, as He is angry
> without being emotionally upset, as He pities without grieving, as
> He is sorry without correcting any fault, so He is patient without
> suffering at all.[35]

What this means is that the impassibility of God functions as a reminder that, although God can experience emotions, we do well not to think of them as analogous to ours.

Be that as it may, the notion of a God who had no emotional register at all was rendered highly problematic by his becoming man. For a God who *genuinely* suffered on the cross was at the heart of the Christian story of redemption. Thus, it was recognised that the issue of the impassibility of God had to be thought through Christologically. The inevitable outcome of this was the assertion of another paradox at the heart of the Christian concept of God: not only a God who became man but also a God who suffered without suffering.

The key to the possible resolution of this paradox was in the relationship between the human and the divine natures in Jesus Christ as it had been laid out by Cyril of Alexandria. As discussed in Chapter 2, Cyril had declared that Jesus was both the Son of God and the son of Mary. But he had also affirmed that the unity between the divine and the human was such that each participated in the properties of the other:

> how can we both attribute suffering to him and yet still hold him impassible as God? It is because the sufferings belong to the economy, with God the Word reckoning those things that pertain to the flesh as his very own because of the ineffable union, and yet remaining outside suffering in so far as pertains to his own nature, since God is impassible.[36]

Thus did the paradox of an impassible God who suffered devolve to the paradox of a person who was both divine and human.

Love in a cold climate

These complex interweavings of a God who cannot suffer with one who can, of the God of the philosophers with the God of the Bible, of an impersonal Absolute with a personal God, of a God who emanates with a God who creates out of nothing, and of a transcendent God 'beyond' the world with an immanent God 'within' it were all to play out in the writings of the Syrian Pseudo-Dionysius the Areopagite (*fl. c.*500 CE).[37] His writings were to become authoritative in both Western and Eastern Christianity, not least because they were assumed to have been written by the Athenian convert of Paul mentioned in Acts of the Apostles (17.34). He was thus to become known as 'the Father of Christian Mysticism'.

Like Augustine, Pseudo-Dionysius was strongly influenced by the emanationism of Neoplatonism, particularly as this had been developed by Proclus (*c.*410–85 CE).[38] But the God of Pseudo-Dionysius was not only one who emanated the world out of himself but also one whose loving, divine nature permeated his creation:

> And we must dare to affirm (for 'tis the truth) that the Creator of the Universe Himself, in His Beautiful and Good Yearning towards the Universe, is through the excessive yearning of His Goodness, transported outside Himself in His providential activities towards all things that have being, and is touched by the sweet spell of Goodness, Love [agape] and Yearning [eros], and so is drawn down from His transcendent throne above all things, to dwell within the heart of all things, through a super-essential and ecstatic power whereby He yet stays within Himself.[39]

Thus did God, who was goodness and beauty, emanate out of himself into angels, humans, animals, plants and finally material things. And it was the presence of his goodness, love and yearning within all things that motivated the desire of all things to return to him. 'Let us declare,' wrote Pseudo-Dionysius,

> that there is but One Simple Power Which of Itself moveth all things to be mingled in an unity, starting from the Good and going unto the lowest of all creatures and thence again returning through all stages in due order unto the Good and thus revolving from Itself, and through Itself and upon Itself and towards Itself, in an unceasing orbit.[40]

In Pseudo-Dionysius, God was apprehended both by knowing and unknowing, both by way of affirmation and by way of negation. The way of knowing or affirmation corresponded to the procession from God, the way of unknowing or negation to the return to God. He was known by affirmation as a result of his presence within all those things that had come from his creative act, particularly as this had been revealed in the Scriptures. Thus, he was known above all in his procession from unity to Trinity and in the Incarnation in Jesus Christ.[41] He was also known by the range of concepts that can be formed of God in the mind – Goodness, Being, Life, Wisdom, Power.[42] God was known too by those images that were drawn from the perception of the world around us through the senses – the figures and instruments proper to him, the places in which he lived and the robes he wore, his anger, grief and indignation, his sleeping and waking, his drinking and even his hangovers.[43] Thus could God be positively known through the great chain of hierarchical being that descended 'downwards' from him.

It was a chain of ever-increasing plurality, from the One to an ever-increasing many. And, we might add, the further we move down the hierarchy of being, the less similarity there was between those things which we perceive through our senses or know through our ideas and the God from whom they were derived. By contrast, the further we move up the chain, along with an ever-decreasing plurality, the greater was the similarity between our perceptions or our ideas and their divine source. Simply put, all things are both similar and dissimilar to God, but some things are more similar than others. Because God is immanent within the world, there is a similarity even between God and the humble worm, although significantly less so than there is between God and the idea of being and goodness. Surely, asked Pseudo-Dionysius,

> it is truer to affirm that God is life and goodness than that He is air or stone, and truer to deny that drunkenness or fury can be attributed to Him than to deny that we may apply to Him the categories of human thought?[44]

Thus, the further we move down the chain, the less analogous are our perceptions and ideas to their divine source.

Simultaneously, however, as affirmations were made about God, it was necessary to deny them. The downward procession of affirmations about God was matched by an 'upward' path of negations, beginning by the negation of the most inappropriate attributes and ascending to that of the least inappropriate. Thus, even though the divine was immanent within the things that could be perceived, he was unlike any of them. The supreme cause of everything capable of being perceived through the senses was not itself perceptible. In other words, God was beyond the realm of space and time.[45] But, further, God was beyond that which could be conceived. Any ideas about God that the mind might consider needed to be negated and transcended. The path of negation ended in a realisation of God within and beyond the self, beyond knowing:

> the Divinest knowledge of God, the which is received through Unknowing, is obtained in that communion which transcends the mind, when the mind, turning away from all things and then leaving even itself behind, is united to the Dazzling Rays, being from them and in them, illumined by the unsearchable depth of Wisdom.[46]

For Pseudo-Dionysius, the ultimately real was thus beyond all possibility of language. Even negations had to be negated as the soul entered into loving union with the God who was beyond Being and Goodness, even beyond both Trinity and unity. The way of negation, declared Pseudo-Dionysius,

> lifts the soul above all things cognate with its finite nature, and, guiding it onward through all the conceptions of God's Being which are transcended by that Being exceeding all Name, Reason, and Knowledge, reaches beyond the farthest limits of the world and there unites us unto God Himself.[47]

Therefore, God transcended both affirmation and negation. As Pseudo-Dionysius summed it up at the end of *The Mystical Theology*, the

Ineffable One 'transcends all affirmation by being the perfect and unique Cause of all things, and transcends all negation by the pre-eminence of Its simple and absolute nature – free from any limitation and beyond them all.'[48]

This was the mystical or hidden theology behind the Scriptures – and sometimes not so hidden. Pseudo-Dionysius found it in the experience of Moses ascending Mount Sinai and finally entering 'the Darkness of Unknowing wherein he renounces all the apprehensions of his understanding and is enwrapped in that which is wholly intangible and invisible.'[49] It was there also, Pseudo-Dionysius believed, in the experience of Paul, who,

> constrained by the Divine Yearning, and having received a share in its ecstatic power, says, with inspired utterance, 'I live, and yet not I but Christ liveth in me': true Sweetheart that he was and (as he says himself) being beside himself unto God, and not possessing his own life but possessing and loving the life of Him for Whom he yearned.[50]

As with Augustine, there was with Pseudo-Dionysius a weaving together of the intellectual path to God with the affective and emotional path. In Augustine, the pre-eminence was given to the affective. The influence of Augustine, in combination with a reading of the Old Testament's Song of Solomon as an allegory of the love between God and the soul and an emphasis on the love of God focused on the crucified Christ, ensured the pre-eminence of a mysticism of love in Western theology (see Plate 20).

In Pseudo-Dionysius, however, while the affective element was present, the intellectual apprehension of God (albeit through 'unknowing') dominated. Thus, when in the twelfth century Western theology began creatively to absorb the Christianised Neoplatonism of Pseudo-Dionysius, it went down two paths. On the one hand, in keeping with the emphasis on love in the West, Pseudo-Dionysius was reinterpreted as a mystic in whom love was dominant. On the other hand, inspired by Pseudo-Dionysius, there developed in the West a tradition of intellectual mysticism.

As exemplary of the former trend, we can take the anonymous fourteenth-century English translation of Pseudo-Dionysius's *The Mystical Theology* entitled *Denis's Hidden Theology* along with *The Cloud of Unknowing* by the same author. In the former, love transcended knowing, and the darkness of unknowing beyond knowing was now an experience of divine affection. Here, Pseudo-Dionysius's stage of unknowing was entered into by love. After being detached from the activities of the mind, 'Moses, *exercising his affection alone* [...] entered by himself into the darkness of unknowing, the darkness which is truly hidden.'[51] So only when both perceptions and ideas were done away with, can you 'be carried up *in your affection and above your understanding* to the Substance beyond all substances, the radiance of the divine darkness.'[52] Thus, God was to be mystically apprehended not in the *intellectual* part of the soul but in its higher, *affective* part. In *The Cloud of Unknowing*, we read: 'By love he [God] can be thought and held but by thinking never.' Thinking had to be transcended and covered

> with a cloud of forgetting. And you are to step over it resolutely and eagerly, with a devout and kindling love, and try to penetrate that darkness above you. Strike that thick cloud of unknowing with the sharp dart of longing love.[53]

The mysticism of love in the Western tradition was Christocentric and Trinitarian. And it endorsed the view that union with God was not so much the consequence of the mystic's own strenuous efforts as, in the final analysis, the result of God's grace. Thus, for example, we find in that most influential of English mystical texts, *The Scale of Perfection* by Walter Hilton (d.1396), a Pseudo-Dionysian framework for the return to the divine, now dominated by the union between God and the soul in love and completely Christianised:

> The third degree of contemplation, which is the highest attainable in this life, consists of both knowledge and love; that is, in knowing God and loving him perfectly. This is achieved when the soul is

restored to the likeness of Jesus and is filled with all virtues. It is then endowed with grace, detached from all earthly and carnal affections, and from all unprofitable thoughts and considerations of created things, and is caught up out of its bodily senses. The grace of God then illumines the mind to see all truth – that is, God – and spiritual things in him with a soft, sweet, burning love. So perfectly is this effected that for a while the soul becomes united to God in an ecstasy of love, and is conformed to the likeness of the Trinity [...] whenever a soul is united to God in this ecstasy of love, then God and the soul are no longer two but one: not indeed in nature but in spirit. In this union, a true marriage is made between God and the soul which shall never be broken.[54]

In this passage, Hilton was at pains to emphasise that, as in the act of human sexual union, although the two became one, yet they were so only for the time of the experience and were not *essentially* so. Thus, within the mysticism of love, the experience was of a oneness that was nevertheless a twoness. This reinforced the theological impossibility of an assertion of *actual* oneness in essence between God and the individual self, even though the divine unity could be experienced at the depths of the soul. This was the consequence of the fundamental Christian doctrine that God, as the creator of the universe *ex nihilo*, was ultimately transcendent to his creation.

The discourse of 'spiritual marriage' also reflected the fact that mystical union between God and the soul could cross into the zone where God became the object of sexual desire. Particularly among female mystics, the union between God and the soul was both in the depths of the soul *and* in the body – a love-making that was both spiritual and physical (see Plates 21, 22). Thus, for example, the thirteenth-century mystic Hadewijch of Antwerp wrote of her vision of Christ while in church at dawn on Pentecost Sunday:

With that he came in the form and clothing of a Man, as he was on the day when he gave us his body for the first time; looking like a

human being and a man, wonderful and beautiful, and with glorious
face. He came to me as humbly as anyone who belongs to another.
Then he gave himself to me in the form of a sacrament […] After
that he came himself to me, took me entirely in his arms, and pressed
me to him; and all my members felt his full felicity, in accordance
with the desire of my heart and my humanity. So I was outwardly
satisfied and fully transported.[55]

Becoming a God

If the translation of the writings of Pseudo-Dionysius into Latin by
John Scotus Eriugena (*c.*810–*c.*877) drew Western Christianity down
one, admittedly rather bumpy, track to a mysticism of love, it flowed
down another, much smoother road to a mysticism of the intellect.
This was the consequence of the incorporation of the thought of
Pseudo-Dionysius into that of the German theologian Albert the
Great (*c.*1200–80), which flowed thence into the speculative German
mysticism of Meister Eckhart (*c.*1260–1327) and his followers Johann
Tauler (*c.*1300–61) and Henry Suso (*c.*1295–1366), as well as to the
author of the *Theologia Germanica* (late fourteenth century).[56]

While the mysticism of love held firmly to the unity-in-difference
between God and the soul, the mysticism of intellect was always
inclined towards the assertion of the substantial identity between
God and the soul at the expense of their essential difference. Even
if Eckhart was not unsympathetic to love occupying a subordinate
place on the intellectual path, his was decidedly a mysticism of the
intellect and one that appeared to express the absolute identity of the
soul with God. For both God and the soul participated in the same
'ground' (*Grunt*): '"Truly you are the hidden God" (Isaiah 45.15), in
the ground of the soul, where God's ground and the soul's ground are
one ground.'[57] This was, for Eckhart, the ultimate hidden truth behind
the surface meaning of the Scriptures. Philosophy and Scripture were
aligned with each other, for Moses, Christ and philosophy all taught
the same thing.

To come to terms with this, however, we need to turn to Eckhart's understanding of the Neoplatonic procession from and return to the One (or 'ground'). Now, according to Eckhart, emanation took place in two simultaneous processes. First, there was an inward emanation of the One in the Trinity itself. Here the One produced something the same as itself. 'This is why,' explained Eckhart, 'the formal emanation in the divine Persons is a type of boiling [*bullitio*], and thus the three Persons are simply and absolutely one.'[58] At the same time, the divine boils out of itself [*ebullitio*] through the eternal Word into the world: 'Therefore the Father speaks the Son always, in unity, and pours out in him all created things.'[59] This boiling out from the divine into the world, through his eternal Logos, the second person in the Trinity, set up the possibility for return to the One. All created things, declared Eckhart, 'are all called upon to return into whence they have flowed out. All their life and their being is a calling and a hastening back to him from whom they have issued.'[60]

The return to God mirrored that of the outflowing from God. It occurred in three stages. The first was that of practising detachment (*Abgeschiedenheit*) from the world as the highest virtue, even above humility, love and mercy. For Eckhart, 'detachment' meant to stand 'as a mountain of lead stands before a little breath of wind'.[61] Second, it was this practice of detachment that made possible the highest uniformity with God by making the soul susceptible to the divine inflowing. More specifically, detachment enabled the participation in the soul of the divine *bullitio*. As the *bullitio* occurred in the divine ground, so it could occur in the soul that shared in this ground. That is, it is within the ground of the soul that the Father gives birth to the Son and is one with the Holy Spirit that proceeds from them both.

> The Father gives birth to his Son in eternity, equal to himself [...]
> Yet I say more: He has given birth to him in my soul. Not only is
> the soul with him and he equal with it, but he is in it, and the Father
> gives his Son birth in the soul in the same way as he gives him birth
> in eternity.[62]

Putting this in a slightly different way, we can say that, for Eckhart, the Son was the true image of God. The soul was also the image of God. Thus, the image of God in the Trinity (the Son who was the divine intellect) was also substantially present in the image of God in the soul (the human intellect).

The third stage of return entailed the breaking through to the divine ground beyond even the Trinity. Thus, Eckhart declared that 'the spark in the soul' that had rejected all created things was not content with the Father, Son or Holy Spirit. Rather, it wanted nothing but the 'naked God, as he is in himself'. Not even content with 'the simple divine essence in its repose', it wanted 'to know the source of this essence, it wants to go into the simple ground, into the quiet desert, into which distinction never gazed, not the Father, nor the Son, nor the Holy Spirit'.[63] Here, the consciousness of the world, of the self and even of God was transcended in an undifferentiated Oneness where neither God nor soul could be distinguished. God and the soul were One: 'Between man and God, there is not only no distinction, there is no multiplicity either – there is nothing but one.'[64]

On 27 March 1329, Pope John XXII condemned some 28 opinions of Eckhart as heretical or dangerous. Eckhart, he declared, 'was led astray by that Father of Lies who often turns himself into an angel of light in order to replace the light of truth with a dark and gloomy cloud of the senses'.[65] At the core of the pope's condemnation was the accusation that Eckhart had closed the gap between the creator and the creature, particularly in his assertion that men could become sons of God. On the face of it, Eckhart was saying, no more than the New Testament, that the Word of God gave Christians 'power to become children of God' (John 1.12), that they were 'participants of the divine nature' (2 Pet. 1.4) and that God had destined them for 'adoption as his children through Jesus Christ' (Eph. 1.5). He was also aligned with the tradition in both Greek and Latin Christianity that God had become man in order that man might become God. Eckhart was drawing on just this tradition when he declared that there was no *essential* difference between the sonship of Christ and the sonship of the believer. That is to say, the believer was divine *by nature*. Why was Eckhart now deemed to be holding heretical opinions?

Simply put, by the time of Eckhart, the majority opinion, following Thomas Aquinas, was against the view that there was a *natural* affinity between the human and the divine. Rather, for Aquinas, the believer came to participate in God – became 'a god' – *not by nature but by grace*. Only through grace did the believer become what the Son was by nature. The soul was thus able to participate in the divine while yet retaining its created place. Participation in the divine was a process that began in this life and reached its fulfilment after death in the Beatific Vision. But it was *participation* in the divine, *not identity* with it. The gift of grace, declared Aquinas,

> surpasses every capability of created nature, since it is nothing short of a partaking of the Divine Nature, which exceeds every other nature. And thus it is impossible that any creature should cause grace. For it is as necessary that God alone should deify [*deificet*], bestowing a partaking of the Divine Nature by a participated likeness, as it is impossible that anything save fire should enkindle.[66]

With the dominance of the theology of Aquinas in Western theology from this time on, the doctrine of deification (in the strong Eckhartian sense of the identity of the soul and God) was to disappear from the mainstream, and 'deification' generally was marginalised.[67]

In contrast to its marginalised role in the Western Latin (Catholic) tradition, deification was at the centre of the Eastern Greek (Orthodox) tradition. This was a consequence of the central role that the writings of Pseudo-Dionysius played in that tradition. Following Pseudo-Dionysius, the East maintained the dominance of the notion that the knowledge of God by negation was a higher 'knowledge' (through unknowing) than that attained by affirmation. It also adopted Pseudo-Dionysius's definition of deification. Theosis (θέωσις), he had written, 'consists of being as much as possible like and in union with God.'[68] Deification became a key focus of the Greek tradition when the Greek theologian Maximus the Confessor (c.580–662) took up the idea and made it the counterpoint to the Incarnation of God in Christ. Thus, God's 'emptying' of himself into finite man made possible man's 'filling' of himself into the infinite God. This was the end that God had intended not only for humankind but for the whole of creation.[69] The likeness to God that was lost at the Fall of Adam was thus restored.

For Maximus, deification was partly the consequence of the pursuit of a life of love of God and neighbour on the part of the believer. But there was nothing natural within man that allowed for his becoming deified. Rather, it was ultimately the result of divine grace. On the return to God, Christ established in the believer an insatiable desire for himself. But there was yet one more step:

> From there he leads us finally in the supreme ascent in divine realities to the Father of lights wherein he makes us sharers in the divine nature by participating in the grace of the Spirit, through which we receive the title of God's children and become clothed entirely with the complete person who is the author of this grace, without limiting or defiling him who is Son of God by nature.[70]

God and man followed the same path, although in different directions. The Incarnation of God (without losing his divine status) in man made possible the deification of man (without losing his created status) in God. This was a unity-in-difference but not an identity between God and the soul. The divine and the human penetrated each other in the believer just as they co-inhered in Christ without becoming (as the Chalcedonian definition had it) confused, changed, divided or separated. It was a deification that also occurred liturgically in the Eucharist. In the sacrament of bread and wine, the communicants became 'gods by adoption through grace because all of God entirely fills them and leaves no part of them empty of his presence.'[71]

This unity-in-difference between God and the soul in the theology of Maximus was reinforced by his account of the mutual love between God and the soul, not merely during the return to God but at its climax.

'Love' and 'unknowing' coincided and the affective and the intellectual paths were interwoven. Thus, for example, Maximus outlined the stages in the return to God in terms of the metaphor of the Sabbath. In the first stage, 'Sabbath' signified the dispassionate soul that had cast off sin through the practice of the virtues. In the next stage, the 'Sabbaths' meant the freedom of the soul that had quelled attachment to the world of the intellect. In the final stage, the 'Sabbath of Sabbaths' signified the final calm of the deified soul, which 'through an ecstasy of love has clothed it entirely in God alone, and that through mystical theology has brought it altogether to rest in God'.[72]

Maximus's greatest contribution to the understanding of God lay in this systematic alignment of deification with Incarnation. He was not the most worldly of monks, and this wasn't his greatest career move. He found himself in the middle of a theological and political brawl that was, in all senses of the word, Byzantine.[73] As a committed supporter of the Chalcedonian determination of the two natures (human and divine) in Christ, he remained determinedly in conflict with those who, while accepting the Chalcedonian definition in principle, were trying to placate the supporters of 'one nature' by declaring that, in the union of the two natures, there was only a single principle of action and 'one will'. Maximus, for his part, saw this as the thin end of a 'one nature' wedge. For him, a fully incarnate Christ must have had a fully human will. Thus, when Christ declared in the Garden of Gethsemane, 'not my will but thine be done' (Matt. 26.39; my translation), he was aligning his human will with God's will.

By 662, Maximus was virtually a lone voice speaking and a lone hand writing in support of the doctrine of two wills. He was tried in that year at Constantinople for heresy. As the two 'instruments' of his heresy, his tongue was cut out and his right hand cut off. He was exhibited thus in every part of the city and then exiled to Lazica in Roman Georgia. Maximus did not live to see his doctrine of two wills ultimately declared the orthodox position at the Third Council of Constantinople (or Sixth General Council) in 680–1: 'we hold that two natural wills [θελήματά] and principles of action [ἐνεργείας] meet in correspondence for the salvation of the human race'.[74]

Sufism

Neoplatonism also provided the intellectual framework within the Islamic tradition for the transcendent God who was also immanent. In spite of the dominance within Islam of a wholly transcendent deity who was 'wholly other' than his creation, the Neoplatonic influence within Islamic mysticism (Sufism) drove it towards, on occasion, an assertion of the identity between Allah and the depths of the self. The Persian mystics Abu Yazid al-Bistami (d.874–5 or 878–9) and Mansur al-Hallaj (c.858–922) typified this drive towards the loss of the boundary between selves and God. In the case of al-Bistami, the Neoplatonic return to the One dovetailed with Muhammad's ascent to heaven (elaborated in the Muslim tradition from Qur'ān 17.1). 'Thou must win release from thy thou-ness,' Allah informed al-Bistami, 'by following my Beloved [Muhammad].'[75] It was a path that led to undifferentiated oneness. As al-Bistami explained,

> Once He raised me up and stationed me before Him, and said to me, 'O Abū Yazīd, truly My creation desire to see thee.' I said, 'Adorn me in Thy Unity, and clothe me in Thy Selfhood, and raise me up to Thy Oneness, so that when thy creation see me they will say, We have seen Thee: and Thou wilt be That, and I shall not be there at all.'[76]

This was the experience that was later to be formalised in the doctrine of annihilation (*fanā'*).

Al-Bistami's 'Glory be to me, how great is my glory' was mirrored in al-Hallaj's 'I am the truth'. Speaking of God in the 'first person' appeared to go well beyond the annihilation of the self in God and to be a declaration of one's own divine status. Al-Hallaj's theology entailed a radical version of the idea that God created man in his own image, that is, God infused his divine spirit into man. This was why God had ordered the angels to 'Prostrate yourselves before Adam' (Qur'ān 2.34). This was not so much the deification of man by his participating in God but deification of man through God's participating in him. God and man were thus essentially identical, according to al-Hallaj:

Glory be to Him whose Humanity manifested
The secret of His piercing Divinity's radiance
And who then appeared openly in his creation
In the form of the eater and the drinker.[77]

To many orthodox Muslims, this looked more like the despised
Christian doctrine of the Incarnation than they could ever be comfort-
able with. Although al-Hallaj would defend himself on the grounds
that he was speaking only of the permeation of the beloved (God)
in the lover (al-Hallaj) and their intimate communion, he was tried
for 'incarnationism' (among other things) in Baghdad in 922. He
was whipped, crucified, beheaded and cremated, and his ashes were
scattered in the River Tigris. This was a pretty clear indication (to say
the least) that the emphasis on the transcendence of God in Islam
rendered a mysticism of essential identity well beyond the borders of
an acceptable orthodoxy.

A compromise was to be found in the unity-in-difference between
God and the self in the Persian Muhammad al-Ghazali (c.1058–1111).
Here the transcendent God of the Qur'ān was aligned with the immanent God of the philosophers. Al-Ghazali was fully aware of the
tradition of the identity of the soul and God, particularly as it was
expressed by both al-Bastami and al-Hallaj. Such mystics, he declared,
having attained a state of undifferentiated oneness with God,

> became intoxicated with such an intoxication that the ruling author-
> ity of their rational faculty is overthrown. Hence, one of them says,
> 'I am the Real!' Another, 'Glory be to me! How great is my station!'
> and still another, 'There is nothing in my robe but God!'[78]

However, that the *experience* was one of undifferentiated unity did
not entail, for al-Ghazali, the conclusion that there was a *real and
essential* identity between the self and God. Rather, he suggested
that, just as the words of lovers when in a state of drunkenness
should be hidden away and not made public, so when the 'drunken'
ecstasy of the mystics abated and reason was restored, they knew

that it was not actual identity but merely a semblance of it, 'like the words of the lover during a state of extreme passionate love: "I am He whom I love, and He whom I love is I."' 'In relation to the one immersed in it,' he went on to say, 'this state is called "unification" [*ittiḥād*, identification], according to the language of metaphor, or [it] is called "declaring God's unity" [*tauḥīd*, divine unity], according to the language of reality.'[79]

Thus, while there may have been, at the heights of experiencing God, a loss of the consciousness of the self, there was no real and essential identity. Rather, the mystics were participating in the eternal divine ground of being from which all impermanent things have arisen. This relationship of unity-in-difference between God and the soul mirrored that between God and the rest of the universe. The many were identical with the One insofar as He was the ultimate source of their being, yet different from him insofar as they had (really) emanated from him. Mystics see, he wrote,

> that there is none in existence save God and that 'Everything is perishing except His face' [Qur'ān 28.88] [...] when the essence of anything other than He is considered in respect of its own essence, it is sheer nonexistence. But when it is viewed in respect of the 'face' to which existence flows forth from the First, the Real, then it is seen as existing not in itself but through the face adjacent to its Giver of Existence. Hence the only existent is the Face of God.[80]

In short, everything in the hierarchy of being was both God and not God. It was God insofar as it existed because it participated in his being. It was not God insofar as, in itself, it had no claim on existence.

Within the Islamic tradition, as in the Christian, the mysticism of the intellect was often interwoven with the mysticism of love, nowhere more so than in the Persian poet and philosopher Jalal al-Din Rumi (1207–73). In the prose and poetry of Rumi, the identity of the self and God became the unity-in-difference between them. The annihilation of the self (*fanā'*) in God was transposed into the dissolution of the lover in the beloved. Thus, for example:

I have been so annihilated within thee that I am full of thee from head to foot. Nothing is left of my own sweet existence but the name. In my existence, oh sweet one, is naught but thee. I have been annihilated like vinegar in an ocean of honey.[81]

This is, in the terms that we have been using, a translation of the central statement of Islamic monotheism – 'there is no God but God' – into the Platonic terms of 'there is no reality but the Real'. This enabled a different reading of the apparent claim of al-Hallaj that *he* was divine. This was not al-Hallaj who was speaking but God in him, who was saying 'I am God'. Thus, wrote Rumi, 'Other than He [God], nothing else existed. Ḥallāj had been annihilated, so those were the words of God.'[82] Thus did the transcendent God manifest himself in the depths of the self:

> O my soul, I searched from end to end: I saw in thee naught
> > save the Beloved;
> Call me not infidel, O my soul, if I say that thou thyself art He.[83]

Kabbalah

The focus of Christian mysticism was the revelation of God in the figure of Christ. In contrast, the focus of Islamic mysticism was the revelation of God in the words of the Qur'ān. So too in Jewish mysticism, the God discovered at the depths of the self was the God who had revealed himself in the words of the Torah (the first five books of the Hebrew Bible). In Christian and Islamic mysticism, Neoplatonism provided the framework for the mystical reading of Christ and the Qur'ān respectively. So too, in Jewish mysticism, the Jewish Scriptures were read through Neoplatonic glasses. Like much Christian and Islamic mysticism in the Neoplatonic register, Jewish mysticism, from the time of the Castilian Kabbalah in late thirteenth-century Spain, was an attempt to explain the existence of the many in the light of their origin in the One, while at the same time attending to the relation of the impersonal One to the personal God of the Torah.

At the core of the Kabbalah was the doctrine of emanation. Unlike the Neoplatonic account of emanation as proceeding from the One to the world, Kabbalistic emanation (analogously to that in Meister Eckhart) took place not only from the One into the world but also within the ultimate reality itself. Thus, the ultimately real, *Ein Sof* (the Endless), formed the will to reveal itself to us in ten emanations (*sefirot*) (see Plate 23). In the foundational Kabbalah commentary on the Torah, the late thirteenth-century *Sefer ha-zohar* (Book of Radiance), known as the *Zohar*, we read:

> In the beginning, when the will of the King [*Ein Sof*] began to take effect, he engraved signs [which become the *sefirot*] into the divine aura. A dark flame sprang forth from the innermost recess of the mystery of the Infinite, *En Sof*, like a fog which forms out of the formless.[84]

This dark flame was the first *sefirah*, the crown or *Keter*, the transformation of the fullness of being into nothingness. It was from this nothingness that the remaining nine *sefirot* (and the world) gradually emerged. Thus was the Neoplatonic doctrine of emanation aligned with the doctrine of God's creating out of nothing.

Out of *Keter* emerged *Hokhmah*, the primal point of real existence, identified with the divine wisdom. The wisdom or inner mind of God then brought forth *Binah*, or understanding. *Binah* and *Hokhmah* also represented the female and male polarities within the divine. This polarity in the divine was reflected in the creation of each human soul in accord with Genesis 1.27: 'In the image of God he created them; male and female he created them.' For its part, *Binah* functioned as the womb out of which flowed the remaining seven *sefirot* of the divine persona. Firstly, there emerged *Hesed*, the grace or love of God, followed by its opposite, *Gevurah*, the aspect of the divine persona before which we tremble – the judgement and wrath of God. Evil was born out of *Gevurah*, a dark and negative principle within God. Evil within the world therefore arose, not independently of the divine, but as the result of an imbalance within the divine itself.

At the very centre of the world of the *sefirot*, there emerged out of both *Hesed* and *Gevurah* the sixth *sefirah*, *Tif'eret* (Beauty). It represented the proper balance of *Hesed* and *Gevurah* within the personal God of the Bible. The personal God of the Bible was thus placed below the impersonal absolute out of which everything arose. This personal God also 'embodied' the opposing and conflicting attributes within the transcendent biblical God – the divine mercy and the divine judgement that calls forth in us both fear and love. This was the personal God whom we are called upon to imitate. The struggle within the divine to appropriately balance love and wrath, mercy and justice, was reflected both within the universe as a whole and within human lives. The next two *sefirot*, *Hod* (Splendour) and *Netsah* (Endurance), the sources of prophecy, were channels for the divine energies into the ninth, *Yesod* (Foundation).

Yesod represented the coming together of all the divine (male) energies above it to be united with the final (female) *sefirah*, *Malkhut* or *Shekhinah*, the union of the celestial bridegroom with the celestial bride. As Gershom Scholem sums it up:

> The ninth Sefirah, *Yesod*, out of which all of the higher Sefiroth
> [...] flow into the Shekinah, is interpreted as the procreative life
> force dynamically active in the universe. Out of the hidden depth
> of this Sefirah the divine life overflows in the act of mystical
> procreation.[85]

The same sefirotic structure was replicated within the human soul, as it was in the Torah and in the world more generally. More broadly, it was the sefirotic structure within the self that enabled the return of self to the God within the soul. Thus, the Kabbalist's experience of the return to the divine followed the sefirotic path. The love between the divine bridegroom (*Yesod*) and the divine bride (*Shekhinah*) also represented the love between God and the individual within the soul. As in Islamic and Christian mysticism, the mysticism of love was interwoven with the mysticism of the intellect. 'Attachment to God, for the *Zohar*,' writes Arthur Green,

> is erotic attachment, whether referring to the kabbalist's own attach-
> ment to God by means of Torah, to *Shekinah*'s link to the upper
> 'male' *sefirot* as God's bride, or in the rare passages where Moses
> becomes the kabbalistic hero and himself weds *Shekinah*, entering
> the Godhead in the male role. The contemplative and erotic aspects
> of attachment to God are just different ways of depicting the same
> reality, quite wholly inseparable from one another.[86]

The tenth *sefirah*, *Shekhinah*, was the passive receptacle of all the male energies above her. But she also gave birth to all the worlds below and was immanently present within them. Perhaps better, we might say, the story of creation told in the first chapter of Genesis was a story about both the relationship between the one and the many within God, a story about the structure of the soul and simultaneously a story about the structure of the world. The creation of man and the world was nothing but the external manifestation of that which occurred within God himself. The physical emanation of the cosmos as a whole mirrored the spiritual emanation of the divine. The Kabbalist mystic thus sought to align himself with the divine flow within himself and within nature more generally, since both were ultimately nothing but processes within the life of God. As Moses de León (*c.*1240–1305), one of the authors of the *Zohar*, put it,

> Everything is linked with everything else down to the lowest ring
> on the chain, and the true essence of God is above as well as below,
> in the heavens and on the earth, and nothing exists outside Him.
> And this is what the sages mean when they say: When God gave
> the Torah to Israel, He opened the seven heavens to them, and they
> saw that nothing was there in reality but His Glory; He opened the
> seven worlds to them and they saw that nothing was there but His
> Glory; he opened the seven abysses before their eyes, and they saw
> that nothing was there but His Glory. Meditate on these things and

you will understand that God's essence is linked and connected with
all worlds, and that all forms of existence are linked and connected
with each other, but derived from His existence and essence.[87]

In sum, we might say that the Kabbalah represents the most complete
attempt to synthesise the God of the philosophers with the God of
the Bible and the transcendent with the immanent divine. It did so
in terms of the emanation of the impersonal Neoplatonic One into
the personal God of the Torah, in terms of the relationship between
the ultimate reality that cannot be known (*Ein Sof*) and the God
who is manifested in the *sefirot*, in terms of the contest between the
opposing and conflicting attributes within the biblical God – love and
judgement, mercy and wrath, male and female – and finally in terms
of the emanating of the transcendent God into the self and the world.

Judaism, Christianity and Islam were as one in trying to hold
together a God who was both personal and impersonal. They were
also as one in attempting to align a God who created the world out of
nothing with a God who emanated it out of himself. This was no
intellectually easy task, not least because the God who created out of
nothing was not immanent within his creation, whereas the God who
emanated was. Nevertheless, those who declared for both God the
creator and God the emanator recognised that both were transcendent
to the world, even if the latter was also immanent within it. In the
Neoplatonic understanding of emanation, the many were ultimately
dependent on the One out of whom they arose and not the One upon
the many.

Even though immanent within the world, the One nevertheless
remained transcendent to it. Within the orthodoxy of the mystical
traditions of Judaism, Christianity and Islam, the paradox of the One
and the many held firm. It was not to be resolved by the collapse of
the One into the many. This would have meant the identification of
God with the world and the denial of God's genuine transcendence
to it. It was tantamount to asserting, 'No world and therefore *really*
no God.' Nor was it to be explained by the absorption of the many
into the One. This would have meant the identification of the world

with God and the denial of the reality of the many apart from God. It was tantamount to asserting, 'God only and therefore *really* no world.' That God was in all things did not mean that all things were in God. Thus, the paradoxical nature of the divine as both One and many was necessary both to the declaration of the transcendent reality of the One and the assertion of the One's (*real* and not merely *illusory*) immanent presence in the many.

4

The God of Reason and Revelation

The fool hath said in his heart, There is no God.

Psalm 53.1 (KJV)

Guides to the perplexing –
Maimonides, Averroes and Aquinas

In Montpellier in December 1232, the French Inquisition burnt *Guide for the Perplexed*. This was the Jewish philosopher Moses Maimonides's (*c.*1138–1204) attempt to reconcile reason and revelation in Judaism. That it was burnt by Christian Dominicans is no surprise. They were always on the hunt for heresy. What was perhaps surprising was that, among those cheering its reduction to ashes were his fellow Jewish religionists – conservative rabbis and proto-Kabbalists. Indeed, his work had been denounced to the Inquisition by his Jewish opponents.[1]

Moses Maimonides was perhaps the greatest philosopher of medieval Judaism (see Plate 24). He was to medieval Judaism what the Christian Thomas Aquinas was to medieval Christianity, and the Muslim Averroes, also known as Ibn Rushd (1126–98), to medieval Islam. All three saw the solution to the problem of the relationship between reason and revelation as the fulcrum of their philosophies and their faiths. In short, all sought an answer to the question, 'What has Athens to do with Jerusalem (or Mecca)?' So all three attempted to align reason with the Hebrew, Christian and Islamic Scriptures, respectively. And all of them came up with distinctively different answers.

Why was it that Maimonides's *Guide for the Perplexed* so incensed his fellow Jews? Simply put, it was because it was believed that Maimonides, in his emphasis on reason, was devaluing the centrality

of Scripture and its traditional interpretation and thereby marginalising
its literal meaning. They were convinced that he was endorsing the view
that the teachings of the Scripture were to be interpreted allegorically
when necessary and that the religious practices endorsed by Scripture
were nothing but custom and not divine law.

There was a fair bit of truth in these accusations. For Maimonides
did privilege reason as the ultimate arbiter of truth. The perplexed
whom Maimonides had in mind was the religious man who, convinced
of the supremacy of reason, was 'lost in perplexity and anxiety' for
'Human reason has attracted him to abide within its sphere', and
who 'finds it difficult to accept as correct the teaching based on the
literal interpretation of the Law'.[2] Moreover, to the severe irritation of
the conservatives who saw the rabbis as the final religious authority,
Maimonides was claiming that the philosopher was the ultimate
authority in matters spiritual.

For Maimonides, although reason and revelation were diverse
sources of truth, truth was a unity. Thus, where there was a conflict
between reason and revelation, this conflict could only be an *apparent*
one and not a *real* one. The conflict could be resolved in either of two
ways. First, it could be resolved by finding the deeper truth in Scripture
that aligned with undoubted philosophical truth. Thus, for example,
Maimonides noted that men had been led to believe that God had a
body as a consequence of the biblical statement that man was made in
the image of God (Gen. 1.26). However, along with the philosophical
truth that God exists, it was also a matter of philosophical truth that
God was an incorporeal spiritual being. Thus, argued Maimonides,
all references to God's bodily features should be reinterpreted in line
with the philosophical truth of his incorporeality. More broadly, any
positive attributes ascribed to God in the Bible should not be taken at
face value. They are not telling us how God really is but merely how
he has affected us.[3]

Along with incorporeality, the unity of God was also a matter
of philosophical certainty. This meant for Maimonides that, since
God admitted of no multiplicity, it could not be said that he had any
attributes at all. In fact, it meant that virtually nothing could be said

about God. This was a form of the way of unknowing or negation that he had inherited from the Neoplatonic tradition. That said (or unsaid, actually), this doctrine of the unity of God did provide for Maimonides a neat opportunity to stick the intellectual knife into Christianity. The doctrine of the unity of God, he wrote, ruled out 'the doctrine of the Christians, who say that He is one and He is three, and that the three are one'.[4]

When philosophical truth was not certain, the apparent conflict between reason and revelation had to be resolved in a different way. According to Maimonides, had Aristotle been able convincingly to demonstrate the eternity of the world, he would have given the biblical account of creation an allegorical reading. However, Maimonides did not accept that the Aristotelian argument for the eternity of the universe was any better than its philosophical opposite.[5] So, in this case, he was able to endorse the general truth of the scriptural account that God was the creator of the universe.[6]

In sum, where there was philosophical certainty, reason trumped revelation and Scripture needed to be reinterpreted in the light of it. Only where there was no *philosophically certain* truth in conflict with revelation could revelation be endorsed. However that may be, there were religious truths beyond those capable of philosophical certainty and therefore a *full* understanding of truth required revelation. As Joseph Buijs neatly puts it: 'Faith necessarily relies on reason for an adequate justification and reason necessarily relies on faith for comprehensive understanding.'[7]

What, then, were the truths of reason and of revelation according to Maimonides? In a number of his works, Maimonides produced a list of 13 principles which he believed all Jews should endorse. These were as follows: (1) the existence of God; (2) the unity of God; (3) the incorporeality of God; (4) the eternity of God; (5) the prohibition of idolatry; (6) the validity of prophecy; (7) the superiority of the prophecy of Moses; (8) the divine origin of the Jewish Law, written and oral; (9) the eternal truth of the Law; (10) God's knowledge of human deeds; (11) rewards and punishments of the good and the wicked; (12) the coming of the Messiah; and (13) the resurrection of the dead.

The first five of these were to be accepted by the masses and philosophers alike. These were intended to impart correct philosophical
knowledge about God. Correct knowledge about God made salvation
possible for all. Thus, immortality would not be restricted to merely
a small intellectual elite. Principles six to nine provided a guarantee
for revelation in general and especially for God's revelation to Moses.
The remaining principles were directed at the masses in particular.
While Maimonides believed that the philosophical elite would do
the good for its own sake, the last four principles presumed that
the masses would not – these were principles that drove virtuous
behaviour in the light of its consequences. Thus, men would do the
good if they believed that God had knowledge of their deeds and that
he would reward or punish them on the basis of their righteousness
or wickedness when the Messiah came and when they arose from
the dead.[8]

In sum, for Maimonides, reason and revelation were complementary
to each other. On the one hand, each was limited and each recognised
the capacity for truth in the other. On the other hand, since truth was
unified, the truth of one could not contradict the other and, where
contradiction occurred, revelation gave way. In the case of Thomas
Aquinas, as we will see, the truth of revelation could be contrary to
reason and then reason gave way to revelation. For Averroes, the reverse
was the case, and where there was conflict between the two, revelation
gave way to reason.

From his grounding in the Neoplatonic tradition, Averroes, like
Maimonides, accepted the unity of truth. That is to say, the truths that
derived from reason were in accord (in some sense of 'accord') with
those derived from revelation and vice versa: 'the Muslim community
know definitely that demonstrative study does not lead to [conclusions]
conflicting with what Scripture has given us.'[9] Thus, indeed, only on
the presumption that the truths of philosophy would not (and could
not) conflict with those of the Qur'ān were the philosophers of Islam
able to appease the opposition of the theologians. Moreover, Averroes
found justification for the pursuit of philosophy in the Qur'ān itself.
'That the Law summons to reflection on beings, and the pursuit of

knowledge about them, by the intellect,' he wrote, 'is clear from several verses of the Book of God.'[10]

Nevertheless, Averroes could not but recognise that truths generated by the use of reason alone would, on some occasions, conflict with those of revelation. In these cases, priority was given to the philosophical, and Scripture needed to be reinterpreted in order to remove its apparent conflict with reason. Averroes argued that, in these instances, Scripture needed to be read *allegorically* in an 'extension of the significance of an expression from real to metaphorical significance' – in other words, from the literal to the philosophical.[11] While the surface meaning of the text may be adequate for the ordinary believer, it may be intellectually inadequate for the educated and, as Buijs remarks, 'an allegorical or hidden meaning, uncovered only by the demonstrative reasoning intelligible to philosophers, provides a more adequate understanding.'[12]

The trick lay in determining which texts required a philosophical reading. When the philosophical reading of the Quranic text was in accord with its literal reading, there was no need to seek a deeper meaning. Thus, for example, the doctrine of the unity of God was verified by philosophy and Scripture. But where there was a conflict between philosophical certainty and the text of the Qur'ān, then the philosopher was obliged to seek its allegorical or hidden meaning. Thus, for example, references in the Qur'ān to the body of God, while they can be taken literally by the ordinary believer, need to be read by the philosopher in a way compatible with his incorporeality.

So reason had the ultimate priority. It was reason that determined whether a text was to be interpreted allegorically, what the interpretation was and, where philosophy could not be determinative, which truths were to be taken as revelatory. This worked well for philosophers within the Sunni Islamic tradition. Unlike Shi'i Islam, in which doctrinal authority was vested in the spiritual head of the community, the Imam, there was no such authority in Sunni Islam. It was into this gap in doctrinal authority that the philosophers could and did step – not surprisingly perhaps, for it was an elitist view of the philosopher that ultimately had its roots in Plato's *Republic*. What it meant was that the philosophers had the final say on matters of doctrine. They were the people, Averroes claimed, who were described in the Qur'ān as 'the ones firmly grounded in knowledge' (3.7).

There were, however, certain limits upon philosophical freedom. The philosopher could neither introduce new doctrines nor reject any already determined. And he was obliged, like everyone else, to subscribe to those doctrines that were indispensable to salvation as they were laid out in the Qur'ān. These were as follows (at least, according to Averroes): (1) the existence of God as creator and sustainer of the world; (2) the unity of God; (3) the divine attributes of knowledge, life, power, volition, hearing, seeing and talking; (4) the perfection of God such that all attributes pertain to him in a pre-eminent way; (5) the creation of the world by God; (6) the validity of prophecy; (7) the divine justice; and (8) resurrection or survival after death.[13] Yet, even here, there was plenty of intellectual space for philosophical argument. On the issue of creation, for example, while it could not be disputed that God created the world, there was room to argue whether he had done so *ex nihilo* and in time. On the issue of the afterlife, philosophers could agree to disagree on whether to take the texts 'in their apparent meaning or interpret them allegorically'.[14] On the issue of the divine attributes, while there was no doubt that God had these attributes, there was plenty of intellectual work to be done on how the divine attributes differed from their equivalent human ones.

Averroes was to have little influence in later Muslim intellectual culture. But he was recognised as a philosopher of the first importance by subsequent Jewish and Christian scholars. This was not least because the Platonic tradition to which all three traditions were heir enabled a common philosophical language in spite of the enormous differences between their respective theologies. But it was also because both Jewish and Christian scholars were indebted to an Islamic philosophical tradition that, like Christianity, from an early period in its history recognised the desirability of engaging with the Greek philosophical tradition. Thus, when in the thirteenth century Thomas Aquinas turned to the issue of the relation between revelation and reason, he did so not only with a history of Christian Platonism to draw upon, but also with an Islamic philosophical tradition that had put Plato's pupil Aristotle (384–322 BCE) at the centre of their Islamic Platonism. The Aristotelian torch was lit in the West by the Islamic flame. It is not a little ironic that the Christian medieval philosophy known as scholasticism, one that attempted to harmonise an Aristotelianised Platonism with Christian revelation, owed much to a religious tradition that, in the very age of the Crusades, the Christian West was determinedly trying to destroy (see Plate 25).

Averroes gave to reason the priority over faith. Thomas Aquinas, perhaps directly rebutting Averroes, did the opposite. A person may err in matters of faith, declared Aquinas, 'if he makes reason precede faith, instead of faith precede reason, as when someone is willing to believe only what he can discover by reason. It should in fact be just the opposite.'[15] This meant that, unlike for Averroes, for Aquinas there were religious truths that lay beyond reason and were independent of it. It meant too that there were religious truths that might be contrary to reason. Thus, for example, that God existed was a truth determinable by reason alone, but that God was three persons in one God, or that God became man, were truths that both lay beyond reason and were contrary to it. This was perhaps an inevitable move for a tradition that had the rational paradoxes of the Incarnation and the Trinity as its defining features. So, we might say, although truth had a unity, there were different ways to it.

More generally, and perhaps most importantly, against the tendency among his more Aristotelian colleagues to hold that philosophy was sufficient for salvation, Aquinas was making a case for its insufficiency in the light of the truths of revelation. Thus, Aquinas began that work for which he is most renowned, the *Summa theologiae* (Summary of theology), with a rebuttal of the argument that, apart from philosophy (*philosophicas disciplinas*), there was no need of any further knowledge. On the contrary, declared Aquinas: 'Although those things which are beyond man's knowledge may not be sought for by man through his reason, nevertheless, once they are revealed by God, they must be accepted by faith.'[16] Ironically (perhaps for us, if not for Aquinas), it was Scripture that gave us the confidence that reason could be trusted

to give us knowledge of God by reason alone. Aquinas quoted the
New Testament to this effect: 'The invisible things of Him are clearly
seen, being understood by the things that are made' (Rom. 1.20). For
Aquinas, it was always a case of faith seeking understanding.

Be that as it may, Aquinas lived in a world that, it was believed,
was shot through with the supernatural. Unlike the modern Western
world, where God's *non-existence* is more likely to be taken as self-evident, Aquinas's was pervaded by the divine and the spiritual. It was
a context in which the existence of God appeared as self-evident and
undeniable to many not least because, as Aquinas pointed out, it had
the authority of the Greek theologian John of Damascus (676–749)
behind it: 'as Damascene says, "the knowledge of God is naturally
implanted in all."'[17] Thus, the first issue that Aquinas tackled was
'Whether the existence of God was self-evident'. For Aquinas, however, in spite of the Damascene tradition, the existence of God was
not self-evident. That anyone *could* deny the existence of God without
being absurd (although only a fool *would* do so – see Psalms 53.1)
meant that his existence was *not* self-evident to everyone and therefore
not self-evident at all. Thus, God's existence could not be assumed,
but rather was *in need* of demonstration. On the other hand, granted
that Aquinas did not think God's existence self-evident, this did not
mean that it was a matter only of supernatural revelation and thus
a matter of faith rather than a matter of reason. For God's existence
could, he argued, be rationally demonstrated. '[It] can be proved,' he
said, 'in five ways.'[18]

From world to God

In attempting to prove the existence of God, Aquinas was drawing on
the philosophy of Aristotle, the pupil of Plato. Aristotle was a believer
in God. Thus, in book 12 of his *Metaphysics*, he wrote:

> God is an eternal and most excellent living being, so that con-
> tinuous and eternal life and duration belong to him [...] it is

without parts and indivisible; for it is moving things throughout an infinite time [...] and plainly it does not change; for change would be for the worse [...] its life is like the best that we can enjoy [...] and its contemplation is of all things the most pleasant and the best.[19]

Simply put, God was, for Aristotle, why the world was as it was – the end of the chain of reason. Beyond God, there was no need of further explanation.

Aquinas followed along the same path as Aristotle – from a universe whose existence did not explain itself to a God whose existence was not in need of explanation. Thus, in his first three ways, Aquinas began from the fact that there are things that are in motion (or change), things that are effects and things that are and eventually will not be. In each case, some other thing is the mover, cause or originator of that which is moved, caused or is. This chain of movements, causes and originators cannot go to infinity. Therefore, there is a first Mover, itself unmoved, that begins the chain of movement, a first Cause, itself uncaused, that begins the chain of causes, a first Being, itself uncreated (and that cannot not be), that begins the chain of things that come to be. This first Mover, first Cause and first Being, Aquinas's fourth argument sets out to show, has to be what everyone understands as God.[20]

The first three ways of Aquinas, generally known as cosmological arguments, can be read as referring to one of two things: a chain of movements, causes or things going back in time, or a chain referring to the present moment. In the former case, the argument aligns with the doctrine of God as creator of the universe. In the latter case, it aligns with the doctrine of God as sustainer and maintainer of the universe.

The temporal form of the argument was put forward by the little-known Alexandrian theologian John Philoponus (*c.*490–*c.*570). His overall theological concern was to support the doctrine of God as a creator *ex nihilo* and creation as an event that had a beginning in time. To this end, against Aristotle's argument for the eternity of the universe, he argued that the notion of an infinite regress in time was impossible.²¹ The importance of Philoponus lies in the fact that his arguments against the eternity of the universe became a key source of both Muslim and Jewish cosmological arguments for the existence of a creator God.

The classical formulation of the Islamic cosmological argument can be found in the Persian philosopher Muhammad al-Ghazali, whom we met in Chapter 3 resisting the mystical identity between God and the soul. He gave the following summary of the argument:

> there are temporal phenomena in the world. And some other phe-nomena are the causes of those phenomena. It is impossible [...] that the series should go on *ad infinitum* [...] So if there is a limit at which the series of temporal phenomena stops, let this limit be called the Eternal.²²

Similarly, within Jewish philosophy, the cosmological argument was the standard one. And, as in Islamic philosophy, it was construed tem-porally. Thus, for example, the father of medieval Jewish philosophy, Saadia ben Joseph (882–942), argued from the absurdity of Aristotle's notion of infinite time, maintaining that there must have been a time when the universe (and time) began. He then argued that, because there was a beginning and because the universe cannot have created itself, there must have been a God who brought it into being.²³ Ironically, perhaps, the cosmological argument to God from the impossibility of an infinite temporal regress came from Philoponus via Islamic philos-ophy back into Christian philosophy with the Franciscan theologian Bonaventure (1221–74). For, following the Islamic philosophers, it was Bonaventure who affirmed what Aquinas denied – that the world had a beginning and that it was not eternal could, he argued, be known by reason independently of faith.

Aquinas's proofs for the existence of God did not depend on the notion that an infinite regress in time was impossible. On the contrary, Aquinas did not accept that it could be rationally shown that there was a time when the world began. That the world did not always exist, and therefore that there was a moment when it was created by God, was a matter not of reason but of revelation: 'By faith alone do we hold, and by no demonstration can it be proved, that the world did not always exist.'[24]

This means that Aquinas was not attempting to prove the existence of God by arguing that the chain of causes backwards in time had to stop somewhere. Rather, the chain of causes that interested Aquinas was not one going back in time but one *in the present.* He was drawing attention to a closed system of interlocking causes each depending *right now* on the one *beyond* it (not *before* it). However, the entire system and its properties (the universe) did not explain itself. Thus, according to Aquinas, if the universe itself were to have an ultimate explanation, it could only do so by reference to something outside it *in the here and now* whose existence required no further explanation. And that, said Aquinas, was what we mean by 'God'.

Thus, for Aquinas, while faith established that God had created the world at *one* point in time, reason could determine that, at *any and every* point in time, God was the sustainer and maintainer of it, a being upon whom the whole and all of its parts ultimately depended. This was a being the existence of whom did not depend upon anything else. That is, God's existence was necessary – he *had to exist.* As such, God was an eternal being and, since time only began at the time of the creation of the universe, God's eternity was timeless.

To Aquinas, therefore, God was a being whose existence did not depend on the existence of anything else. From the perspective of belief in God, there was, on the face of it, little problematic in going from the fact that the universe was not self-explanatory to a God upon whom the universe depended and a God whose existence was self-explanatory. Here, reason was illuminating faith. To be sure, Aquinas's argument was not compelling to an unbeliever. Nevertheless, he was in effect confronting his readers with an ultimate choice: either the universe was just there and had no ultimate meaning, and that's all there was to it (as Bertrand Russell and like-minded atheists would have it), or there was a solution to the problem of why there was something rather than nothing, as a result of which the universe had a meaning. This was a key moment in the history of God, for it demonstrated that, outside faith, there was no *compelling reason* to believe that God existed. It was very much a toss of the coin.

That said, there might be matters other than reason that would dispose us to believe in God rather than not. This was the issue that the French philosopher Blaise Pascal (1623–62) took up in his *Pensées*. On the question of the existence of God or its opposite, Pascal declared: 'Reason cannot make you choose either, reason cannot prove either wrong.'[25] There were not sufficient signs of a divinity in the world to merit belief and too many to deny him. Still, a choice had to be made and, at the far end, 'a coin is being spun which will come down heads or tails.'[26] It was a matter of weighing the gain against the loss in betting that God existed, of determining on which side of the coin the most happiness was to be gained. Thus, if you call heads that God exists, 'if you win you win everything, if you lose you lose nothing. Do not hesitate then; wager that he does exist.'[27] In short, in belief there is everything to gain and nothing to lose; in disbelief there is everything to lose and nothing to gain. Whether God would be ultimately impressed with faith in him based on a bet is another matter again. Odds on, he wouldn't.

From 'God' to God

For Thomas Aquinas, the Psalmist's words 'The fool hath said in his heart, There is no God' (Ps. 53.1, KJV) meant that the existence of God was not self-evident to the fool or, for that matter, to the man of wisdom. Like Aquinas, the Benedictine monk Anselm of Canterbury (1033–1109) was a man of faith seeking understanding. 'I believe,' he wrote in his *Proslogion*, 'so that I may understand' (*credo ut intelligam*).[28] More than that, he was a man passionately seeking God. But for Anselm, in contrast to Aquinas, only a fool would deny that God's existence was self-evident. And, unlike Aquinas, Anselm's argument for the existence of God did not go from the world to God but from the meaning of the word 'God' to God. Anselm believed that to understand the meaning of the word 'God' was to know that God existed.[29] Thus,

Anselm's argument for the existence of God was intended for both the reasonable believer and the reasonable unbeliever. His was the first in a family of arguments that are now known as ontological arguments for the existence of God.

Anselm's argument for the existence of God was in two phases. In the first, the argument ran like this. Although God is always a being greater than our comprehension of him, he is nonetheless 'something than which nothing greater can be thought'. The idea of God as 'something than which nothing greater can be thought' exists in the mind (*in intellectu*). But it is greater to exist in reality (*in re*) as well as in the mind. Therefore, if something exists *only* in the mind, it cannot be 'something than which nothing greater can be thought'. Therefore, 'something than which nothing greater can be thought' exists not only in the mind but also in reality.

The first criticism of Anselm's argument quickly arrived in the form of a short work entitled *Pro insipiente* (On behalf of the fool), traditionally ascribed to Gaunilo, an eleventh-century Benedictine monk of Marmoutiers. Gaunilo attempted to reduce Anselm's argument to absurdity by demonstrating that, on Anselm's logic, an island that 'always excels that of all the lands which men occupy' exists.[30] Reshaped to mimic Anselm's argument, Gaunilo's argument went along these lines. There is an island than which nothing greater can be thought. The idea of this island exists in the mind. But it is greater to exist in reality as well as in the mind. Therefore, if the island exists *only* in the mind, it is not an island than which nothing greater can be thought. Therefore, the island than which nothing greater can be thought exists not only in the mind but also in reality.

Gaunilo's point was that, granted that the argument for the existence of the lost island was absurd, so too was Anselm's for the existence of a 'something than which greater cannot be thought'. As Gaunilo concluded, if someone were to argue that, on the basis of this argument, it is no longer to be doubted that such an island truly exists,

I would either believe him to be joking, or not know whom I might consider more stupid, myself, if I should concede the point to him,

or him, if he should think that he had established the existence of
that island with some kind of certainty.[31]

Anselm was to attempt to answer all of Gaunilo's criticisms. The
key to his answers lay in demonstrating that the parallel between
his 'something than which nothing greater can be thought' and
Gaunilo's 'island than which nothing greater can be thought' did
not hold because Anselm's 'something' was a special case. It was
unique because, unlike islands (or anything else for that matter),
which can be thought not to exist, it cannot be thought not to exist.
This was the result of phase two of his argument, which he had in
fact already laid out in his *Proslogion*. That argument went something
like this. It is possible to think of 'something that cannot be thought
not to exist'. This is greater than something that can be thought not
to exist (like islands or sticks and stones). The idea of 'something
that cannot be thought not to exist' is in the mind. If the 'something
that cannot be thought not to exist' exists *only* in the mind, it cannot
be 'something greater than which cannot be thought'. Therefore,
something than which nothing greater can be thought truly exists
in such a way that it cannot be thought not to exist. 'And You are
this thing, O Lord our God,' declared Anselm. 'Therefore, O Lord
my God, You truly exist in such a way that You cannot be thought
not to exist.'[32]

The divine persona

More philosophical ink than can be thought has been spilt on arguments for and against Anselm's ontological argument and its later
variant in the writings of the French philosopher René Descartes
(1596–1650). Debate has continued in progressively more complex
forms into the twenty-first century.[33] If the validity of Anselm's ontological argument gives you sleepless nights, philosophy is the career
for you. The rest of us can doze happily, content in the recognition
that the distinctive contribution of Anselm lay in his clarifying of the

concept of God. For what he undoubtedly showed was that, unlike everything in the universe, if God exists, then he exists as a being who is not dependent on anything else for his existence or any of his attributes. He cannot not be. He is 'self-existent' and 'self-sufficient'. He is therefore a being upon which the existence of everything else depends and is therefore the creator. And Anselm made yet another move: since a being that created the universe out of nothing is greater than one that created it out of some pre-existent material, God created the world *ex nihilo*: 'What are You,' asked Anselm, 'if not that which, the highest of all things, alone existing through itself [*solum existens per se*], made all other things from nothing?'[34]

A further attribute flows from God's self-sufficiency ('aseity'), namely, his simplicity. As a 'simple' being, God cannot be distinguished from his attributes (or parts) but is identical with them. And his parts cannot be distinguished from each other. Thus, for example, rather than 'goodness' being an 'attribute' of God, God is identical with 'goodness'. As Anselm put it:

> Therefore, there are no parts in You, Lord, nor are You several things, but You are one thing [...] More precisely, You are unity itself, divisible by no understanding. Therefore life and wisdom and the rest are not parts of You, but they are all one, and each one of them is all that You are and all what the rest are.[35]

On this account, God was, for example, goodness itself, and his goodness was identical with his perfect knowledge. Anselm admitted that how this could be so was not something that we could grasp with our limited understanding. He got that right!

Be that as it may, what we can say is that the divine attributes can be divided into two sets. First, there are those that are unique to God, notably his aseity, his simplicity, his eternity, his impassibility, his unchangeability and his incorporeality. We have looked at all of these already. Second, there are those that are personal and that he holds in common with us: states of the intellect such as knowledge (which he has to the greatest degree possible – omniscience) and power (which he has to the greatest degree possible – omnipotence), and states of the appetite (desires and wants) such as love, which he *is* perfectly, and goodness, which he *is* pre-eminently (thanks to Plato).

That God's knowledge was vast had biblical precedents. 'O the depth of the riches and wisdom and knowledge of God' (Rom. 11.33), Paul reminded us. But, granted that, does God know what will happen in the future? For Augustine, the answer was an emphatic yes: 'For, to confess that God exists, and at the same time to deny that He has foreknowledge of future things, is the most manifest folly [...] For one who is not prescient of all future things is not God.'[36] But it was the philosopher Boethius (*c*.480–*c*.524) in his *De consolatione philosophiae* (On the consolation of philosophy), written while imprisoned in Ticinum for treason before being executed (whether cut down with swords or throttled until his eyes bulged before being clubbed to death remains uncertain), who set the pattern for the subsequent medieval discussion.[37]

Boethius was in no doubt that God had foreknowledge of future things. At the same time, he recognised that God's knowledge of the future, being infallible, conflicted with human free will. 'It seems,' he wrote,

> too much of a paradox and a contradiction that God should know all things, and yet there should be free will. For if God foresees everything, and can in no wise be deceived, that which [Divine] providence foresees to be about to happen must necessarily come to pass. Wherefore, if from eternity He foreknows not only what men will do, but also their designs and purposes, there can be no freedom of the will, seeing that nothing can be done, nor any sort of purpose be entertained, save such as a Divine providence, incapable of being deceived, has perceived beforehand.[38]

Boethius was unwilling to forgo the doctrine of God's foreknowledge. To do so would be impious. He was just as unwilling to give up on the idea of human free will. For on that depended the possibility of morality and, with that, the possibility of the reward of the righteous and the punishment of the wicked after death:

> Vainly are rewards and punishments proposed for the good and bad, since no free and voluntary motion of the will has deserved either one or the other [...] And therefore neither virtue nor vice is anything, but rather good and ill desert are confounded together without distinction.[39]

The human race, he believed, would as a consequence fall into ruin.

To enable belief in both God's foreknowledge and human free will, Boethius provided two solutions. First, knowledge depended not on what was known but on the capacity of the knower. Thus, in order to understand the problem, we need to view it from the standpoint not of what 'knowledge' means to us but rather of what 'knowledge' means for God:

> Wherefore let us soar, if we can, to the heights of that Supreme Intelligence; for there Reason will see what in itself it cannot look upon; and that is in what way things whose occurrence is not certain may yet be seen in a sure and definite foreknowledge.[40]

Thus, second, to understand the nature of divine knowledge it was necessary to understand the nature of God, particularly his eternity. Everyone agreed, declared Boethius, that God was eternal. But in what did God's eternity consist? It followed from God's simplicity that he lived in an eternal present (or timelessly): God saw all times – past, present and future in a timeless present. Consequently, his knowledge was of all things *in the present*:

> Since God abides for ever in an eternal present, His knowledge, also transcending all movement of time, dwells in the simplicity of its own changeless present, and, embracing the whole infinite sweep of the past and of the future, contemplates all that falls within its simple cognition as if it were now taking place.[41]

Boethius thus attempted to resolve the conflict between God's fore-knowledge and human freedom by dissolving it. God's foreknowledge was transformed into God's observation of the present. And since it was no longer knowledge of what was yet to come, it could not be causing in advance what was yet to come. The consequence was that it was not in conflict, and could not be in conflict, with human freedom of choice:

> The freedom of man's will stands unshaken [...] Therefore, withstand vice, practice virtue, lift up your souls to right hopes, offer humble prayers to Heaven. Great is the necessity of righteousness laid upon you if ye will not hide it from yourselves, seeing that all your actions are done before the eyes of a Judge who seeth all things.[42]

And with those (perhaps not especially) consoling words, Boethius ended *De consolatione philosophiae*.

As with the doctrine of omniscience, the doctrine of God's omnipotence had no shortage of biblical testimony. Thus, the prophet Jeremiah declared that God had created the world 'by [his] great power and out-stretched arm': 'Nothing is too hard for you' (Jer. 32.18), he concluded. The Gospel of Matthew said simply, 'for God all things are possible' (Matt. 19.26). While it was clear that God could do anything, it wasn't so clear that he could do everything. Thus, for example, Augustine held that God could not die or fall into error. But this, he argued, did not affect his omnipotence. His being able to die or to be deceived would not be a sign of more power but of less. God was called omnipotent 'on account of doing what He wills, not on account of suffering what he wills not'.[43] Thus, God was omnipotent just because he *cannot* do some things. Anselm went a step further. God, he declared, cannot be corrupted, lie or cause something that is true to be false. For God to be able to do such things, argued Anselm, would be disadvantageous to himself. This would be 'not a power but a lack of power'.[44]

Medieval Jewish philosophy wrestled with the same problem. Saadia ben Joseph, for example, wrote that 'omnipotence' did not mean 'the bringing back of yesterday and causing the number five to be more than ten'.[45] Similarly, Moses Maimonides said that 'it is impossible that God should produce a being like Himself, or annihilate, corporify, or change Himself'.[46] Aquinas added to these lists. Thus, without it affecting his omnipotence, God cannot walk, fail, tire, create square circles, make the past not to have been, make something equal to himself, make himself not be, make himself not good or happy or will evil.[47] All that said, 'God is called omnipotent,' said Aquinas, 'because He can do all things that are possible absolutely.'[48] Moreover, his omnipotence entailed that he did not require any assistance in implementing his power. In short, within the bounds of the absolutely possible, God had both maximal strength and maximal range in the exercise of his power. Aquinas's was to become the consensus medieval account of omnipotence.[49]

As well as all-knowing and all-powerful, God was also said to be 'all-present' (omnipresent). The Psalmist had asked of God, 'Where can I go from your spirit? Or where can I flee from your presence? If I ascend to heaven, you are there; If I make my bed in Sheol, you are there' (Ps. 139.7–8). Anselm had wrestled with the issue of what God's omnipresence might mean in a work that preceded his *Proslogion*, namely, the *Monologion*. On the one hand, he argued to the conclusion that the Supreme Being existed in no place. On the other, he argued to the conclusion that God existed in every place. Anselm's aim was to resolve the apparent contradiction between these by demonstrating how each could be true.

There was no question that, with respect to space and time, God was outside them. The Supreme Being was in no place or time because 'it does not receive into itself distinctions of place and time – as for example, *here, there*, and *somewhere*, or *now, then*, and *sometime*'.[50] Thus, God was not bound by space or time. It was also certain that, although the Supreme Being was not *in* any place (in the sense of being contained by it), it was present in every place inasmuch as 'all other existing things are sustained by its presence in order that they not fall away into nothing'. Thus, God was present everywhere, not as *what is contained* but as that which *contains* all things by its pervasive presence: 'You do not exist in space and time, and all things exist in You. For nothing contains You, but You contain all things.'[51] In sum, God was not in space or time. Rather, space and time were in him. The

Supreme Being 'is in every place and time', declared Anselm, 'because it is absent from none; and it is in no [place or time] because it has no place or time.'[52] It was a solution that held to both the transcendence and immanence of God.

For Anselm then, God was *literally* everywhere. But for Aquinas, he was only *metaphorically* so. This was because Aquinas rethought omnipresence in terms of omnipotence, omniscience and God's essence. Thus, he declared,

> God is in all things by His power, inasmuch as all things are subject to his power; He is by His presence in all things, as all things are bare and open to His eyes; He is in all things by His essence, inasmuch as He is present to all as the cause of their being.[53]

This was a much-reduced reading of omnipresence. It meant that God was *not present everywhere*. Rather, he was *only* present in all existing things. And to be present in *all* existing things meant only that he had power over them, knew what was happening with them and was the cause of their existence. Here, God's omnipresence was not so much explained by God's power, knowledge and essence but explained away by them – *it was nothing but these things*. To his credit, Aquinas had resolved the paradox of being both nowhere and everywhere. But he had done so at a cost, namely, the emptying of the notion of God's omnipresence of any real meaning. As Nicholas Everitt aptly puts it: 'if this is how omnipresence is interpreted, one might well think that God is not omnipresent at all.'[54] This was a God who was not omnipresent as a result of his real presence or immanence within the world. Rather, this was a version of omnipresence that pertained to a God who, ironically, was transcendent to the world but not genuinely present in it at all.

God and evil

The persona of God outlined above was the one endorsed by Thomas Aquinas. But Aquinas recognised that, while some features of the world pointed to God's existence, another counted against it. This was the existence of evil. Aquinas saw the issue clearly: 'the word God means that He is infinite goodness. If, therefore, God existed, there would be no evil discoverable; but there is evil in the world. Therefore God does not exist.'[55] Aquinas was here drawing attention to a problem that had been recognised since the time of the Greek philosopher Epicurus (341–270 BCE). Epicurus had expressed it, according to the Christian theologian Lactantius (c.250–c.325 CE), as a problem that arose from God's goodness along with his power. God, he wrote,

> either wishes to take away evils, and is unable; or, He is able, and is unwilling; or He is neither willing nor able, or, He is both willing and able. If He is willing and is unable, He is feeble, which is not in accordance with the character of God; if He is able and unwilling, He is envious, which is equally at variance with God; if He is neither willing nor able, He is both envious and feeble, and therefore not God; if He is both willing and able, which alone is suitable to God, from what source then are evils? Or why does he not remove them?[56]

Within the Christian tradition, the nature of evil has been primarily understood in terms of its origins. Simply put, there are two dominant stories of the origin of evil: a theological story derived primarily from the Bible and a philosophical story derived from Neoplatonism. In the first, evil was a consequence of the disobedience of Adam and Eve. The whole of creation was infected with both natural and moral evils, along with the loss of immortality. This story was itself part of a larger cosmic drama consisting of God's creation of the world *ex nihilo*, the Fall of Adam and Eve and their expulsion from the Garden of Eden, the atonement for man's sin made by God who became man in Jesus Christ through his life, death and Resurrection, and finally the end of the world, when the dead will arise, Christ will return and God will judge the living and the dead, some for the joys of eternal life in heaven, others for the sufferings of an eternity in hell.

The theological story was embedded in the doctrine of God as the creator. The alternative philosophical story was implicit within the concept of God as the emanator. As we recall from Chapter 3, according to the Neoplatonist philosopher Plotinus, the world originated in a process of emanation from the One that was, at the same time, a process of the emanation of the Good. At the furthest point of emanation from the One and the Good, therefore, matter existed both at the limits of being and at the limit of the good. And thus matter, construed as the absence of good, was evil:

> Given that the Good is not the only existent thing, it is inevitable that, by the outgoing of it [...] there should be produced a Last, something after which nothing more can be produced: this will be evil [...] This Last is Matter, the thing which has no residue of good in it: here is the necessity of Evil.[57]

To sum up: evil was not so much something in itself but rather an absence of the good, the process of emanation as it reached its final end.

Thus, there was, on the one hand, a 'horizontal' biblical story that went through time successively, and, on the other a 'vertical' philosophical one that was always in the present time without beginning or end. Since the third century CE, these two stories have been woven in and out of each other in various and varyingly complex ways. They were also combined with 'maximal' and 'minimal' accounts of the Fall. On the one hand, influential in the Greek Eastern tradition, there were those accounts of the Fall that saw it as a *deprivatio* – a loss of something good that was recoverable. Alternatively, dominant within the Latin Western tradition, there were those that viewed it as a *depravatio* – a wicked corruption with goodness irrecoverable.[58]

A 'minimal' account of the Fall, combined with a Platonised theology, is to be found in a third-century CE account of the origin of evil in Origen. He began with the recognition of the inequities within the world. Why, he asked, 'do we find some new-born babes to be blind, when they have committed no sin, while others are born with no defect at all?'[59] The existence of such apparently unwarranted injustices threatened the goodness and omnipotence of God. Origen's answer was twofold.

First, he removed the apparently arbitrary injustices of this world by locating the origin of individual suffering in a pre-existent life. Thus, according to Origen, all souls came into existence before the creation of the world in a state of unity and harmony. Souls were unable to maintain themselves in that state. Through 'sloth and weariness of taking trouble to preserve the good, coupled with disregard and neglect of better things, [they] began the process of withdrawal from the good'.[60] In such a state, they fell victim to the Devil, who had been the first to fall away from the good.[61] Some souls sinned so lightly that they became angels in ethereal bodies, others so heavily that they became demons in aerial bodies. Others who had not sinned so heavily as to become demons nor so lightly as to become angels, were to become men and women, their souls bound in material bodies. Philosophically, they descended down the chain of being; biblically, they descended down Jacob's ladder (Gen. 28.10–17). Thus did Origen explain the present evils in the world as, on the one hand, cosmic evils brought about by the Devil and, on the other, personal evils as the result of the sins of pre-existent lives. In a scriptural reading that was simultaneously literal and allegorical, Origen declared that there were two 'creations' of humans: first the creation of souls (Gen. 1.26), and second their coming to be located in material bodies (Gen. 2.7).

Second, this fall was not inevitable. Rather, it was the consequence of the misuse of divinely given free will. All souls were created with the capacity to choose good or evil:

> every rational soul is possessed of free will and choice [...] There follows from this the conviction that we are not subject to necessity [...] to act either rightly or wrongly, as is thought to be the case by those who say that human events are due to the course and motion of the stars.[62]

Thus, according to Origen, our fate in our pre-existent life, this life and the next was down to us. Our sufferings were of our own making and not directly attributable to God, albeit in accord with divine justice.

More positively, freedom of choice made possible the cultivation
of the good. This was a happy Fall (*felix culpa*). On this account, the
world became not so much a vale of tears as a divinely created 'vale
of soul-making' as the poet John Keats put it.[63] All this suggests that
the evils of this world were not only punitive but remedial, reflective
of the divine goodness. The world was a place where souls could be
restored to health. God was the physician of souls:

> God our physician, in his desire to wash away the sins of our souls,
> which they have brought on themselves through a variety of sins
> and crimes, makes use of penal remedies of a similar sort, even to
> the infliction of a punishment of fire on those who have lost their
> soul's health.[64]

Thus, suffering was to our ultimate advantage and was, consequently,
an expression of God's love rather than his anger, both in this life and
the next.

Thus, for Origen, the soul can reascend the chain of being until
finally reunited with God, restored to the place that it enjoyed before
its fall. As evil did not exist when souls were first created, neither
would it when they were restored. It was a view of the journey of the
soul that, in principle, meant that, ultimately, all could be saved were
they to choose the good. Moreover, when reunited with God, the soul
would no longer desire to choose anything but the good: 'For if the
soul shall have ascended to this state of perfection, so that it loves God
with all its heart and with all its strength, and loves its neighbour as
itself, what room will there be for sin?'[65]

Origen's account of the origin of evil was consistent with the
goodness of God. Granted that evil and suffering conduced towards
an ultimate good – the ultimate salvation of all souls (perhaps even the
Devil and his minions) – the divine goodness was vindicated. There
was, however, a price to be paid for the free-will defence, namely, that
in his creating of beings that he could not subsequently control, there
was a further diminution in God's omnipotence.[66]

This was a price that Augustine too was willing to pay. Like

Origen, Augustine saw evil as a loss of something good. At the core of Augustine's account of the origin of evil was his refutation of the notion of evil within the tradition of the religion founded by the Persian prophet Mani (216–74 CE). In Manichaeism, a religion to which Augustine once belonged, the problem of evil was solved in terms of an eternal struggle between good and evil. Thus was the world, and humanity in particular, a battleground between two powers or of one divided against itself. To Augustine, it was a 'shocking and detestable profanity, that the wedge of darkness sunders not a region distinct and separate from God, but the very nature of God.'[67]

Mani's was, of course, an account of the nature of God completely at odds with Augustine's Platonist view, which saw God as both Being and Goodness, the one indistinguishable from the other. For Augustine, theologically, the goodness of God was manifest in his gracious and voluntary act of creation *ex nihilo*; philosophically, it was shown in the overflowing of the divine fullness into the world, 'pouring itself outwards and downwards in a teeming cascade of ever-new forms of life until all the possibilities of existence have been actualized and the shores are reached of the unlimited ocean of non-being.'[68] Thus, for Augustine, God created a universe in which all possible forms of being have been produced – from archangels to worms.

Consequently, with a God who in Neoplatonic style maximised his goodness in the creation of all possible forms of being, there was no possibility of the source of evil lying in the divine itself. Augustine thus looked for its origin in the misuse of free will, initially by Satan and the angels, and subsequently by Adam and Eve, the parents of all of us, in the Garden of Eden: 'when the will abandons what is above itself, and turns to what is lower, it becomes evil – not because that is evil to which it turns, but because the turning itself is wicked.'[69] From this misuse of free will came all the moral evils in the world. How, on this free-will account of the origin of moral evils, were natural evils not attributable to the actions of humans to be accounted for? These too were explicable as a misuse of free will, not by us but rather by those angels who, having been created by God with free will, turned away from God and became demons as a consequence.[70]

Unlike Origen's, Augustine's story of the Fall in the Bible was no mere allegory of the fall of 'everyman'. Rather, it was a historical event, one that not only deprived Adam and Eve of the happiness for which they were intended, but so radically corrupted and depraved human nature that all were damned from birth. All had been infected with the original sin of Adam:

> for we were all in that one man, since we all were that one man, who fell into sin by the woman who was made from him before the sin [...] And thus, from the bad use of free will, there originated the whole train of evil, which, with its concatenation of miseries, convoys the human race from its depraved origin, as from a corrupt root, on to the destruction of the second death, which has no end, those only being excepted who are freed by the grace of God.[71]

Thus were the sufferings of individuals the consequence not only of sins committed but sin inherited. As a result of the Fall of Adam and Eve, all were, consequently, in Augustine's eyes, depraved and justly condemned (see Plate 27).

So, on Augustine's reading of the results of the Fall, that God saved anyone at all was an act of graciousness on his part since no one deserved it. God's goodness was vindicated by his making redemption available through his redemptive activity in becoming man (although his activity was not sufficient to save everyone). Thus, the redeemed sinner was of more ultimate value than the innocent, who, not having sinned, did not require redemption. In the case of Origen, divine goodness was demonstrated in God's allowing, in principle, for the salvation of all through freely turning their will towards him. The case was otherwise for Augustine. Regardless of their choices for virtue or vice, God had predestined only some souls for salvation; the remainder (who were in the majority by far) were eternally damned. This is not to be seen as God's willing the damnation of most. Rather, it was a case of his being willing to let happen that which they justly deserved as the consequence of their original sin. This may have been divine justice for most, kindness for a select few. But it does seem to annul

God's goodness, although it was undoubtedly a demonstration of his sovereign divine power. On this account, God had given us free will, but our use or misuse of it was a matter of little importance to God, since our virtues or our vices had no relevance to our ultimate salvation. God seems something of an arbitrary despot on this account.[72] But more of this anon.

The best of all possible worlds

Still, all that said, there was in the thought of Augustine a tension, which he never quite resolved, between the origin of evil on the one hand and the origin of sin on the other. It flowed out of the strain between a philosophy that accounted for evil in terms of 'the absence of good' and a theology that looked to its origins in human (and demonic) sin and especially in that historical act of turning away from God that totally corrupted human nature from that moment on. In each case, the goodness of God was differently explained.

Philosophically, the goodness of God was vindicated, in spite of evil in the world, by the harmony of the whole. That the higher parts of the great chain of being were better than the lower was without question. That the natural evils of the universe were problematic was undeniable. Yet they were all part of a divinely created, ultimately benevolent harmony: 'And to Thee is there nothing at all evil,' wrote Augustine,

> and not only to Thee, but to Thy whole creation; because there is nothing without which can break in, and mar that order which Thou hast appointed it. But in the parts thereof, some things, because they harmonize not with others, are considered evil; whereas those very things harmonize with others, and are good, and in themselves are good [...] I did not now desire better things, because I was thinking of all; and with a better judgement I reflected that the things above were better than those below, but that all were better than those above alone.[73]

In short, the universe was more perfect for the presence of evil than for its absence.

Theologically, the goodness of God was vindicated, in spite of his foreseeing that man (and some angels) would misuse free will, by having planned that the ensuing moral (and natural) evils would fit into the overall harmonic perfection of the universe:

> For God would never have created any, I do not say angel, but even man, whose future wickedness He foreknew, unless He had equally known to what uses in behalf of the good He could turn him, thus embellishing the course of the ages, as it were an exquisite poem set off with antitheses.[74]

In other words, the universe was more perfect for the presence of sin than for its absence. Thus, for Augustine, the origins of both sin and evil lay uneasily poised between philosophy and theology. This opened up the possibility for later accounts of evil to peel off in two directions: one that would optimistically view all evil as a necessary aspect of an ultimately harmonious universe, and another that would pessimistically see all evil as the inevitable consequence of the original act of sin on the part of Adam and Eve.

With its emphasis on biblical revelation rather than Neoplatonic philosophy, this latter, pessimistic position dominated the sixteenth-century Protestant Reformation. The Swiss reformer John Calvin (1509–64), for example, followed Augustine's theological account of the origin of evil: it was the result of the misuse of free will by the first man. As a consequence, he lost his original freedom and all his descendants were enslaved to sin. 'Therefore,' declared Calvin, 'all of us, who have descended from impure seed, are born infected with the contagion of sin. In fact, before we saw the light of this life we were soiled and spotted in God's sight.'[75] Calvin, however, made two important variations to the Augustinian account. The first of these concerned the relation between free will and predestination that we will examine in Chapter 5. The second went to the origin of natural evil. For Augustine, natural evil was the result of the activities of the fallen angels and the consequence of their Fall. For Calvin, natural evil was the result of the activities of the original man. It was the sin of Adam that brought about both the Fall of Man and a more general cosmic fall.

Thus, according to Calvin, God brought natural evils into the world as a result of Adam's sin:

> For ever since man declined from his high original, it became necessary that the world should gradually degenerate from its nature. We must come to this conclusion respecting the existence of fleas, caterpillars, and other noxious insects. In all these, I say, there is some deformity of the world, which ought by no means to be regarded as in the order of nature, since it proceeds rather from the sin of man than from the hand of God. Truly, *these things were created by God, but by God as an avenger.*[76]

At best, Calvin's God was a God of justice, duly punishing man by introducing pain and suffering into a world that he had originally created perfectly good. At worst, he was an angry, punitive despot, worthy of our respect, even of our fear, but not of our love. In either case, he was a God whom, after the Fall, on Calvin's account, it was difficult to see as essentially good. That's probably the way Calvin intended. God was powerful, certainly, but hardly good. It may have been the best of all possible worlds before the Fall, thanks be to God. But afterwards – no thanks to God – far from it!

If Augustine's pessimistic theological solution to the problem of evil dominated that of John Calvin, it was Augustine's philosophical account that resonated with the German philosopher Gottfried Wilhelm Leibniz (1646–1716). Like Calvin, he attributed the existence of evil, both natural and moral, to the misuse of free will. But for its ultimate origin, Leibniz fell back upon the Neoplatonic Augustine. The origin of evil, he declared, was to be found neither within the divine nor as a 'something' independent of him, but in the *absence of good* within every created being by virtue of its created status.

Nevertheless, in spite of evils both moral and natural, this was still the best of all possible worlds and the best that God could have made, not least because it had the greatest variety of things and the simplest laws of nature. Evils natural and moral, Leibniz declared, were part of an overall universal good: 'if the smallest evil that comes to pass in the world were missing in it, it would no longer be this world; which, with nothing omitted and all allowance made, was found the best by the Creator who chose it.' While he admitted that it was possible to imagine worlds without sin and without unhappiness, 'these same worlds would be very inferior to ours in goodness.'[77] He was, in other words, the perfect gardener, in spite of the weeds.

So it was that, before bringing this world into existence, God compared all possible worlds in order to choose the one that was best – one that was, like Augustine's, all the more harmonic for some pain, acidity and darkness rather than all pleasure, sweetness and light. That it was so could not be demonstrated from the world. Leibniz saw that the 'appearances' of evil in the world strongly counted against God's goodness and justice. However, to allow the evils of the world to count *decisively* against God was to confuse the surface of the world with its depth. Thus, he did not argue from knowledge of the 'appearances' of the world; rather, Leibniz believed, the defender of God should proceed from a faith that the world, in spite of its obvious evils, was ultimately good by virtue of its foundation in the goodness of God. Calvin took evil so seriously he was willing to sacrifice God's goodness. Leibniz had Platonically vindicated the goodness of God. But had his unfailing eighteenth-century optimism and his firm belief in divine goodness failed to take evil seriously?

The French philosopher Voltaire (aka François-Marie Arouet, 1694–1778) believed so. He thought natural and moral evil far too serious to be taken seriously. It could only be treated satirically. Thus, for example, in his *Candide* (1759), he wrote:

After the earthquake [in 1755] had wiped out three quarters of Lisbon, the learned men of the land could find no more effective way of averting total destruction than to give the people a fine *auto-da-fé*; the University of Columbra had established that the spectacle of several persons being roasted over a slow fire with full ceremonial rites is an infallible specific against earthquakes.[78]

Voltaire's Leibniz was Dr Pangloss, an instructor in 'metaphysico-the-ologico-cosmoloonigology'.[79] Pangloss was a committed believer in this world as the best of all possible ones, in spite of its natural evils and the moral evils perpetrated in particular by those of religious faiths (Christian, Jewish and Muslim). Whatever happened in the world, Pangloss like Leibniz was able to rationalise it as compatible with its being eventually for the best.

If Leibniz's view of the world was a consequence of faith in God and blind faith in the pre-established harmony of the world, Voltaire's was the result of seeing the horror of evil and human suffering for what it was – completely inexplicable. 'The origin of evil,' declared Voltaire in his *Philosophical Dictionary* (1764), 'has always been an abyss whose bottom nobody has been able to see.'[80] The solution? Not despair, but rather a quiet resignation. This meant the quiet cultivation of the Garden as God had originally intended for man, an avoiding of airy philosophical speculations on how to justify the ways of God to man, and the doing of a little good in the hope of becoming a little better.

It was not the existence of evil as such that rendered God's goodness questionable and the notion of the best of all possible worlds problematic. Rather, it was the sheer quantity and quality of evil:

This system of *All is good* represents the author of nature only as a powerful and maleficent king, who does not care, so long as he carries out his plan, that it costs four or five hundred thousand men their lives, and that the others drag out their days in want and in tears. So far from the notion of the best of possible worlds being consoling, it drives to despair the philosophers who embrace it. The problem of good and evil remains an inexplicable chaos for those who seek in good faith.[81]

This was a loss of faith not only in biblical revelation but in Neoplatonic reason too. It was a problem that went to the very heart of the persona of the divine. Or at least it seemed so to do, unless God's wrath and justice could be said to be more determinative of his nature than his mercy and compassion.

1. 'Then one of the seraphs flew to Isaiah holding a
live coal with a pair of tongs' (Isaiah 6.6).

2. 'God saw everything
that he had made, and
indeed, it was very
good' (Genesis 1.31).

3. 'In the image of God he created them' (Genesis 1.27).

4. A very human God.

5. A 'naturalistic' God the Father supports his crucified Son with the Holy Spirit as a dove suspended between them.

6. 'And all flesh died that moved on the earth' (Genesis 7.21).

7. God appears to Abraham as one of three men (Genesis 18.2).

8. Ezekiel's vision of God (Ezekiel 1.26–8).

9. Abraham sacrifices his son Isaac (Genesis 22.1–14).

10. Moses receives the tablets of the Law (Exodus 34.1–10).

11. Job and his comforters (Job 16.2).

12. God becomes man in Jesus Christ.

13. Christ crucified.

14. Muhammad and
the Archangel Gabriel
(Qur'ān 53.5–12).

15.
The Christian
God – a unity
and a Trinity.

16. The Council of Nicaea (325 CE).

17. Mary Theotokos – the God-bearer.

18. 'Divided tongues, as of fire, appeared among them' (Acts 2.3).

19. Plato's cave.

20. The soul united to God in an ecstasy of love.

21. The ecstasy of St Teresa.

22. The ecstasy of St Catherine of Siena.

23. The *sefirot* in the Kabbalah.

24. Maimonides and the philosophers.

25. Thomas Aquinas, with Plato and Aristotle
on each side, confounds Averroes.

26. The Last Judgement.

27. The Fall of man.

28. Demons and the damned in hell.

29. Tintern Abbey and a sense 'of something far more deeply interfused'.

30. William Blake's God as Satan, with cloven hoofs and entwined by a serpent.

5

The God of Wrath, Mercy and Justice

But God is the judge: he putteth down one, and setteth up another.

Psalm 75.7 (KJV)

Athens in decline

The great virtue of the world, as conceived with Platonism generally, and Christian Platonism in particular, was that it was utterly rational and undeniably good. The world, we might say, was read in the light of the goodness of God. Voltaire read in the reverse direction – from the quantity and quality of evil in the world to God. In this reading, grounding a fundamentally and deeply flawed world in a being whose essence was goodness – and more particularly one whose goodness had flowed out of itself into the universe – was little short of grotesque. The Platonic God who was both transcendent and immanent could not be squared with the evidence of evil in the world. And, in this light, while God could still be transcendent to the world, he could no longer be considered immanent within it.

John Calvin was no Neoplatonist. Consequently, for him, the presence of evil in the world had no bearing on God's immanence since he had, as the transcendent creator of it out of nothing, never at any time been immanent within it. But Calvin, like Voltaire, took evil seriously, and he too read from the enormity of evil in the world to God. Calvin's God was not one whose essence was goodness. Rather, he was a punitive deity who had introduced evil into the perfect world that he had originally created as a consequence of human sin. Calvin's view of God was emblematic of the sixteenth-century Reformation more generally.

Until the time of the Reformation, and for the previous 1,500 years, philosophical theologians within Judaism, Christianity and Islam had all attempted to align the God who had revealed himself in the Torah, in Jesus Christ and in the Qur'ān, respectively, with the God of Platonic philosophy. They had tried to hold together, however awkwardly, a creating with an emanating deity. While Catholicism held to the alignment between the biblical and Platonic deity forged in the theology of Augustine (and has continued to do so until relatively recent times), the Protestant Reformation created a gap between the God of revelation and the God of Platonic reason that was unbridgeable.

Sola scriptura – Scripture alone – with authority vested in the enlightened reader thus became the battle cry of the Reformation. The printed Bible in vernacular languages made this possible both in theological theory and in popular practice. A democratised Bible was no longer the exclusive possession of ecclesiastical, theological and philosophical elites. At the least, this meant a rejection of alternative sources of knowledge of God such as those embedded in the Platonic tradition. Theologically, these alternative sources depended for their trustworthiness on reason as the image of God. For the reformers, the image of God in man was so besmirched by the Fall that, after it, reason could not be relied upon as a source of knowledge of God. But more importantly, *sola scriptura* meant the rejection of possible readings of the Bible 'behind' its literal (historical, plain, grammatical) meaning. Martin Luther (1483–1546) put it simply. The literal sense, he declared, was 'the highest, best, strongest, in short, the whole substance, nature and foundation of the holy scripture'.[1]

The literal sense had always been recognised as of first importance, ahead of its mystical, allegorical and hidden meanings. Aquinas had written that 'all the senses [of Scripture] are founded on one – the literal – from which alone can any argument be drawn, and not from those intended in allegory'.[2] In spite of that, the recognition that there were multiple meanings of Scripture meant accepting that the meaning of Scripture was indeterminate. But the Protestant insistence that the literal meaning was not merely the foundational but the *only* one entailed that Scripture (at least in principle) had but one fixed, determinate meaning. Thus, Scripture could no longer be read Platonically, the God of the Bible could not be identified with the God of Scripture, and, in Protestantism, Jerusalem and Athens were now going their separate ways.[3]

Thus, the God of Protestantism became pre-eminently the biblical God, the key player in a historical drama that began with his creation of the world *ex nihilo* and ended when Christ returned and God judged the living and the risen dead, some for eternal joy in heaven and others for eternal misery in hell (see Plate 28). Within Protestantism, God's story became exclusively a 'horizontal' one that went through time successively, rather than a 'vertical' one, always in the present time without beginning or end. The Protestant God was one who moved in history rather than one who resided in an eternal present.

The problematic relation between his biblical persona as a merciful and merciless, benevolent and malevolent, just and unjust God would now come to the fore – and this nowhere more so than on the Last Day! Then there would be the final separation between the saved and the damned. Christ would appear to all, declared Calvin,

> with the ineffable majesty of his Kingdom, with the glow of immortality, with the boundless power of divinity, with a guard of angels. From thence we are commanded to await him as our Redeemer on that day when he will separate the lambs from the goats, the elect from the reprobate. No one – living or dead – shall escape his judgement. The sound of the trumpet will be heard from the ends of the earth, and by it all will be summoned before his judgement seat, both those still alive at that day and those whom death had previously taken from the company of the living.[4]

But how was God to separate the saved from the damned? The criteria by which he was to do so were less than clear, not least because they embodied a conflict within the history of Christian thought on the nature of the divine justice, one that had been present in Christian thought since at least the time of Augustine.

Damned if you do and...

The Christian doctrine of the afterlife served, among other things, to redress the injustices on this side of the grave by justice on the other. Put simply, because there was no apparent connection between virtue and reward, vice and punishment, in this life, God rewarded the virtuous for their good works and punished the wicked for theirs in the next. The *iustitia Dei* (here the 'justice of God') thus consisted in God's rewarding people for what they deserved as a consequence of their actions in this life. In a word, men were saved by their merits or works. One consequence of this was the development within the church of an economy of the afterlife. Late-medieval Catholicism had given the not unwarranted impression, much to Martin Luther's chagrin, that salvation was for sale and could be purchased for a price. As the indulgence seller Johann Tetzel (1465–1519) was reputed to have put it: 'As soon as the coin in the coffer rings, the soul out of Purgatory springs.' The church was the key player in a medieval consumer culture, although one based on the afterlife rather than this one.

On the other hand, there had been an alternative understanding of the *iustitia Dei* within the Christian West. This was to the effect that salvation was not the consequence of any accumulation of merit on the part of men, but the result of God's grace. Here, the *iustitia Dei* was the 'righteousness of God' by which he justified sinners and imparted righteousness to them. The good works that followed, which earned salvation, were nevertheless God's, not man's. As Augustine put it:

> It follows then, dearly beloved, beyond all doubt, that as your good life is nothing else than God's grace, so also the eternal life which is the recompense of a good life is the grace of God; moreover, it is given gratuitously [freely].[5]

Luther's concerns about salvation by works were driven in part by the abuses within the Catholic penitential system. But they were embedded in his familiarity with the Augustinian theological tradition. Luther believed that, were merit a precondition of salvation, and were God to judge on that basis, all humanity was doomed, and himself before all others. 'Although I lived blamelessly as a monk,' he wrote, 'I felt that I was a sinner with an uneasy conscience before God; nor was I able to trust that I had pleased him by my satisfaction [works].'[6] And then he realised, he tells us, that the *iustitia Dei* (here the 'righteousness of God') consisted in 'that by which the righteous lives by the gift of God'.[7] Thus, the God of Christianity was not a harsh God of justice who punished the sinner according to his demerits, but a merciful and gracious God who bestowed righteousness upon the sinner as a free gift *in spite of* his demerits. Men remained sinners, but in the eyes of God they were righteous (*simul iustus et peccator*). For Augustine, man became righteous in justification. But, for Luther, man became, if anything, more aware of his own sinfulness.

As for good works, they were no longer a cause of justification, but a consequence of it. In short, regardless of good works, men were saved by God's grace. Little wonder then that the church reacted so vehemently. For Luther had made redundant the whole paraphernalia of the penitential system of late medieval Catholicism – prayer to the saints and martyrs, penances, suffrages, indulgences – and the profits generated by an economy based on them.[8]

With his doctrine of justification by grace, Luther had created a large gulf between Protestantism and Catholicism. Augustine, and the Western Catholic tradition after him, had understood 'justification' as meaning the sinner's being both declared righteous by God *and* made righteous (justified and sanctified). For Luther, justification did not entail sanctification. Thus, Luther had, in effect, separated salvation and sanctification. The works done by the justified sinner had no relevance to his salvation. God saved individuals regardless of their deserving to be or not.

This was a chasm made even deeper by the doctrine of predestination. It was one thing for God to determine one's eternal destiny during life or at death regardless of merit, but quite another to have it predestined before birth. The consequence of Augustine's account of justification was that, since God had made some righteous and not others, God had selected those who were to be saved, leaving others to be condemned through their own choices and actions. God had predestined some to salvation but omitted to save others.

Calvin went one step further. God's grace now became a function of the divine sovereign will. The consequence of this was that God actively, and apparently quite arbitrarily, predestined some to salvation and *others to damnation.* 'As Scripture, then, clearly shows,' wrote Calvin,

> we say that God once established by his eternal and unchangeable plan those whom he long before determined once for all to receive into salvation, and those whom, on the other hand, he would devote to destruction. We assert that, with respect to the elect, this plan was founded upon his freely given mercy, without regard to human worth; but by his just and incomprehensible judgment he has barred the door of life to those whom he has given over to damnation.[9]

In marked contrast to the understanding of the *iustitia Dei* that would see God bound to judge persons according to a principle of lawfulness outside himself (and thus according to their merits), Calvin's God was not bound by anything external to himself. The creator was not bound by his creation. Still, as Calvin recognised, God's devoting to destruction whomever he pleased did appear 'more like the caprice of a tyrant than the lawful sentence of a judge'.[10] However, for Calvin, God's will was so much the standard of righteousness that whatever he willed, 'by the very fact that he wills it, must be considered righteous', regardless of how it might appear to us.[11] The will of God was the law of all laws, inscrutable as it may be to us. Moreover, since all men inherited the corruption of sin from Adam, 'we can only be odious to God, and that not from tyrannical cruelty but by the fairest reckoning of justice,' for all are drawn from a corrupt mass.[12] From the perspective of original sin, all men deserved damnation anyway. That any at all were saved, and not all damned, was itself a sign of God's infinite mercy.

Except within an understanding of the human condition as one determined by the original sin of Adam, and of a God who does what he pleases, it is hard to take this seriously. A less pessimistic view of human nature than that of either Luther or Calvin might lead to the conclusion that a God acting according to a law of justice, tempered with mercy, might find reason to grant salvation to most, if not all. Still, granted this highly pessimistic view of human nature, predestination did provide a beacon of hope for those who believed that, whatever they did even to the good, *they* could never merit salvation. There is, after all, a certain comfort in fatalism, theological or otherwise. The early modern age was, after all, a pretty melancholic one. As Robert Burton (1577–1640) wrote in his *The Anatomy of Melancholy* in 1621, melancholy was 'a disease so frequent […] in these our daies, so often happening […] in our miserable times, as few there are that feele not the smart of it'.[13]

The idea of predestination to damnation was perhaps both cause and effect of sad times. Certainly, it provided an additional ground for deep melancholy among those who believed that, whatever *they* did to the good and regardless of their moral strivings, they were inevitably doomed to the eternal torments of hell. The key point is that a belief in predestination could cut either way: it could increase or alleviate anxiety. This was a conundrum through which Calvinist preachers needed to find a way.

The Norfolk Calvinist preacher John Yates (d.1657) was one of the first Protestants to explore this problem. He recognised the danger that the doctrine of predestination held for those who were melancholic. Such people, he declared, are never able to live with their sins when the 'narrow point of reprobation and election' is 'propounded unto their melancholic braines and hearts, and most miserable polluted souls'.[14] He told of a melancholic virtuous gentlewoman Mary Honeywood who, doubting her salvation, fell 'into the gulfe of Gods secret counsels' seeking intellectual certainty about that which was beyond that which can be known.[15] Her minister, John Foxe (1516–87), the famous English 'historian' of the Protestant persecutions under the Catholic Queen Mary I, counselled her against going beyond the Scriptures and to trust 'assuredly that shee might conclude her salvation out of Gods word'.[16]

She went way beyond his advice and

the temptation grew upon her, insomuch that having a *venice glasse* in her hands [...] presently breakes forth into lamentable words: You have often told mee that I must seeke no further than Gods word, but I have been long without comfort, and can indure no longer; therefore if I must be saved, let this glasse be kept from breaking; and so she threw it against the walls [...] yet the Lord that is rich in mercie, having stamped her with the seale of his election, was content to satisfie the languishing soule with a miracle: the glasse rebounds againe, and comes safe unto the ground.[17]

Thus can the doctrine of predestination cause harm to the melancholic soul when wrongly construed. In itself, Yates went on to say,

it is the most strong rock of assurance, in al storms of temptations that can befall unto bodie or soule; because predestination is Gods immutable will, the cause and rule of all justice, and uttermost of all reason in his workes.[18]

On the face of it, the doctrine of double predestination was hardly an incentive to lead a life of virtue. Because salvation or damnation was an individual's lot regardless of his behaviour in this life, it mattered little how he behaved. Granted that, the possibility of moral libertinism necessitated Calvinism reinventing a link between ethics and eternal destiny. It did so in response to the question, 'How can I be assured that God has determined that I am among the elect and not the reprobate?' This was a question at the very core of predestinarian piety. And there was another problem: if some were predestined to salvation and others to damnation, what difference did the atoning work of Christ make to it all?

The Puritan Stephen Denison (d.1649), minister of St Katharine Cree church in London, was a committed predestinarian. Election and reprobation were at the top of his theological agenda. Election, he declared, 'is the eternall and unchangeable decree of God, whereby of his free grace and favour he hath made choice of some rather then of others, to bestow upon them eternall life and happiness'. Reprobation, he continued, is also the eternal decree of God 'whereby he hath rejected others, leaving them in the fall of Adam, to their eternall destruction, and that to the praise of his power and justice'.[19]

As a consequence, Denison supported the doctrine of limited atonement, namely, that Christ died to save only the elect, and not all persons. As for the elect, they could and would continue to sin. They must nonetheless persevere in faith. This in itself would lead them towards an assurance of their salvation. Perseverance in faith was one sign of their election. Another was good works: 'Faith must be tried by the Fruits: for faith without good works, is but a carkeise of faith […] For howsoever faith alone doth justifie the person, yet works must necessarily justifie the faith'.[20]

That said, if faith without works was dead, so too was its converse. Thus did good works need to be balanced by the cultivation of inward piety and personal godliness. This was not salvation by works so much as the *personal* conviction of salvation through the cultivation of inward piety, the maximising of virtue, the minimising of vice, a strong conviction of the different destinies of the godly and the ungodly, and a persuasion of the arbitrariness of God's will. As Max Weber (1864–1920) eloquently put it in his *The Protestant Ethic and the Spirit of Capitalism* (1950), this personal conviction 'cannot, as in Catholicism, consist in a gradual accumulation of individual good works to one's credit, but rather in a systematic self-control which at every moment stands before the inexorable alternative, chosen or damned'.[21] The prospect of damnation, no doubt, sharpened the mind wonderfully.

Nevertheless, expectations of being among the elect can never have been very high. Whether it was a case of salvation by grace or by works, the general expectation was that the number of the damned would be far greater than the number of the elect. There were strong biblical grounds for the small proportion to be saved. 'Enter through the narrow gate,' declared Jesus,

> for the gate is wide and the road is easy that leads to destruction, and there are many who take it. For the gate is narrow and the road is hard that leads to life, and there are few who find it. (Matt. 7.13–14)

'Many are called,' he said elsewhere, 'but few are chosen' (Matt. 22.14).

Augustine had been a passionate supporter of the damnation of the many by an unconcerned God. Thus, in a letter to a Mauretanian bishop called Optatus in 418 CE, he wrote of the reprobates who

> by an incomparable multitude outnumber those whom God has deigned to predestine as children of promise in the glory of his kingdom, in order that it might be shown, by their very multitude, that the number of those who are most justly damned, whatever it may be, is of no concern with the righteous God.[22]

This was to be the default position in both early modern Catholicism and Protestantism.

Thus, for example, the Jesuit Jeremias Drexel (1581–1638) asserted that the 100,000 million destined for hell would be contained within a cubic German mile at the centre of the earth, where they would be closely thronged together 'like grapes in a wine-press, or salt herrings in a barrel, or bricks in a kiln [...] or like sheep butcher'd in the shambles'.[23] Not to be outdone by any 'Papist', the Copernican and Anglican Tobias Swinden (1659–1719) declared Drexel to be far too soft. Drexel's calculation, he said, was 'a poor, mean and narrow Conception both of the numbers of the Damned, and of the Dimensions of Hell'.[24] How infinitely short, he continued, 'is that Computation to those Multitudes who, as many, are set in Opposition by Christ to the few Saints, which, yet no Man can number?'[25] And one of his main reasons for transferring the location of hell from beneath the earth to the sun was that the inside of the earth could not contain the vast number of lapsed angels and the infinite number of the damned.[26] If not sufficiently large, it would certainly be hot enough. Loving in name if not by nature, the Puritan Christopher Love (1618–51), in his sermon on the terrors of hell, followed geographers in dividing the world into 31 parts: 19 possessed by the doomed Jews and Turks, seven by the heathen worshipping 'stocks and stones', who were similarly destined for hell, and the remainder populated by Papists and Protestants, the former likewise damned.[27]

All this was difficult to square away with a God of love and mercy, one who 'so loved the world that he gave his only begotten Son, that whosoever believeth in him should not perish but have everlasting life' (John 3.16, KJV). The German philosopher Leibniz analysed the problem clearly in his *Theodicy* in 1709. It is a terrible judgement, he wrote,

> that God, giving his only Son for the whole human race [...] yet saves so few of them and abandons all others to the devil his enemy, who torments them eternally and makes them curse their Creator, though they have been created to diffuse and show forth his goodness, his justice and his other perfections. And this outcome inspires all the more horror, as the sole cause why all these men are wretched to eternity is God's having exposed their parents to a temptation that he knew they would not resist; as this sin is inherent and imputed to men before their will has participated in it; as this hereditary vice impels their will to commit actual sins; and as countless men, in childhood or maturity, that have never heard or have not heard enough of Jesus Christ [...] die before receiving the necessary succour for their withdrawal from this abyss of sin [...] though in essence they have not been more wicked than others, and several among them have perchance been less guilty than some of that little number of elect, who were saved by a grace without reason, and who thereby enjoy an eternal felicity which they had not deserved.[28]

A very particular judge

The God who arbitrarily predestined some for salvation or damnation regardless of their virtues or vices was juxtaposed within the Christian tradition to a God who meted out rewards and punishments in the afterlife in accord with moral deserts. This was epitomised in the conflict between salvation by grace and salvation by works that had been a source of conflict in Christianity since the time of Augustine in the early fifth century and was resurrected by Martin Luther 1,100 years later.

While, on the face of it, a God who distributed reward and punishments in the afterlife according to the principle of individual merit went some way to mitigating the apparent arbitrariness of a predestining God, it created a whole new set of problems. The first of these concerned the time when the destiny of each individual was determined. There was general agreement that God determined an individual's destiny at the time of their death. Thus, the *general* judgement of all the resurrected dead on the Day of Judgement merely confirmed the *particular* judgement that God made when the soul departed its body (see Plate 26). As Aquinas rather elegantly put it:

> Accordingly the soul will remain perpetually in whatever last end it is found to have set for itself at the time of death, desiring that state as the most suitable, whether it is good or evil. This is the meaning of Ecclesiastes 11:3: 'If the tree fall to the south or to the north, in what place soever it shall fall, there shall it be.' After this life, therefore, those who are found good at the instant of death will have their wills forever fixed in good. But those who are found evil at that moment will be forever obstinate in evil.[29]

New Testament support for the particular judgement was found in the key passage that dealt with life immediately after death, namely, the parable of the rich man and Lazarus (Luke 16.19–31). Not only were the rich man and Lazarus allocated to places of agony or torment respectively, but it is clear that there was no possibility of transfer from the one to the other. Thus, Abraham told the rich man, 'between you and us a great chasm has been fixed, so that those who might want to pass from here to you cannot do so, and no one can cross from there to us' (16.26).

By the year 400 CE, there was a general consensus on the 'particular judgement'. In 419 CE, in his *On the Soul and Its Origin*, in a discussion about the parable of the rich man and Lazarus, Augustine agreed unquestioningly with the view that

souls after quitting the body are judged, before they come to that
final judgement to which they must submit when their bodies are
restored to them, and are either tormented or glorified in the very
same flesh wherein they once lived here on earth.[30]

Thus, God irrevocably fixed the eternal destiny of individuals at the
time of death. And it was fixed according to their merits or otherwise.
Individuals could not subsequently alter their destiny.

From the time of Clement of Alexandria (*c.*150–*c.*215 CE), there
had been attempts to mitigate the apparent harshness of God's distinguishing only between two groups of people – the wicked and the good,
the former destined to hell, the latter to heaven. It was the consequence
of the realisation that the division of people into two classes only at the
time of death was too strict. It was clear that some (the saints, martyrs
and confessors) merited heaven immediately after death while others
deserved an eternity in hell. It was just as clear, however, that there
were those who, although they had died with unremitted sins, were
neither sufficiently evil nor sufficiently incorrigible to merit eternal
punishment, yet not sufficiently good to deserve eternal happiness.
Most of us, it was realised, had not been sufficiently good at being
really bad, nor sufficiently bad at being really good. Thus, by the end of
the thirteenth century the harshness of this eternal either/or had been
somewhat mitigated by the development of the doctrine of Purgatory.

This allowed for a period of purgation between death and the Last
Judgement that both punished and purified those not sufficiently
wicked to merit eternal punishments in hell, nor sufficiently virtuous
to gain immediate rewards in heaven.[31] Its virtue lay in its squaring
God's justice with his mercy. Justice was apparent in God's giving the
saints and martyrs immediate eternal happiness in heaven, the incorrigibly wicked immediate eternal torments in hell and those in between
purgatorial torments proportionate to their (un-forgiven) sins prior
to their eventual admission into heaven.

This doctrine of the *particular* judgement ensured that the afterlife was morally static. There was neither motive nor opportunity
for post-mortem moral improvement. Even Purgatory was a place

where vice was purged rather than virtue acquired. But during the
seventeenth century, those Protestants who were dissatisfied with the
fixing of the destiny of the soul at death began to opt for a morally
dynamic state between death and the Last Judgement. That is to say,
the possibilities of individual repentance, of moral and spiritual growth,
and consequently of divine forgiveness and the gift of salvation, were
extended beyond the grave. Protestantism had rejected the doctrine of
Purgatory. But the doctrine of a morally dynamic afterlife amounted
to a Protestant rethinking of Purgatory. More importantly, in opting
for progress beyond the grave, it effectively rejected the doctrine of
God's particular judgement at death.

It is not perhaps surprising that an early example of the morally
dynamic afterlife was provided by a Platonist – Henry Hallywell
(1641–1703) – committed to the return of *all* souls to an essentially
good God. According to Hallywell, there were rewards for the good
immediately after death, and shame and misery for the impious. But
he was not persuaded that the Scriptures held that the good went
to heaven and the wicked to hell. Rather, he suggested, on rational
grounds, it would be more appropriate were *all* to go to an intermediate state after death until the Day of Judgement. He carefully
distinguished this state from Purgatory, primarily because, whereas
Purgatory was penitential, his intermediate state was purificatory and
morally dynamic. 'By this middle State,' he wrote,

> I mean no such condition of Being, as that wherein a man from his
> impious transactions in this life, shall undergo very sharp and acute
> torments, the protraction or abbreviation of which yet, depend upon
> the will and pleasure of his Holiness [the pope] and mercenary
> priests; and after such a time of penance and purgation, be delivered,
> and translated into heaven: but, such a state, wherein, by a due puri-
> fication of their minds, and subjugation of those stubborn lusts and
> desires which exalt themselves against the life of God, and which
> were not thoroughly tamed in this life, the Soul of man becomes
> wholly dead to every inordinate affection, and daily kindles that fire
> of Divine Love, till at last it arise to a perfect flame.[32]

In particular, Hallywell found it unsatisfactory that 'the infinitely far greater part of men are damned'.[33] And, as a Platonist, he found it inconsistent with the goodness of God to allow the majority to be born into circumstances where there would be little hope of recovering the lost image of God in their souls with only everlasting damnation the inevitable outcome. Consequently, free will was extended beyond the grave and time was allotted for moral improvement: 'surely it would be a great eye-sore and blemish in Heavens righteous Oeconomy and dispensation in the World, if there were really no time or means allowed for the recovery of these lapsed Souls.'[34] Hallywell did not deny the possibility of eternal torments after the Day of Judgement. But he did make it possible that all could be saved through diligent application in this world and the next before that final day.

The idea that God allowed for the possibility of the dead growing towards perfection in the afterlife was an innovation in the history of Christian thought that was to reach its fulfilment in the German philosopher Immanuel Kant (1724–1804). He argued that, although we are imperfect human beings, we rationally aspire for perfection. It was as obvious to Kant as to the rest of us that moral perfection was unattainable in this life. Thus, he argued in his *Critique of Practical Reason* (1788) that it was reasonable to postulate an infinitely enduring existence immediately after death and before the Last Judgement in which the individual 'may hope for a further uninterrupted continuance of this progress, however long his existence may last, even beyond this life'.[35] Thus may the soul progress endlessly towards God, who is the highest good. That the soul may progress after death entails that it could do so. Thus, the soul was free, both on this side of the grave and the other, to progress in virtue. In the afterlife, God imparted happiness as the result of virtue. In a version of Luther turned upside down, perhaps inspired by Kant's own grounding in Lutheran Pietism, Kant's salvation was by works. Grace (the gift of happiness) did not precede works as in Luther but, rather, followed the acquisition of virtue.

That said, moral progress in the afterlife was not for eternity. It was dependent on time. After the Day of Judgement, declared Kant, there would be no more time. Our eternal destiny – salvation or damnation – would be fixed on that day according to our merits or otherwise. The Last Day, declared Kant in *The End of All Things* (1794),

> is a *Judgement Day*: the decision of the World-Judge in favour of salvation or damnation is, therefore, the proper end of all things in time and the beginning of (blissful or miserable) eternity in which the fate that has fallen to each man endures as it was allotted to him in the moment of its pronouncement [by God].[36]

God the terminator

In believing in the possibility of moral progress *after death*, Hallywell and Kant were in the minority. But in accepting that, *after the Last Judgement*, the damned had no further chance for salvation, they were still among the majority of both Protestants and Catholics in the seventeenth and eighteenth centuries. As much as the torments of hell themselves, it was the emphasis on the eternity of them that was intended to provoke horror, effect repentance and act as an incentive to a good and holy life in the here and now. Unlike punishments in this life, the awesome ceremonies of hell went on forever. It was 'the eternity of the Punishment', declared the Anglican divine Matthew Horbery (1706–73), 'which gives its chief weight and Edge, and makes it pierce deepest into the Hearts of Sinners.'[37]

Within the Christian tradition, that the punishments of the damned in hell would be eternal had always been the majority opinion. But from the latter part of the seventeenth century and into the eighteenth, there were a small number by whom it was privately disbelieved, publicly (although discreetly) questioned or anonymously challenged. This was done in the name of the conviction that God would either annihilate all those in hell or save them after an appropriate period of punishment. In either case, punishment was only temporary.

In keeping with the Protestant emphasis on Scripture, the debate about whether God would annihilate the wicked after an appropriate period of punishment or torment them for eternity turned in part on the literal meaning of the term 'eternal' (αἰώνιος) in the New Testament. Did it mean what it suggested or merely 'of long duration'? Both annihilationists and universalists mined Scripture for support for their respective positions. 'Scripture alone' was a unifying factor among Protestants. But granted the possible variety of literal readings, it was also grounds for disunity. Such was the diversity of opinions on the eternity of hell torments that could be generated by appeal to Scripture that, on occasion, reason was invoked against it. Thus, the English scientist and theologian Thomas Burnet (c.1635–1715) argued that, granting the ambiguities within the debate,

> every Man is at Liberty to embrace that Opinion which his Conscience shall pronounce to be most agreeable to sound reason; and let him adhere to that Interpretation of the Sacred Scripture upon this Point which the weighty Reasons of the Cause before us will be best able to bear.[38]

It would be simplistic to suggest that the debate over eternal torments in the seventeenth and eighteenth centuries simply reflected a dispute between reason and the Bible. 'Reason over Scripture' was certainly a manifesto for those who perceived themselves progressive and enlightened in contrast to the hidebound traditionalists who supported the eternal punishment of the wicked. For these, 'reason' implied not so much the power of the human mind to arrive independently at truth as a commitment to avoid intolerance, bigotry and extremism. But opponents and advocates of eternal torments alike provided rational arguments that nonetheless orbited within a biblical space. At the same time, the meaning of the Bible was itself determined within the context of debates about the nature of God. These went particularly to the relationship between the divine attributes of mercy, wrath and justice, and the implications of these for the destiny of the damned.

The wrath of God was, for some, sufficient reason to punish the wicked eternally. The Calvinist Thomas Goodwin (1600–80) wrote his discourse on the punishment of sin in hell in 1680, as the subtitle indicates, to demonstrate 'the Wrath of God to be the immediate

Cause Thereof'. Eternal punishment, he exclaimed, is 'an act of aveng-
ing Wrath'.[39] America's most famous eighteenth-century Calvinist
theologian, Jonathan Edwards (1703–58), imagined sinners 'in the
hands of an angry God'.[40] For Goodwin and Edwards, as for many
others, vengeance and retributive justice were closely combined. The
doctrine of eternal torments retained a medieval element of the law of
vengeance combined with an early modern sense of retributive justice.
The wicked, proclaimed Edwards,

> *deserve* to be cast into hell, so that divine justice never stands in the
> way, it makes no objection against God's using his power at any
> moment to destroy them. Yea, on the contrary, justice calls aloud
> for an infinite punishment of their sins.[41]

It was difficult to reconcile the concept of eternal retribution with
God's goodness and mercy. The English theologian Matthew Tindal
(1657–1733), in his *Christianity as Old as the Creation* (1730), for example, lamented those who impute such actions to God 'as [to] make him,
resemble the worst of beings, & so run into downright *Demonism*'.[42]
As a consequence of this kind of critique, those who argued for eternal
torments were forced to reinterpret the goodness and mercy of God
accordingly. With the Catholic Francis Blyth (c.1705–72), it is difficult to distinguish his rhetorical assertion of the mercy of God from
what is in effect a denial of it. For Blyth, the mercy of God can only
be understood from the primacy of his retributive justice:

> It is unmerciful, you say, for God to give sinners their desert; is it
> mercy then for worms, for wretches, to rob God of his due? And
> must God be more merciful than becomes him as God to be, merely
> to prove him less just than he really is, and must be?[43]

The implication that, in the light of eternal torments imposed by
God, divine mercy was not up to much could be mitigated by arguing
that the penalties for sins were something that followed naturally
and inevitably upon the sinner – self-inflicted wounds rather than

externally imposed tortures. They were, after all, the consequence of the misuse of free will. But arguments of this sort did little to solve the issue of God's apparent lack of mercy. As D. P. Walker has pointed out, although a God who allows punishments to happen is less cruel than one who actively imposes them, 'there is little if any moral difference between allowing the occurrence of a disaster together with the resultant suffering, which you could prevent, and actively causing the disaster and the suffering.'[44]

William Whiston (1667–1752) would have agreed. He was Isaac Newton's successor as Lucasian Professor of Mathematics at the University of Cambridge. To Whiston, the doctrine of the love of God was absolutely inconsistent with those 'common but barbarous and savage opinions' of eternal torments,

> as if much the greatest part of mankind are under a state of reprobation, unalterable reprobation, and must inevitably be damned: and that such their damnation is to be *coeternal* with the duration of their Creator himself; and that the torments, the exquisite torments of these most numerous and most miserable creatures, are determined without the least pity, or relenting, or bowels of compassion in their Creator, to be in the flames of Hell; without abatement, or remission, for endless ages of ages. And all this for the sins of this short life; fallen into generally by the secret snares of the Devil, and other violent temptations; which they commonly could not wholly either prevent, or avoid; and this without any other advantage to themselves or to others, or to God himself, than as instances [...] of the absolute and supreme power and dominion of the cruel and inexorable author of their being; for all the infinite ages of eternity.[45]

For his part, Whiston was, at the end of the Last Day, an annihilationist. When he was a student at Cambridge from 1686 to 1691, he was a supporter of eternal torments. But by 1709, perhaps under the influence of the English philosopher John Locke (1632–1704), he had changed his mind. A temporary period of punishment followed by annihilation, he suggested, reflected both the divine (retributive) justice and goodness. The punishments were eternal, he maintained, only in the sense that they would 'continue the whole Duration of the Wicked, who are the subjects of it'.[46]

Whiston's annihilationism was informed by his scientific researches. Before the Last Judgement, he believed, the wicked were confined beneath the earth. The Astronomer Royal Edmund Halley's and his own researches demonstrated, he claimed, a large cavity between the internal and external parts of the earth, thus vindicating the biblical and traditional descriptions of Hades being beneath the earth. During this period, the wicked would be confined there with the opportunity for repentance. The majority would grab that last chance. Whiston even hoped that Satan and his evil angels might eventually choose to repent and be saved. The incorrigibly wicked, however, would be resurrected on the Last Day with physical bodies that would be punished in flames (fire), and with the same diseases they had at death (worms). Moreover, he surmised, they would then be located on a comet (like Halley's):

> I cannot but think the Surface or Atmosphere of such a Comet to be that Place of Torment so terribly described in Scripture, into which the Devil and his Angels, with wicked Men their Companions, when delivered out of their Prison in the Heart of the Earth, shall be cast for their utter Perdition or second Death; which will be indeed a terrible but a most useful spectacle to God's rational creatures.[47]

The period of time that the wicked would spend in this hellish comet would be proportionate to their sins, to be followed by their 'second death' – annihilation.

Whiston's belief that the wicked would have a 'second death' after an appropriate time of punishment in hell, although without his geology and cometology, remained the standard pattern for theologically driven annihilationist views from this time on. The most significant variation on this theme occurred only in the second half of the nineteenth century, among those who were influenced by the Darwinian challenge to the Christian idea of man as unique in the animal world by virtue of his immortal soul. Darwinism served to reinforce the assumption implicit within annihilationism that the soul was not naturally immortal, that immortality was a consequence of divine grace and that man was naturally mortal.[48]

The Darwinist notion of the survival of the fittest also served to align the annihilationists' account of the afterlife with the belief that those not fit for salvation would, like many species, just disappear. Thus, for example, the Anglican evangelical Henry Constable (1816–91), in his highly successful *The Duration and Nature of Future Punishment* (1868), declared:

> We find in nature that death and destruction are God's usual agents in removing from their place things animate and inanimate as soon as they cease to discharge the part for which they were intended [...] Whole races of living things have long ceased to exist [...] Lower creatures know not God, and fade away out of life. Higher intelligences knew Him, turned from Him, made themselves like beasts, and like beasts are treated. Hell will add its fossil remains to those of the quarries of the earth.[49]

God the saviour of all

Advocates of both annihilationism and universalism no doubt comforted themselves with the thought that, even if God's justice was manifested in the punishments the wicked endured in hell, his mercy was demonstrated in the torments of hell being only temporary and not eternal. For universalists, however, in contrast to annihilationists, the end of punishments brought salvation rather than destruction, if only after a period of punishments intended to reform the sinner. Within the history of Christian thought, universalism was a minor tradition, generally viewed with suspicion. Since it was often believed that universal salvation would act as a disincentive to the virtuous life among the riff-raff, some held it to be a secret doctrine for the few, an esoteric truth not to be revealed to the masses to whom the eternity of hell's torments still needed to be preached lest they run morally

amuck. Not surprisingly, focused as it was on the essential goodness
of God, it was implicit in the Platonic tradition of the early church,
particularly with Origen. It re-emerged among some of the English
Platonists in the seventeenth century (Peter Sterry, George Rust and
Jeremiah White), and among supporters of the radical Reformation
(John Denck, Gerrard Winstanley and Richard Coppin).[50] It was
during the nineteenth century, however, that it became a matter of
mainstream controversy.

The German liberal Protestant theologian Friedrich Schleiermacher
(1768–1834) was the first major modern theologian to accept universalism. In his case, oddly enough, it was combined with a commitment to predestination and a rejection of eternal damnation.
According to Schleiermacher, God did not predestine some to salvation
and others (the vast majority) to eternal misery. Rather, he foreor-
dained the salvation of all humanity. In contrast to the view that some
obtained the highest bliss while others were lost in irrevocable misery,
Schleiermacher proclaimed, we ought to admit 'the equal rights of the
milder view [...] that through the power of redemption there will one
day be a universal restoration of all souls'.[51]

Schleiermacher's liberal view on salvation was to have little impact
on nineteenth-century German theology. In England, by contrast,
controversy about universalism was a constant feature of the theological landscape of the second half of that century. We can take
the Broad Church Anglican cleric Frederic W. Farrar's (1831–1903)
collection of sermons entitled *Eternal Hope* (1878) and the arguments
it generated as emblematic of the debate around universalism in the
mid-Victorian period.[52] It was the third of these sermons, 'Hell – what
it is not', that was to provoke the most controversy, not least because
Farrar had the virtue of being able not only to preach *to* but to write
for a large crowd.

Farrar was vehemently opposed to the doctrine of eternal punishment. 'I know nothing,' he declared,

> more calculated to make the soul revolt with loathing from every
> doctrine of religion than the evil complacency with which some

cheerfully accept the belief that they are living and moving in the midst of millions doomed irreversibly to everlasting perdition.[53]

He deemed it a doctrine of 'judicial terrorism', 'a blasphemy against God's exceeding and eternal love'.[54] And of the biblical texts that appeared to endorse it? 'I protest at once,' he wrote,

> and finally against this ignorant tyranny of isolated texts which has ever been the curse of Christian truth, the glory of narrow intellects, and the cause of the worst errors of the worst days of the corrupted Church [...] The devil, as we know, can quote texts for his own purpose.[55]

The words 'hell', 'everlasting' and 'damnation' should be expunged, he declared, from all English Bibles as mistranslations.

It is also clear that, along with eternal torments, he rejected annihilationism. This, on the face of it, would leave universalism as the only remaining option. Yet, he wrote, 'I cannot preach the certainty of Universalism.' There were, no doubt, practical and theoretical grounds for this uncertainty. Practically, Farrar wished to avoid accusations of teaching an unorthodox doctrine. Theoretically, he was agnostic not only about universalism but also about all the options for those who did not merit eternal life at the time of death. God has given us 'no *clear and decisive* revelation on the final condition of those who have died in sin'.[56]

Nevertheless, he did go on to sail very close to the winds of heresy. He had no doubt that the will of God was that all would eventually be saved. He believed that there would be a period of time after death when man would continue in that spiritual death that is alienation from God, although how long that might be – 'that is one of the secret things which God hath not revealed.'[57] Without asserting that *all* would be saved, he did express the hope that the *vast majority* of the lost would be. And he strongly hinted that there would be a period of time when those who were not yet ready for salvation 'may have to be purified in that Gehenna of aeonian fire beyond the grave'.[58]

Farrar, like many a Victorian, was driven by a moral seriousness that was rebelling against some parts of Christian orthodoxy. A God whose nature was such that he happily consigned the vast majority of humankind to an eternity of torments in hell was looking very ethically dodgy. As early as 1825, the poet Samuel Taylor Coleridge (1772–1834) had analysed the theological disquiet among his acquaintances:

> I have found the far larger number of serious and inquiring persons little, if at all, disquieted by doubts respecting Articles of Faith, that are simply above their comprehension. It is only where the belief required of them jars with their *moral* feelings; where a doctrine in the sense, in which they have been taught to receive it, appears to contradict their clear notions of right and wrong, or to be at variance with the divine attributes of goodness and justice; that these men are surprised, perplexed, and alas! not seldom offended and alienated. Such are the Doctrines of Arbitrary Election and Reprobation; the Sentence to everlasting Torment by an eternal and necessitating decree; vicarious Atonement, and the necessity of the Abasement, Agony and ignominious Death of a most holy and meritorious Person, to appease the wrath of God.[59]

Thus, the God of eternal damnation was becoming morally repugnant to many both inside and outside the church. It sat awkwardly with an ethical optimism that saw virtue in all regardless of their state in life. As Don Cupitt puts it:

> The Victorians thought it a moral duty to believe that no one was quite beyond redemption; they did not like the doctrine of Reprobation, and if a Broad Church clergyman questioned the doctrine of eternal punishment he might […] be reviled by the theologians, but he was sure of the sympathy of a large public of liberal-minded laymen.[60]

Almost at the end of the nineteenth century, the English statesman William Gladstone (1809–98) commented that the doctrine of hell had been 'relegated [...] to the far-off corners of the Christian mind [...] there to sleep in deep shadow as a thing needless in our enlightened and progressive age'.[61] This was an exaggeration. The doctrine of hell remained the orthodoxy within Christianity and that of the eternal torments of the damned continued within both conservative evangelical Protestantism and conservative Roman Catholicism. But gentler souls were increasingly uncomfortable with a God who could act so vindictively or whose idea of physical punishments was now well outside secular norms of justice and punishment. For these, hell was no longer a *place* but a *state* of psychological and not physical punishment – one that consisted primarily in the soul's despair at its separation from God.

The nineteenth century's belief in the possibility of progress for individuals and humanity as a whole also saw a decline in the acceptance that the destiny of individuals was fixed at death (or at birth for that matter). Salvation by grace and predestination to salvation or damnation (or both) were countered by an emphasis on the individual being able freely to create his ethical self and his eternal destiny. Thus, on the other side of life, the individual became free to turn towards God after death, morally to advance, and finally to attain salvation. Kant had established philosophical reasons for this. But it was also reinforced by the decline in expectations of the Last Judgement. At least among liberals, both Catholic and Protestant, there was no expectation of the imminent return of Christ. The eschatology of the Last Day with its assertion of the end of history, its harsh judgemental God meting out eternal happiness or eternal misery, and its increasingly incredible expectations of the resurrection of the physical body, while still theoretically endorsed, was practically ignored. God's justice was no longer determined by wrath but was tempered with mercy, and this not just for a chosen few but for all.

6

The Designer God

The Heavens are telling the glory of God;
and the firmament proclaims his handiwork.

Psalm 19.1

Reason revisited

Until the Protestant Reformation in the sixteenth century, Judaism, Christianity and Islam had attempted, each in different ways as we have seen, to align the God of revelation with the God of Platonic philosophy. But the Reformation created an unbridgeable gap between the God of the theologians and the God of the Platonic philosophers, not least because the God of Protestantism became pre-eminently the personal God of a biblical drama that began with creation and concluded with the final judgement. God was no longer the impersonal Platonic absolute that had flowed out of itself thus emanating the universe.

However, within Protestantism itself, there now developed a new understanding of reason. This was one that was no longer inflected by Platonism but couched in biblical imagery. We might say that, whereas before the Reformation it was a matter of aligning the Bible with reason, it was now a matter more of aligning reason with the Bible. Thus, for example, Protestant natural philosophers (or the 'new scientists', as we might call them) took seriously the idea of reason as the image of God in man and therefore saw reason as God's revelation of himself within man. Reason was now to become not so much the means by which God could be found in the depths of the self but rather the means by which he could be discerned outside the self in the depths of the natural realm. As Joseph Addison put it in 1712:

The unwearied Sun from day to day
Does his Creator's power display;
And publishes to every land
The work of an Almighty hand.[1]

At the same time, natural philosophers did take seriously the corruption of reason through the Fall. But they did not do so to the extent of its no longer being revelatory of the divine or of its no longer being a means of access to knowledge of God. Similarly, they took seriously the corruption of the world as a consequence of the Fall but, again, not at the expense of its no longer being revelatory of divine design and purpose.

That the Fall had seriously damaged man and the creation over which God had given him dominion was never doubted. But it was not irrevocable. Indeed, a key motivation for the development of the sciences was to restore that which had been damaged by the Fall and to return the earth to its perfect primeval state. Thus, for Francis Bacon (1561–1626), the father of English empirical science, the investigation of nature was driven by the quest to restore to man the pure contact with nature, and the knowledge that went with it, that Adam had before the Fall. Bacon's project for a new science was motivated by the question of 'whether that great commerce between the mind of man and the nature of things [...] might by any means be restored to its original condition.'[2]

To restore what was lost at the Fall was the hope of many of the new scientists. For Robert Hooke (1635–1703), first curator of experiments for the Royal Society,

> as at first, mankind fell by tasting of the forbidden Tree of Knowledge, so we, their Posterity, may be in part restor'd by the same way, not only by beholding and contemplating, but by tasting too those fruits of Natural Knowledge that were never yet forbidden.[3]

In contrast to Calvinist theology, among the new scientists, the effects of man's sin were minimised. There was, as a consequence, an optimism

that man was able, by his own efforts, to restore nature to its ideal
state before the Fall. As John Passmore simply puts it, 'What sin had
shattered, science could in large part restore.'[4]

Ironically, in the century in which science was emerging, the boundaries between philosophy and theology, far from becoming sharper,
were becoming more blurred. This was, in part, because the natural
philosophers saw theology as part of their professional remit. More
importantly, in an age in which theology had become confessionalised
and divided – between Catholicism and all sorts of Protestantisms –
theological authority was shifting towards those for whom confession-
alism was not decisive, namely, the new scientists.

The new science was thus, in this sense, a theological programme.
There was now the Book of Nature alongside the Book of Scripture,
God's works alongside God's words. Both demonstrated his existence
and attributes. There were some who sought to unite the two books
in one organic synthesis. The Czech philosopher John Comenius
(1592–1670), for example, employed the term 'Pansophia' to indicate his ideal of the unification of all knowledge. But, in principle,
the natural philosophers saw the two books as separate – although,
crucially, equal. Each revealed the divine, and each led to knowledge
of God.

To be sure, the borders were insecure and often crossed. The Book
of Nature did sometimes serve to illuminate the Book of Scripture.
William Whiston was perhaps the most outstanding example of a
scientist willing to blur the boundaries virtually beyond recognition.
For Whiston, Moses was no longer a Hebrew Greek philosopher
but an English scientist. Here science has replaced Platonism as the
true meaning of the Scriptures: 'The Mosaick account of creation,'
he declared,

> is not a Nice and Philosophical account of the origin of all things,
> but an Historical and True Representation of the formation of
> our single earth out of a confused Chaos, and of the successive
> and visible changes thereof each day, till it became the habitation
> of Mankind.[5]

While Isaac Newton (1643–1727) believed that religion and philosophy should be kept separate, he was an inveterate boundary crosser.[6]

Ideally, however, it was Francis Bacon's division between the Books
of Nature and Scripture that informed, at least rhetorically, the scientific experiments of the natural philosophers: 'let no man upon a
weak conceit of sobriety or an ill-applied moderation,' declared Bacon,

> think or maintain that a man can search too far, or be too well
> studied in the book of God's word, or in the book of God's works,
> divinity or philosophy; but rather let men endeavour an endless
> progress or proficience in both; only let men beware that they apply
> both to charity, and not to swelling; to use, and not to ostentation;
> and again, that they do not unwisely mingle or confound these
> learnings together.[7]

So while nature and Scripture should not be mingled, science was
nonetheless a very 'hands-on' way of worshipping God. As Frank
Manuel eloquently writes:

> Rhetorically [...] science was integrated into the life of the literate
> English upper classes through a baroque elaboration of a theology
> of glory, arguments backed up by profuse illustrations of the mar-
> vellous design, beauty, harmony, and order of nature as revealed by
> scientific inquiry.[8]

More importantly, a new theology was emerging out of the new science:
'natural theology'. This was theology turned towards contemplation
of the rational and moral law within and the natural laws without.
Before the Reformation, Platonism was the glue that held together
Christianity – both East and West – Judaism and Islam. It provided a
philosophical unity to the variety of revelations. It enabled a common
discourse among the likes of Aquinas, Averroes and Maimonides. After
the Reformation, the new natural theology became the glue that was in
principle able to hold together not only Christianity, Judaism and Islam,
but also the ever-increasing varieties of Protestantism, now divided as

much as united by their doctrine of *sola scriptura*. Where Scripture divided, natural theology united. It thus provided an account of the theological unity beneath the various religious faiths that had been constructed since the Reformation, not in terms of inner piety, but as conflicting sets of religious propositions that required intellectual assent.[9] It thus provided the grounds for toleration not only between the religions but also between the Catholic and Protestant confessions. This was no bad thing in a Europe weary of endless violence over matters theological.

Unlike Platonism, which read the world in terms of God, natural theology did the reverse. It read God in terms of the evidences provided by investigations, observations and experiments in the natural world. Isaac Newton's friend William Derham (1657–1735) laid out the intentions of this theology in the subtitle of his 1713 book *Physico-Theology: Or a Demonstration of the Being and Attributes of God, from His Works of Creation*, as did William Paley (1743–1805) in 1802 in his *Natural Theology: Or Evidences of the Existence and Attributes of the Deity, Collected from the Appearances of Nature*. The God revealed in natural theology was a very 'English' and even-handed 'Anglican' God. Quite the gentleman, really. Not the wrathful, vengeful God of Calvinism, but a benevolent, 'humane', supremely ethical and rational deity – a God you could rely upon not to make too many demands in this life and to be generous in the next, and one who was revealed in the moral law within and the natural laws without.

The God of everything

The God revealed by natural philosophy or the new science and in natural theology was the creator and the designer. Unlike the emanating God of Platonism, who was *both* transcendent and immanent, this God was *only* transcendent. But there was one exception to this, namely, the God of the Dutch ('Jewish') philosopher Baruch de Spinoza (1632–77). I place 'Jewish' in inverted commas because, while Spinoza was a Jew by descent, he was not one by faith. Indeed, in 1656, he had been thrown out of the synagogue of Amsterdam for heresy. No longer considering himself Jewish and remaining free of any further religious commitments, Spinoza became, in effect, Europe's first secular Jew (by descent). Indeed, he was anti-Judaic. He wanted nothing to do with the transcendent God of Judaism. As Steven Nadler sums it up:

> Spinoza rejected the providential God of Abraham, Isaac, and Jacob as an anthropomorphic fiction; he denied the divine origin of the Torah and the continued validity of the Law of Moses; and he argued that there is no theologically, metaphysically, or morally interesting sense in which the Jews are a chosen people.[10]

More generally, the transcendent and personal creator God or gods of the religions were, in Spinoza's view, nothing but human inventions. Thus, people came to believe that all natural things were to their advantage and that such things had not made themselves. They concluded that 'there was some governor or governors of Nature, endowed with human freedom, who have attended to all their needs and made everything for their use.' The nature of God or the gods was then constructed on the basis of human nature. And hence

> they asserted that the gods direct everything for man's use so that they might bind men to them and be held in the highest honour by them. So it came about that every individual devised different methods of worshipping God as he thought fit in order that God should love him beyond others, and direct the whole of Nature so as to serve his blind cupidity and insatiable greed.[11]

Rather than being the personal, transcendent creator, Spinoza's God was purely an impersonal immanent deity. Spinoza referred to 'Deus sive Natura' – 'God or [in other words] Nature'. God is Nature in the sense that God underlies, is present within and unifies all things. God is Nature and Nature is God. Thus, everything is in God. 'Whatever is,' wrote Spinoza, 'is in God, and nothing can either be or be conceived without God.'[12] Outside Nature, there is nothing.

Unlike the transcendent creator God, Spinoza's God did not create as the consequence of a spontaneous act of free will. God for Spinoza was not the kind of being of whom it made sense to talk of having a free will. Rather, everything that occurs within the world is absolutely and necessarily determined. Thus, there is no transcendent being with a purpose for the universe and there is no grand plan for it. Things just and can only happen because of God or Nature and according to the necessary laws of nature. For Spinoza, there can be no departures from these laws. God cannot do miracles, not least because 'miracle', as 'an abrogation of the laws of nature', is a concept that makes no sense. To 'take refuge in the will of God', in the face of naturally inexplicable events, is to flee to a 'sanctuary of ignorance'.[13] Our only option is to know that we are part of God, to cultivate an intellectual love for God (although he will not love us in return) and accept philosophically (both intellectually and emotionally) whatever hand the impersonal God, Nature or (what amounts to the same thing) Fate should deal us.

'Pantheism' is a notoriously fluid term. But the common identification of Spinoza's understanding of God with pantheism provides an opportunity to clarify it as a possible understanding of the relationship between God and the world. At its most general, pantheism is the view that God is identical with the universe. On this broad definition, Spinoza was a pantheist. He rejected the transcendent God who existed apart from the world. He also rejected the God of Christianised Platonism, who was both transcendent to and immanent within the world. But was Spinoza divinising Nature or naturalising God – or was he doing both? It is best to come at this question not by asking about Spinoza's view of God, but by asking about his view of Nature.

There are, according to Spinoza, two aspects to Nature. First, there is *natura naturans* ('nature naturing'). This is the 'creative' or (better) 'emanative' part of Nature, out of which everything else comes. Second, there is *natura naturata* ('nature natured'). This is the universe, the effects of Nature's naturing. For Spinoza, God is both what 'natures' and what is 'natured'. 'The more we understand particular things,' he wrote, 'the more we understand God.'[14] Insofar as *God* is that which brings about everything else, Nature has been divinised for it, as *natura naturans*, functions like God in Spinoza's theology. On the other hand, since what God, as *natura naturans*, brings about is himself, as *natura naturata*, God is naturalised in the form of the universe. In sum, on this account, Spinoza was both divinising Nature and naturalising God. Thus, Spinoza was a pantheist and, since all of Nature was divine and not merely a part of it, a 'strong' pantheist at that. We might take this one step further and ask: if there were no world, would God still exist? It is hard to see, on this account of Spinoza, how, were there no world, God could be said to exist.[15]

An innate God

In contrast to Spinoza's immanent deity, the new natural religion and natural theology looked to the transcendent God. This God may not have been immanent within the natural world but he was nonetheless evidenced by it. But the transcendent God was also 'revealed' through introspection. God was, as it were, an innate idea. Thus, for example, for the philosopher Edward Herbert of Cherbury (1583–1648), since the mind was 'the best image and specimen of divinity', rational introspection was the key to knowledge of God and of the fundamentals of religion more generally.[16] Thus, in 1624 in his principal work *De veritate* (On truth), he devoted a chapter to 'Common notions concerning religion' that were an imprint or inscription of God on the mind. Herbert was thus mounting a defence against all those Protestant theologies that, in their attacks upon other theologies, were not only undermining reason in general but also creating scepticism about religious truth more generally.

These common notions were five in number: (1) there is a supreme God; (2) this God ought to be worshipped; (3) virtue and piety are the most important part of religious practice; (4) wickedness must be repented; (5) there is reward or punishment after this life. These common notions could be added to by revealed truths. Nevertheless, Herbert declared, the book, religion or prophet 'which adheres most closely to them is the best'.[17]

These common notions were evidenced in the history of religions beneath the layers of superstitions, conventions and particularly priest-craft that had accrued. They thus comprised the philosophical essence of all the historical religions and therefore their inner unity. The history of religions, read through their eyes (not all that surprisingly perhaps), verified them. They also underpinned the religions and confessions of Herbert's time. What divided contemporary religions and confessions – namely, superstitions, conventions and priestcraft – was the corruption of what united them all, namely, the common notions. Herbert was thus discerning the religion of 'nature' behind or within the religions of culture.

All religions in the past and all future religions, Herbert declared, have acknowledged the existence of a supreme deity, although known by different names – Jehovah, Allah, Optimus Maximus, and so on. This supreme being was good, just, eternal, free, all-powerful, and so on. In addition, proof that this God was to be worshipped was to be found in every type of religion 'from every age, country and race.'[18] While there was universal disagreement about rites, ceremonies and revealed truth, all agreed that conscience, guided by the common notions, produced virtue and piety, from which sprang hope, faith, love, joy and blessedness. In addition, the religions generally agreed that God's goodness and our conscience told us that our sins could be washed away by true repentance and that we could be restored to union with God (no predestination here!).[19]

While Herbert recognised that there were considerable differences within the religions over the nature of post-mortem rewards and punishments, all religions taught that there would be punishment or reward after death. Implicit here was the radical notion that the redemptive act of God in Christ was unnecessary (and for that matter, so was the doctrine of the Trinity). So while not every religion was good, and while salvation was not open to every man in every religion, Herbert was convinced that in every religion and in every individual conscience, 'sufficient means are granted to men to win God's good will.'[20] In short, the pious and virtuous practice of the common notions brought heavenly rewards. This was salvation through pious and virtuous works for everyone – Catholic, Protestant, Jew, Muslim and pagan.

This was a radical move. For, on the face of it, Herbert was the first to say that salvation was possible for everyone *outside revelation* and that it was available through rational introspection and a pious and virtuous life. The God of reason and the God of revelation were thus beginning to part company. We are witnessing in Herbert the beginnings of a rational or natural religion sustainable independently of revelation. Revelation was becoming the handmaiden of reason.

Revelation 'naturalised'

Thus it was that the English philosopher John Locke (1632–1704) set out to demonstrate in 1695, as the title of his work showed, *The Reasonableness of Christianity, as Delivered in the Scriptures*. In Locke, unlike in Herbert, reason was not turned inward but outward – to the Books of Scripture and Nature. Christianity, not as delivered in the dogmas, traditions and confessional conflicts but as delivered *in the Scriptures*, was reasonable simply because, practically, it was the most reliable means for fallen humanity to obtain the immortality that had been lost at the Fall. That said, this was not the Scriptures read through Platonist eyes or, for that matter, through Protestant eyes. Rather, or so at least Locke claimed, it was the Scriptures read as 'the plain man' would read them (for which read 'sensible Englishman'), 'without such learned, artificial, and forced senses of them, as are sought out, and put upon them in most of the Systems of Divinity'.[21] The requirements of the Scriptures were twofold. First, it was necessary to accept Jesus Christ as the Messiah. Second, it was necessary to obey the moral law and lead a virtuous life. 'These two,' declared Locke, 'Faith and Repentance; i.e. believing Jesus to be the Messiah, and a good Life; are the indispensable Conditions of the New Covenant to be performed by all those who would obtain Eternal Life.'[22]

If salvation depended on faith and repentance, what was to become of those who had not heard of Christ and neither accepted nor rejected him? That would depend on what use they had made of natural religion. God had revealed, wrote Locke,

> by the Light of Reason [...] to all Mankind, who would make use
> of that Light, that he was Good and Merciful. The same spark of
> the Divine Nature and Knowledge in Man [...] shewed him the
> Law he was under as a Man; Shewed him also the way of Attoning
> the merciful, kind, compassionate Author and Father of him and
> his Being, when he had transgressed that Law. He that made use of
> this Candle of the Lord, so far as to find what was his Duty, could
> not miss to find also the way to Reconciliation and Foregiveness.[23]

In other words, reason properly used could bring salvation.

Locke, of course, realised that, in principle, this made Christ redundant. But, he argued, although the works of nature sufficiently evidence the existence of God, yet did man make such little use of his reason, that he failed to see God. This was, in the final analysis, down to the wickedness of priests who, in order to preserve their power, excluded reason from religion. Even those who found God through the right use of their reason dared not teach it to the multitude. For the same reason, the moral law was hidden from the masses: 'natural Religion in its full extent, was no where, that I know, taken care of by the force of Natural Reason.'[24]

Thus, the role of Christ was to make clear that which had become hidden beneath the priests' subversion of natural religion and the philosophers' cowardice to proclaim it. As a result, the masses were able to accept the moral law as taught by Christ. His authority so to teach was evidenced by his miracles and reinforced by the prospect of heavenly reward for those who humbly worshipped God and lived pious and virtuous lives. All the duties of morality were apparent in the Scriptures. Christ's was teaching that,

> as it suits the lowest Capacities of Reasonable Creatures, so it
> reaches and satisfies, Nay, enlightens the highest. The most elevated
> Understandings cannot but submit to the Authority of this Doctrine

as Divine; Which coming from the mouths of a company of illiterate men, hath not only the attestation of Miracles, but reason to confirm it; Since they delivered no Precepts but such, as though Reason of itself had not clearly made out.[25]

In a word, Christ was the teacher of natural religion (rather than the Saviour) and Christianity was natural religion for both the intellectual elite and the simple folk. No need here for complicated esoteric readings of Scripture to satisfy the cultivated appetites of philosophers – just plain home cooking.

The implication of Locke's account of the difference between what was revealed and what was natural was that there wasn't much of one – or, at least, not one that mattered. That there *was* no difference that mattered was the central theme of the major work in 1730 of English theologian Matthew Tindal (1657–1733).[26] The title rather gave the game away: *Christianity as Old as the Creation: Or the Gospel, a Republication of the Religion of Nature.* Tindal's theology epitomised the 'naturalising' direction in Anglicanism since the time of Herbert. It was, in effect, a radical reframing of Christianity in line with reason. Christianity became, in Tindal's view, a re-establishing of the original religion of humanity, before it had been corrupted by superstition:

Men, if they sincerely endeavour to discover the Will of God, will perceive, that there's a *Law of Nature*, or *Reason*; which is so call'd, as being a Law which is common, or natural to all rational Creatures; and that this Law, like its Author, is absolutely perfect, eternal, and unchangeable: and that the Design of the Gospel [i.e. Christianity] was not to add to, or take from this Law; but to free Men from that Load of Superstition which had been mix'd with it: So that TRUE CHRISTIANITY is not a Religion of Yesterday, but what God, at the Beginning, dictated, and still continues to dictate to Christians as well as others.[27]

This natural religion promoted by Tindal consisted of two things: first, belief in the existence of an absolutely perfect God who was the

source of all other beings; second, the practice of the moral duties
that arise from this belief. Religion, on this account, was a pretty
plain and simple business: 'we may define True Religion to consist
in a constant Disposition of Mind to do all the Good we can; and
thereby render ourselves acceptable to God in answering the End of
his Creation.'[28]

The religion of nature was, consequently, the absolutely perfect
religion, no more and certainly no less than anything revealed by God.
Moreover, it was the religion of nature, written in the hearts of everyone
from the time of creation, that provided the criteria upon which any
apparent revelation was to be judged. If any revealed religion varied
from the religion of nature 'in any one Particular, nay, in the minutest
Circumstance, That alone is an Argument, which makes all Things else
that can be said for its Support totally ineffectual'.[29] Moreover, anything
that was false by reason could not be true by revelation, simply because
'nothing unreasonable, nay, what is not highly reasonable, can come
from a God of unlimited, universal, and eternal Reason'.[30] Thus, the
precepts of revealed religion could not be different from those of natural religion, not least because, unlike the despotic God of Calvinism,
God was the kind of God who also acted only according to the reason
and nature of things.

This was far removed from the Catholic view (inherited from
Aquinas) that 'unreasonable' revelation could supplement reasonable
religion. But it was also distanced from the Protestant doctrine of
sola scriptura. Tindal was suggesting that reason should be the judge
of revelation not only because reason provided a more likely access
to religious truth but also because Scripture itself was flawed. Its
disputed books, various translations and uncertain meanings were
themselves, he argued, the cause of Christian disunity. Misreading
literally what Scripture intended figuratively, he declared, can 'run
Men into monstrous Absurdities'.[31] He drew attention too to various
unacceptable aspects of the Bible – particularly its anthropomorphic
God and his often-contemptible breaches of the moral law. Even the
precepts of Jesus, he wrote, 'are not to be taken in the plain, obvious,
and grammatical Meaning of the Words; but are to be explain'd, limited,

and restrain'd, as best serve to promote human happiness.'[32] Faith in
reason was now allied with scepticism about the Bible.

Tindal was thus proclaiming the need for yet another Protestant
Reformation. This was one that no longer held unalloyed belief in the
primacy of Scripture but subjected the Bible not only to philosophical
and theological criticism but also to historical and philological scrutiny – not *sola scriptura* but rather *sola natura et ratio*.

Tindal was in fact part of a developing liberal Protestantism
that had begun, since the 1650s, to differentiate itself from both
a Catholic scholasticism grounded in Platonism and a conservative Protestantism founded on the Bible alone. It was, at the same
time, distinguishing itself *both* from a conservative Catholicism that
based its claims to truth on evidence of the miracles performed in
its name *and* from a radical Protestantism that was declaring religious legitimacy on the basis of the miracles and divine healings
performed on its behalf.

God, providence and the cessation of miracles

Tindal's new religion of nature was radical indeed. For unlike that
of John Locke, which allowed for God's intervention in the natural
world, Tindal's excluded it. 'God,' he declared, 'will not, in this Life,
miraculously alter the Course of Things [...] nor break in upon the
ordinary Methods and Laws of his Providence.'[33] Ironically, however,
Tindal's rejection of miracles was the philosophical heir of a theological doctrine that was firmly based on the Protestant principle of *sola
scriptura*. This was the doctrine of the cessation of miracles.[34]

The doctrine of the cessation of miracles held that miracles had
ceased after the time of the New Testament or, at the latest, soon
after the 'establishment' of the church in the fourth century CE. It
was the most important of an array of arguments against miracles in
sixteenth-century Protestant theology which were intended to criticise
the claims of the Catholic Church to sole religious truth and legitimacy
on the grounds of the miracles that were performed within it. It was

certainly a declaration that God no longer intervened supernaturally in the affairs of men and that therefore Catholic claims that he still did so were spurious.

At the same time, Protestant claims that apparent miracles were the fraudulent acts of a priesthood comprising charlatans, the works of Satan or part of the end-time activities of the papal Antichrist helped to establish Protestant self-identity as a reaffirmation of New Testament Christianity, one that looked around Christendom to Christ. The Protestant critique of Catholic miracles along with the ritualistic paraphernalia that accompanied them – saints, pilgrimages, relics, shrines, exorcisms, indulgences – was at the heart of the Protestant invention of itself as a distinct tradition. The Anglican bishop of Gloucester John Hooper (*c.*1495–1555) summarised the English Protestant position in 1550:

> I believe that this holy doctrine of the gospel in the very time by God appointed was confirmed and approved by heavenly miracles, as well by Jesus Christ himself, the prophets and Apostles, as also by other good and faithful ministers of the same Gospel; and that after such a sort, that for the confirming thereof there is now no more need of new miracles; but rather we must content ourselves with what is done, and simply and plainly believe only the holy scriptures without seeking any further to be taught; watching and still taking heed to ourselves, that we be not beguiled and deceived with the false miracles of Antichrist, wherewith the world at this day is stuffed; which miracles are wrought by the working of Satan, to confirm all kinds of idolatry, errors, abuses, and iniquities, and thereby to blind the poor and ignorant.[35]

Generally, English Protestant theologians were following the lead of the major European reformers in accepting that, although God could still do miracles if he so wished, he did so no longer (or very rarely). Martin Luther, for example, accepted that God did miracles to establish Christianity and that, as the faith became established, miracles gradually ceased. While he accepted that the 'miracle' of the soul transformed by faith would continue until the Last Day, the much rarer miracles of the body, as exemplified in Christ's healing miracles, were no longer needed since the Christian faith had come to rest securely on the Scriptures. This excused the absence of miracles within Protestantism, though it did not go to a critique of their apparent continuation in Catholicism.[36]

More than Luther, Calvin engaged directly with the Catholic claim that miracles validated Catholicism and their absence falsified Protestantism. Against this claim, Calvin mounted a counterargument from Scripture that miracles, far from pointing to the truth of doctrines, pointed far more to false prophets and Antichrists.[37] Miracles, he declared, nourished idolatry, drawing people away from the true worship of God. Their [Catholics'] miracles are 'so foolish and ridiculous, so vain and false!'[38] And he hinted that Catholic doctrine, far from being confirmed by miracles, was actually disconfirmed by what were really illusory Satanic wonders: 'Satan has his miracles, which, though they are deceitful tricks rather than true powers, are of such sort as to mislead the simple-minded and untutored.'[39]

Still, Satanic wonders aside, Calvin's considered opinion was that miracles had probably ceased in the time of the early church. No doubt he thought it better to criticise all Catholic miracles as fraudulent, on the basis of the cessation of *all* miracles, than to argue for the possibility of Protestant ones. Thus, he declared,

Though Christ does not expressly state whether he intends this gift to be temporary, or to remain perpetually in his Church, yet it is more probable that miracles were promised only for a time, in order to give lustre to the gospel, while it was new and in a state of obscurity [...] I think that the true design for which miracles were appointed was, that nothing which was necessary for proving the doctrine of the gospel should be wanting at its commencement. And certainly we see that the use of them ceased not long afterwards, or at least, that instances of them were so rare as to entitle us to conclude that they would not be equally common in all ages.[40]

All this was not to imply that, from the time of creation, God had gone into very early retirement and that all that had since happened was the consequence of blind fate or indiscriminate fortune. Quite the contrary! Calvin's God was no distant unmoved mover, as Aristotelians would have had it; nor was he indifferent to what happened in the world, as the Epicureans would suggest. Rather, he was a transcendent yet active ruler and governor of the world.

So, in spite of appearances at times to the contrary, God really was working his purposes out as year succeeded to year. This doctrine of divine providence meant that, as Calvin put it, God 'sustains the world by his energy, he governs everything however remote, so that not even a sparrow falls to the ground without his decree'.[41] In short, God so attended to the regulation of individual events according to a set plan that nothing took place by chance. '[W]e make God the ruler and governor of all things,' wrote Calvin,

> who in accordance with his wisdom has from the farthest limit of
> eternity decreed what he was going to do, and now by his might
> carries out what he has decreed. From this we declare that not only
> heaven and earth and the inanimate creatures, but also the plans
> and intentions of men, are so governed by his providence that they
> are borne by it straight to their appointed end.[42]

That said, granted the changes and chances of this fleeting world, God's purposes are not comprehensible to us, so much so that a sceptic might say that they seem little different from mere serendipity or happenstance. Calvin himself admitted as much:

> But since the order, reason, end, and necessity of those things
> which happen for the most part lie hidden in God's purposes,
> and are not apprehended by human opinion, those things which
> it is certain take place by God's will, are in a sense fortuitous. For
> they bear on the face of them no other appearance, whether they
> are considered in their own nature or weighed according to our
> knowledge or judgement.[43]

This strongly suggests that there is little difference between those who fatalistically believe that what will be, will be, and those who providentially accept that what is is God's will. But, for Calvin, there was a difference, although it was only a psychological one: providentialists found comfort, he said, where fatalists felt only anxiety. Those who tried to overturn the doctrine of providence, declared Calvin,

> depriving the children of God of true joy and tormenting their minds with a wretched disquiet, create for themselves hell on earth. What more horrible torment can there be than endlessly to tremble in anxiety? We will find no rest until we learn to recline in the providence of God.[44]

Better stoically to accept the slings and arrows of outrageous fortune as part of God's great plan than to wallow melancholically in the Slough of Despond.

For Calvin, God's providential action, incomprehensible as it often was to us, nevertheless had a moral meaning. For the sufferings of this present time were not only unworthy to be compared with the glories yet to come but also served both as a divine punishment for vice and as a godly incentive to virtue – to foster humility, to demonstrate God's authority, to cultivate patience, to point out human weaknesses, to indicate our hidden vices and to show our need for his mercy. Little wonder, then, that Calvin was able to underplay the notion of miracle considered as an occasional intervention into the world by God. The notion of providence entailed that there was never anything in the world that occurred in which God was not already active. In this sense, miracles were everywhere. Thus, providence not only informed how one was to understand the world but also how one was to live within it. As the Anglican John Pelling put it in a sermon in 1607,

> It is so profitable a doctrine, that well learned and well used, it informes a mans understanding with the knowledge of God and himselfe; it conformes the will to religious resolutions, it reformes the courses of a mans life, to christian obedience, it armes a distressed

and an injured man with patience, it humbles a man full of pros-
peritie, that he burst not with pride; it tempers a man given to his
lascivious and luxurious appetite that hee shall abstaine: it cooles,
nay it quenches a mans fierie and sudden furie, that he shall do
no mischiefe: it pacifieth ones deepe conceived displeasure, and
otherwise implacable offense taken, that a man neither workes
nor meditates revenge; it makes men make a conscience of their
doings, for their gaine, for their delight, for their preferment, for
any way having their will, their purpose. It makes men remember
whence they came, consider where they are, what they doe, and
whither they shall; it keeps men the more innocent that they doe
no harme; it makes men the more warie that they take no harme;
it teacheth men how to live well, and how to die well, which
is next to eternall felicitie; live he poore or rich, in high or low
estate, die he in his flourishing or decrepit age, of what disease,
by what meanes, at home or abroad, at sea or land, when, where,
and howsoever.[45]

Did God work miracles?

That God had always worked miracles and continued to do so in the
present remained a part of the Catholic tradition, although the Council
of Trent (1545–63), Catholicism's attempt to rethink itself in response
to the rise of Protestantism, brought the verification of miracles under
episcopal control (and ultimately medical control).[46] Within Protestant
modes of thinking, in spite of, and partly as a result of, the Protestant
critique of miracles, 'miracle' became a contested category. Miracles,
particularly those of healing, remained a part of popular Protestant
piety and practice and a bulwark against an overemphasis on reason.
In less combative contexts than the conflict with Catholicism, some
Calvinist theologians even held open a place for miraculous occurrences
now rebadged as 'extraordinary and unusuall' providences over against
the 'ordinary and usuall' providences that did service as demonstrations
of God's all-powerfulness.[47]

In addition, the distinction between miracles (*miracula*) as the result of direct supernatural interventions by God, wonders (*miranda*) as extraordinary events entirely explicable in natural terms (which included the demonic and the angelic) and providential events (whether ordinary or extraordinary) was becoming increasingly uncertain. Hence the problem, as Alexandra Walsham notes, 'of deciding whether bizarre and puzzling phenomena should be attributed to diabolic guile, human cunning, the creativity of Nature, or the ingenuity of the Almighty'.[48]

Most importantly, during the latter part of the seventeenth century and into the eighteenth, the term 'miracle' was shifting its intellectual context from the theological to the naturalistic. That is to say, miracles were becoming located within the context of a world understood scientifically rather than theologically. As such, God's activity in the world (whether ordinary or extraordinary) now became a matter of *philosophical* debate rather than *theological* argument and *confessional* dispute – a matter for rational discussion, not scriptural quarrel. It pertained more to the European Enlightenment than to the European Reformation. And it became more problematic as the new science came to focus on nature's orderliness, simplicity, decorum, regularity and uniformity. Miracles thus became defined as violations of the laws of nature. As the Anglican theologian William Fleetwood (1656–1723) put it in 1702, a miracle was 'an extraordinary operation of God, against the known course, and settled Laws of Nature, appealing to the senses'.[49]

As a consequence, the question – on the face of it a simple one – then became: did God work miracles? Granted that miracles were now seen primarily as violations of the laws of nature, there were two refinements of this question. As Jane Shaw puts it:

First, *would* God violate the laws of nature? And secondly, *could* God violate the laws of nature? [...] To suppose that God *would* not violate the laws of nature was to make an argument from divine character and purpose: that God is of consistent purpose, God thinks through what kind of world he wants to begin with, and then opts for the laws of nature he wants. To suppose that

God *could* not violate the laws of nature was to develop Spinoza's argument, that it was metaphysically impossible for those laws to be contravened.[50]

Matthew Tindal, in his *Christianity as Old as the Creation*, exemplified the former position.[51] For Tindal, although God could supernaturally intervene in the world, he chose not to. That he did not do so was the consequence, for Tindal, of God's wisdom and goodness. The wise and benevolent deity created a world that operated according to laws that did not require alteration or suspension: 'as his Wisdom is always the same, so is his Goodness; and consequently from the Consideration of both these, his Laws must always be the same.'[52] God governs all his actions according to the dictates of reason and 'does not act arbitrarily, or interpose unnecessarily'.[53] Tindal's strong doctrine of benevolent divine providence, as a consequence of which all was as well in the world as it could possibly be, ruled out the necessity for God ever to interfere with the natural order of things. Why would he?

Of course, a miracle was at the absolute core of Christianity. This was the Resurrection of Christ from the dead on the third day after his crucifixion. So while it was feasible to argue that, since the time of early Christianity, God no longer did miracles (although he could if he wished) and remain within the bounds of orthodoxy, to suggest that God had *never* done miracles because he *never could*, and therefore to deny the truth of the Resurrection, was to question the very foundation of the Christian tradition. Thus, when the schoolmaster Peter Annet (1693–1769) attacked the credibility of the evidence for the Resurrection in his book *The Resurrection of Jesus Considered* in 1744, he did so as an explicit unbeliever.

That the evidence for the miracle of the Resurrection was not credible was the consequence of Annet's belief that miracles *could not* happen.[54] His argument was a simple one. The laws of nature were inviolable. A miracle could only be defined as a violation of the laws of nature. Therefore, miracles could not happen. Moreover, miracles were inconsistent with the attributes of God. For their occurrence, as violations of the laws of nature, implied a changeability in God that was incompatible with his immutability. 'To suppose that God can alter the settled laws of nature,' declared Annet,

> which he himself formed, is to suppose his will and wisdom mutable; and that they are not the best laws of the most perfect being; for if he is the author of them, they must be as immutable as he is; so that he cannot alter them to make them better. And will not alter them to make them worse.[55]

Thus, along with the Resurrection of Christ were thrown out the biblical miracles of the sun standing still at the command of Joshua (Josh. 10.13), Moses parting the Red Sea (Exod. 14.21), Jonah living in the belly of a whale (Jonah 1.17), Jesus feeding the multitudes with a few loaves and fishes (Matt. 14.13–21), Satan showing Jesus all the kingdoms of the world from a mountain top (Matt. 4.8), the followers of Jesus speaking in languages unknown to them on the day of Pentecost (Acts 2.6–13), and so on.[56]

For his subversive ideas, Peter Annet was sentenced at the age of 68 in 1762 to stand in the pillory and to serve a prison sentence of one year's hard labour. Unlike Annet, the Scot David Hume (1711–76) was no humble schoolmaster. By the time he published his essay 'Of miracles' in his *An Enquiry Concerning Human Understanding* in 1748, he was recognised as one of Europe's greatest philosophers and immune from either legal prosecution or ecclesiastical persecution. His was an argument that would be, at least to the wise and learned, he declared, 'an everlasting check to all kinds of superstitious delusion and consequently, will be useful as long as the world endures'.[57] It was just as much an attack on the Resurrection of Christ as that of Annet. But Hume was more circumspect in his presentation of it. Thus, without mentioning any names, as his exemplar of a miracle that was 'a violation of the laws of nature', he gave that of a dead man coming to life 'because that has never been *observed* in any age or country'.[58]

Hume did not accept that the laws of nature could not be violated. Thus, in principle, miracles could occur. But his argument was that there could never be sufficient evidence for the reasonable man, who proportioned his belief to the weight of evidence, to believe that such a violation had occurred. The evidence that a violation of a law of nature had occurred (from the testimony that a man had risen from the dead, for example) could never outweigh the enormous weight of evidence that had established the law (that men do not rise from the dead) in the first place. There must, therefore, Hume wrote,

> be a uniform experience against every miraculous event, otherwise the event would not merit that appellation. And as a uniform experience amounts to a proof, there is here a direct and full *proof* [...] against the existence of any miracle.[59]

Moreover, Hume believed, the testimony in favour of miracles was never really up to much. First, we do not have, in all history, any miracle attested by men of such good sense, education and learning as to secure us against their being deluded. So much for the biblical writers! Second, men like strange and miraculous tales and the miraculous fosters the agreeable emotions of surprise and wonder. Third, it is a strong presumption against miracles that they 'abound among ignorant and barbarous nations' and, where they are still admitted among the civilised, they will have been inherited from ignorant and barbarous ancestors.[60] Fourth, the different religions (of Rome, Turkey, Siam and China) appeal to miracles in support of their truth. In so doing, they discredit the miracles appealed to by other faiths and indirectly thereby discredit those of their own. In sum, in spite of any quantity of evidence, the quality of the evidence for miracles was pretty suspect.

All of this was not to say that Christ did not rise from the dead. He may well have done so. Hume's point was that, *on the evidence*, it would not be reasonable to believe that he had. Hume tried to apologise for his rational critique of miracles by suggesting that he was attempting to confound those dangerous friends or disguised enemies of Christianity who were defending Christianity by appeal to the principles of reason. 'Our most holy religion,' he declared, 'is founded on *Faith*, not on reason.'[61] Really? Hume as a staunch defender of

Jerusalem against Athens? It just doesn't ring true, particularly in the light of the concluding sentences of his 'Of miracles', which suggested that to believe in the Christian religion required an internal miracle, so subversive of all reason and so against all experience was it:

> So that, upon the whole, we may conclude, that the Christian Religion not only was at first attended with miracles, but even at this day cannot be believed by any reasonable person without one. Mere reason is insufficient to convince us of its veracity; and whoever is moved by Faith to assent to it, is conscious of a continued miracle in his own person, which subverts all the principles of his understanding, and gives him a determination to believe what is most contrary to custom and experience.[62]

God, providence, watches and evolution

The reformer John Calvin, as we noted above, discerned the activity of God in all events in the world. Whether good or evil, the providence of God was in play and God was the primary cause of all worldly happenings. Beneath the doctrine of God as creator of the world lay that of God as its ruler. '[F]aith ought to penetrate more deeply,' wrote Calvin,

> namely, having found him Creator of all, forthwith to conclude he is also everlasting Governor and Preserver – not only in that he drives the celestial frame as well as its several parts by a universal motion, but also in that he sustains, nourishes, and cares for, everything he has made, even to the least sparrow.[63]

The consequence of this was that Calvin tended to minimise secondary or natural causes. These were for him a distraction from the appropriate emphasis on God's all-powerful government of the world and his activity as the primary cause of all that happened. Calvin was suspicious of natural philosophy (or what we would call 'science') for this reason.

Not all were as committed as Calvin to such a 'hot' version of providentialism as his. Most probably thought that life was too short for that. Thus, for example, Arthur Gurney complained in 1581 of a scepticism about providence such that, when God imprinted his warnings in the sky and upon the earth, people were prone to 'dasell and devise' of Mother Nature and ascribe 'eche thing unto her lawes'.[64] There were no doubt times when events that seemed to some to cry out for a providential reading were taken by others merely as matters of serendipity.

'Cooler' versions of providence were also to arise with the new science that focused explanations of what happened in the world primarily on natural causes. The doctrine of providence now had to be aligned with a new philosophy in which natural rather than providential explanation of the world was becoming dominant. The question was: how was the doctrine of providence – that nothing happens in the world that is not a message from God of some sort or other – to be understood in a world that operated according to divinely instituted laws of nature, was much less a theatre of theological and moral drama and was consequently no longer quite so divinely communicative?[65]

Thomas Sprat (1635–1713) was a fellow of the Royal Society, later bishop of Rochester and author of *The History of Royal Society*. His view is representative of those who constructed a 'cool' doctrine of providence to cohere with the new experimental science that the Royal Society exemplified. His was a moderating account of providences, intended to restrain the excesses of the hotter kind of providentialist. Thus, according to Sprat, the 'experimental philosopher' will not conclude that *all* extraordinary events are 'the immediate Finger of God' because he knows from his familiarity with the workings of nature that 'the common instruments of nature' can produce those wonders that appear to the ignorant to have a providential meaning.[66]

Moreover, the finger of God was not to be found in that which excited fear but rather in that which incited a calm admiration of the ordinary and not the extraordinary workings of nature. Even extraordinary events needed to be interrogated for a natural explanation. Thus,

If they [the new scientists] take from the Prodigies, they add to the ordinary Works of the same Author. And those ordinary Works themselves, they do almost raise to the height of Wonders by the exact Discovery, which they make of their excellencies.[67]

Thus did the new scientist become a new kind of Christian, one who discerned the providence of God in the everyday workings of the world rather than in any extraordinary doings. As Lorraine Daston and Katharine Park neatly put it: 'Natural philosophers fought fire with fire, pitting the calm wonder of admiration against the fearful wonder of awe.'[68]

And thus back to the rise of the natural theology with which this chapter began. This was a theology that found God's providential activity not in the unnatural and unusual but, above all, in the natural and usual order of things. The regularity, harmony and order in the world that the new science promoted were evidence too of the essential goodness of the world, a goodness that remained discernible in spite of any corrupting effects of the Fall. The natural world revealed by the new science thus served to stress not only the goodness of the world as originally created but also the goodness of its creator. For the new science, this was not the God of Platonism, whose goodness had flowed out of itself into the world. Rather, it was the transcendent God of the Bible, who 'saw everything that he had made, and indeed it was very good' (Gen. 1.31).

It was the 'design argument' (often called the 'teleological argument') for the existence of God that philosophically united the intricate design of nature revealed by the new science with its transcendent designer.[69] The argument from design to a divine designer was first proposed by the Stoic philosopher Quintus Lucilius Balbus (*fl. c.*100 BCE). His strongest reason to believe in God, it was reported, was

drawn from the regularity of the motion and revolution of the heavens, the distinctness, variety, beauty, and order of the sun, moon, and all the stars, the appearance only of which is sufficient to convince us they are not the effects of chance.[70]

Thomas Aquinas gave a version of it as the fifth of his five ways. But its heyday was in the eighteenth and nineteenth centuries as the new science provided ever more examples of the intricacies of nature from the tele- to the macro- to the microscopic.[71]

William Paley's *Natural Theology: Or Evidences of the Existence and Attributes of the Deity, Collected from the Appearances of Nature* in 1802 gave the argument its most famous rendition in the story now known as 'Paley's watch':

> In crossing a heath, suppose I pitched my foot against a *stone*, and asked how the stone came to be there; I might possibly answer, that, for anything I knew to the contrary, it had lain there for ever: nor would it perhaps be very easy to show the absurdity of this answer. But suppose I had found a *watch* upon the ground, and it should be inquired how the watch happened to be in that place; I should hardly think of the answer which I had before given, that, for any thing I knew, the watch might always have been there. Yet why should not this answer serve for the watch as well as for the stone? Why is it not as admissible in the second case, as in the first? For this reason and for no other, viz. that, when we come to inspect the watch, we perceive (what we could not discover in the stone) that its several parts are framed and put together for a purpose, *e.g.* that they are so formed and adjusted as to produce motion, and that motion so regulated as to point out the hour of the day; that, if the different parts had been differently shaped from what they are, or placed after any other manner, or in any other order, than that in which they are placed, either no motion at all would have been carried on in the machine, or none which would have answered the use that is now served by it.[72]

The conclusion to be drawn from this was that the watch must have had a maker and that there must have existed at some time somewhere an artificer who designed and constructed it for the purpose it actually answered. The connection between watches and watchmakers established, Paley extended the principle to nature generally:

for every indication of contrivance, every manifestation of design, which existed in the watch, exists in the works of nature; with the difference, on the side of nature, of being greater and more, and that in a degree which exceeds all computation. I mean that the contrivances of nature surpass the contrivances of art, in the complexity, subtlety, and curiosity of the mechanism; and still more, if possible, do they go beyond them in number and variety: yet, in a multitude of cases, are not less evidently mechanical, not less evidently contrivances, not less evidently accommodated to their end, or suited to their office, than are the most perfect productions of human ingenuity.[73]

The upshot of all this was obvious: as the watch could not but point to a watchmaker, so the world – infinitely more complex in its design – could not but point to a cosmic maker: 'The marks of *design* are too strong to be got over. Design must have had a designer. That designer must have been a person. That person is God.'[74] Moreover, the design pointed to a designer who was omnipotent, omniscient and benevolent. And, in spite of incidental evidence to the contrary, the overall design was ultimately beneficial. As Paley, in Panglossian mood, put it: 'It is a happy world after all' – even if this was not always obvious to us.[75]

Saturday, 30 June 1860, and some of England's leading scientists gathered in the Museum of Natural History in Oxford to discuss Charles Darwin's (1809–82) work *On the Origin of Species by Means of Natural Selection*, published in the previous year. The audience had gathered not least because the rumour had circulated that the bishop of Oxford, Samuel Wilberforce (1805–73), intended a diatribe against Darwin's account of evolution. His talk was to be followed by that of Thomas Huxley (1825–95), Darwinism's most vehement and eloquent defender. Wilberforce ended his address provocatively, to roars of approval from his supporters in the audience, by asking Huxley whether it was through his grandfather or his grandmother that he traced his descent from an ape. To Sir Benjamin Brodie, sitting near him, waxing biblical, Huxley remarked, 'The Lord hath delivered him into my hands.' Having risen to reply, Huxley declared that this was not a topic that he would have brought forward himself but that he was quite prepared to meet the bishop even on that ground. 'If then,' Huxley said,

> the question is put to me would I rather have a miserable ape for a grandfather or a man highly endowed by nature and possessed of great means and influence and yet who employs those faculties for the mere purpose of introducing ridicule into a grave scientific discussion – I unhesitatingly affirm my preference for the ape.[76]

What was it about Darwin's account of the history of nature that was able to provoke such passions? On the face of it, there was nothing obviously contradictory between the understanding of God as creator and the proposition that nature, rather than being static, was evolving and therefore changing over time. Although he could not accept that the diversity of organic life was as explained in the book of Genesis, Darwin saw no incompatibility between creation and evolution. Thus, he prefaced the first edition of *On the Origin of Species* with Bacon's words about the books of God's words and works (quoted earlier in this chapter) and concluded the second edition with his own words:

> There is grandeur in this view of life, with its several powers, *having been originally breathed by the Creator into a few forms or into one*; and that, whilst this planet has gone cycling on according to the fixed law of gravity, from so simple a beginning endless forms most beautiful and most wonderful have been, and are being, evolved.[77]

To Darwin, evolution was the process of change in nature determined by God from the beginning.

However, while evolution as such may not have been incompatible with creation, it jarred with the notion of God's providence. For, as it seemed to many, that there was this rather than that was not, on Darwin's reckoning, a matter of divine providence but of mere chance, or at least of a set of natural laws that could not be providentially construed.[78] And the consequence of this was that nature was an instance not of providential design but of natural selection, of a struggle for existence, of the survival of the fittest and the extinction of unviable forms of life. Thus did the higher forms of life evolve, remarked Darwin, 'from the war of nature, from famine and death'.[79] This was Tennyson's 'Nature, red in tooth and claw' gone evolutionary. Hardly Paley's 'it is a happy world after all'!

It was a darker vision of nature that William Blake had similarly evoked in his poem 'The Tyger' some 66 years earlier, in 1794:

> Tyger, Tyger, burning bright
> In the forests of the night;
> What immortal hand or eye
> Could frame thy fearful symmetry?

The tiger, both terrifying and fascinating, reflected its creator, a being who could be just as fearsome and captivating, as loving as a lamb yet as lethal as a tiger. Blake's image of God was of a deity both good and evil, just as his creation appeared to be – ethically ambivalent and providentially ambiguous. Thus, between God and Satan, Blake fixed no great distance. This was epitomised in his illustration to the book of Job entitled 'Job's evil dreams' showing a God who has become Satan with a cloven hoof and entwined by a serpent (see Plate 30).

Charles Darwin's own dark vision of the natural world was later to lead him to reflect on Paley's argument:

> Although I did not think much about the existence of a personal God until a considerably later period of my life, I will here give the vague conclusions to which I have been driven. The old argument of design in nature, as given by Paley, which formerly seemed to me so conclusive, fails, now that the law of natural selection has been discovered. We can no longer argue that, for instance, the beautiful hinge of a bivalve shell must have been made by an intelligent being, like the hinge of a door by man. There seems to be no more design in the variability of organic beings and in the action of natural selection, than in the course which the wind blows.[80]

In *On the Origin of Species*, Darwin sat lightly on the issue of human evolution. In the distant future, he remarked, 'Light will be thrown on the origin of man and his history'.[81] But the implication of his work was clear, as Wilberforce and Huxley had noted, namely, that the human species had not been independently and specially created but had itself evolved (albeit not from monkeys but from a common ancestor). Darwin made his own position clear in his *The Descent of Man* in 1871. That man had evolved was a matter too of chance:

> we have given to man a pedigree of prodigious length, but not, it may be said, of noble quality. The world, it has often been remarked, appears as if it had long been preparing for the advent of man; and this, in one sense is strictly true, for he owes his birth to a long line of progenitors. If any single link in this chain had never existed, man would not have been exactly as he now is.[82]

At its most general, this meant that man could no longer be considered to have any unique status relative to the rest of creation. Theologically, it made problematic any notion that man was made in the image of God. Darwin could not have named his book *The Ascent of Man* for he made it clear in its closing pages that, while some men may have morally progressed beyond their lowly origins, there were others, of whom the Fuegians were an example, who had signally failed to progress as far as some apes.[83] Although man (or at least some men) had attained, although not through his own efforts, to the very summit of the organic and moral scale, concluded Darwin, he 'still bears in his bodily frame the indelible stamp of his lowly origin'.[84]

Since the time of Copernicus, Christianity had not been backward in making theological virtues out of scientific necessities and in adjusting itself to the discoveries of science. So some apologists for Christianity saw evolution itself as a welcome return to the God immanent within the processes of nature that natural theology seemed to have banished from the world. Thus, as the Christian Darwinian Aubrey Moore (1848–90) put it in 1889:

The one absolutely impossible conception of God, in the present
day, is that which represents him as an occasional visitor. Science has
pushed the deist's God further and further away, and at the moment
when it seemed as if He would be thrust out altogether, Darwinism
appeared, and, under the disguise of a foe, did the work of a friend.[85]

For many proponents and opponents of Darwinism, suggesting as it
did the compatibility of providence and chance, this was stretching the
friendship a little too far. And if God had indeed designed the world
such that it would, from the time of creation, proceed by chance, it
said little for his goodness in designing one that proceeded in such a
callous and wasteful way. As Darwin himself recognised, the pain and
suffering evidenced in the natural world was more readily explicable
in terms of a process driven by the struggle for existence than the
downside of the providential plan of a benevolent deity.

As much as some Christian supporters of Darwin were committed to blurring the boundaries between Christianity and evolution,
Wilberforce and Huxley, albeit from opposite sides of the border, were
just as determined to deny any overlapping territory. Huxley drew up
the battle lines as early as 1860 in his review of *On the Origin of Species*
in the *Westminster Review*:

> Everybody has read Mr. Darwin's book [...] bigots denounce it with
> ignorant invective; old ladies of both sexes consider it a decidedly
> dangerous book, and even savants, who have no better mud to throw,
> quote antiquated writers to show that its author is no better than an
> ape himself; while every philosophical thinker hails it as a veritable
> Whitworth gun in its armoury of liberalism; and all competent
> naturalists and physiologists, whatever their opinion as to the ulti-
> mate fate of the doctrines put forth, acknowledge that the work in
> which they are embodied is a solid contribution to knowledge and
> inaugurates a new epoch in natural history.[86]

For his part, in his review in the same year, Wilberforce recognised
that this was not simply a dispute between a natural theology and a

naturalised biology. It was infinitely more than that. Darwinism was a threat to the whole Christian drama of creation, Fall and redemption, to the doctrines of the Incarnation and the Trinity – indeed, to the credibility of revelation more generally. For Wilberforce, evolution, especially that of man,

> is absolutely incompatible not only with single expressions in the word of God on that subject of natural science with which it is not immediately concerned, but, which in our judgment is of far more importance, with the whole representation of that moral and spiritual condition of man which is its proper subject-matter. Man's derived supremacy over the earth; man's power of articulate speech; man's gift of reason; man's free-will and responsibility; man's fall and man's redemption; the Incarnation of the Eternal Son; the indwelling of the Eternal Spirit – all are equally and utterly irreconcilable with the degrading notion of the brute origin of him who was created in the image of God, and redeemed by the Eternal Son assuming to himself his nature.[87]

This was, on the face of it, a struggle for survival between competing world views that has lasted until the present day. It was construed on both sides as a do-or-die battle in the history of the warfare between science and Christianity, not merely between evolution and providence, but between reason and revelation, faith and philosophy. Hostilities between Athens and Jerusalem had once again broken out.

7

The Known and Unknown God

Athenians, I see how extremely religious you are in every way. For as I went through the city and looked carefully at the objects of your worship, I found among them an altar with the inscription, 'To an unknown god'. What therefore you worship as unknown, this I proclaim to you.

Acts 17.22–3

Agnosticism

In 1889, Thomas Huxley was led to reflect on his understanding of the term 'agnosticism', the coining of which has been long attributed to him. When he reached intellectual maturity, he declared, he began to ask himself whether he was an atheist, a theist, a pantheist, a materialist, an idealist, a Christian or a free thinker. The one thing that separated him from all of these (except perhaps the last) was that they 'were quite sure that they had attained a certain "gnosis" – had, more or less successfully, solved the problem of existence; while I was quite sure I had not, and had a pretty strong conviction that the problem was insoluble'.[1] Thus it was that Huxley conceived the title of 'agnostic' as 'suggestively antithetic to the "gnostic" of Church history, who professed to know so much about the very things of which I was ignorant'.[2]

Simply put, 'agnosticism' meant 'follow reason and the evidence as far as possible'. It was a method, as Huxley put it, and not a creed. But, in spite of Huxley's claims, it was really much more than that. At its simplest, it meant that the existence of God could no longer be taken as a simple matter of fact. God had moved into the realms of the unknowable, not least because, in a Darwinian world in which the argument from design was no longer persuasive (at least to Huxley), there was no way of inferring a designer God from any seeming cosmic design. And although Huxley, as befitted an agnostic, could never in principle conclude that God did not exist, he nevertheless saw no reason to believe that the personal God of Christianity did. Little wonder that he was accused of being an atheist and an infidel:

> I know that I am, in spite of myself, exactly what the Christian would call, and, so far as I can see, is justified in calling, atheist and infidel. I cannot see one shadow or tittle of evidence that the great unknown underlying the phenomenon of the universe stands to us in the relation of a Father [who] loves us and cares for us as Christianity asserts.[3]

Thus, in more general terms, Huxley was no idealist. He did not believe that reality was ultimately 'idea' or 'spirit' and that matter was merely an attenuated form of it. On the other hand, he was no materialist either. He did not believe that ultimate reality was material and that idea or spirit was completely explicable in terms of it. Consistent in his agnosticism, ultimate reality – whether spiritual or material – was simply unknowable. Mind you, he sailed on occasion pretty close to the winds of materialism. Thus, as early as 1869, in a lecture entitled 'On the physical basis of life', he declared that the best minds of these days

> watch what they conceive to be the progress of materialism, in such fear and powerless anger as a savage feels, when, during an eclipse, the great shadow creeps over the face of the sun. The advancing tide of matter threatens to drown their souls.[4]

No doubt, the terminology of materialism was to be preferred to that of idealism. Yet he believed that materialism as an explanation of ultimate reality was a 'grave philosophical error', one 'likely to paralyze the energies and destroy the beauty of a life'.[5] His was the union of a materialistic scientific method with the repudiation of both mate-rialistic and spiritualistic philosophies. For Huxley, the fundamental doctrines of materialism, like those of idealism, lay *outside the limits of philosophical inquiry*.[6]

Huxley saw his agnosticism as part of an intellectual tradition that went back to the Scottish philosopher David Hume and the German philosopher Immanuel Kant. More than a quarter of a century before William Paley's *Natural Theology*, Hume had subjected the argument from design to a fairly withering critique in his *Dialogues Concerning Natural Religion*. He admitted that the universe may have arisen from something like design. But beyond that there was only fancy and hypothesis. For all we know, declared Hume, this world

> is very faulty and imperfect, compared to a superior standard; and was only the first rude essay of some infant deity, who afterwards abandoned it, ashamed of his lame performance: it is the work only of some dependent inferior deity; and is the object of derision to his superiors: it is the production of old age and dotage in some super-annuated deity; and ever since his death, has run on at adventures, from the first impulse and active force, which it received from him.[7]

Thus, while it was possible to infer from the world to some sort of designer or other, to infer from the world to a God who was personal, all-powerful, all-knowing and good was impossible. Reason could not lead us from the nature of the world to affirm the existence of the orthodox God of Christianity.

Does this possibly lead us nonetheless to a God who is minimally the creator, governor and maintainer of the universe? It does. Hume concedes that 'a purpose, an intention, a design strikes everywhere the most stupid thinker'.[8] Elsewhere, he admitted that 'the cause or causes of order in the universe probably bear some remote analogy to human intelligence'. But he went on to add that this left us in what amounted to a state of 'profound ignorance' that 'affords no inference that affects human life'.[9] Thus, the difference between the believer and the non-believer made little difference to anything that mattered. Here there was only a fine line between a religious scepticism that said there was nothing to know and an agnosticism that said there was nothing that could be known. As Hume put it in the last paragraph of his *Natural History of Religion*: 'The whole is a riddle, an enigma, an inexplicable mystery. Doubt, uncertainty, suspence of judgment appear the only result of our most accurate scrutiny, concerning this subject.'[10]

Kant, like Hume, had subjected the traditional arguments for the existence of God to pretty devastating criticism. After the critiques of Hume and Kant, that it was possible to prove the existence of God by reason alone became a matter of doubt rather than certainty, a matter for philosophical debate and not a theological presupposition. But Kant went further than this. For not only did he argue that the existence of God was not an item of knowledge, but also that the existence of God was unknowable in principle.

This was a consequence of his more general theory of knowledge. According to Kant, existence can be divided into two 'realms': the realm of things as they appear to us (phenomena) and the realm of things as they are in themselves (noumena). The realm of phenomena or the empirical world is that which can be known through the senses, structured by our minds into a realm of time, space and causal relations. In a word, our minds, at least in part, *constitute or construct* reality. The noumenal realm, on the other hand, is the world *as it really is* outside space, time and causal relationships. Although we have knowledge of the phenomenal realm by means of the constitutive nature of the mind constructing the data received by the senses into spatial, temporal and causal relations, we have no knowledge of the noumenal realm, that is, 'things' as they are in themselves (*Dinge an sich*). Since God is part of the noumenal realm and not part of the world as it appears to us, God is unknowable. This is the key to Kant's criticism of the arguments to God from the being or nature of the world, namely, that it is impossible to argue from relationships that pertain to things within the world to anything that is beyond it. In short, the existence of God was among those things that could not be known.

On the face of it, this seems to place Kant in the intellectual tradition that derived from the negative theology of Pseudo-Dionysius that we examined in Chapter 3. There, too, God was beyond the realm of space and time. There, too, God was the God beyond knowing.

But there was a significant difference between Kant and the negative theology of such as Pseudo-Dionysius and, one might say, between religious thinking about God before Kant and religious thinking about God after him. In this difference there lay a key moment within the history of God.

In thinking about God before Kant, while there was complete certainty that God existed, there was just as complete agreement that the nature or essence of God was unknowable. Basil of Caesarea summed it up neatly: 'I do know that He exists; what His essence is, I look at as beyond intelligence.'[11] By contrast, for Kant and for thinking about God after him, it was God's essence or nature that *was* knowable. We have a clear and certain idea of God formed by our reason. But now it was not his nature but his *existence* that was unknowable.[12]

For Kant, then, God was no longer an object of knowledge. But Kant did invite his readers to consider the idea of God as one that was necessary to make sense of morality. Simply put, Kant's account of morality amounted to doing the right thing because it was the right thing to do. Practical reason, the realm of reason that had to do with how we ought to act, demanded it. So there was no expectation of reward here (on either this or the other side of the grave) for virtuous behaviour (or at least not as the reason for doing good).

Central to this account was Kant's notion of the 'highest good' (*summum bonum*) – the ideal goal for every human life in which the highest degree of virtue was combined in equal proportion with the highest degree of happiness. It was clear to Kant that the attainment of the highest degree of virtue was never reached in this life. Thus, the attainment of perfect virtue was possible only on the assumption of 'an infinitely enduring existence and personality of the same rational being'.[13] Thus, it was necessary to postulate the immortality of the soul in order that perfect virtue could be realised.

But while immortality was necessary for the attainment of the *summum bonum*, it was not sufficient. Practical reason also demanded the possibility of attaining perfect happiness. Kant realised that there was no connection between virtue and happiness such that the attainment of the former guaranteed the realisation of the latter. Thus, it was necessary to postulate a being with sufficient will, intelligence and power to bring about, in the afterlife, the proportionate combination of morality and happiness. Therefore, concluded Kant, 'it is morally necessary to assume the existence of God,' even if his existence could not be theoretically known nor demonstrated by reason.[14] Thus were immortality and God essential to the highest good of human life.

In declaring God's existence unknowable, Kant had cut the link between faith and reason that Christian, Muslim and Jewish philosophers in the Platonic tradition had held to so firmly. After Kant, faith could no longer rely on reason to shore it up. Indeed, the severing of the link meant not only that faith could not rely upon reason, but that there was now the intellectual possibility for faith to be opposed by reason. It was a possible conflict between faith and reason that Kant himself recognised: 'I have therefore found it necessary,' he wrote, 'to deny *knowledge*, in order to make room *for faith*.'[15] But in making room for belief, Kant also opened up the possibility of unbelief. Denial of God's existence on the grounds of reason was now on the intellectual agenda, as the story of God for the next two centuries was to prove.

The return of immanence

To the enlightened sceptics at the end of the eighteenth century, the God whom Kant had disposed of was a distant and nebulous transcendent deity who appeared at the end of a philosophical argument, one who, having created and designed the world, left it pretty much to itself. To these 'cultured despisers of religion', as the German Romantic philosopher Friedrich Schleiermacher (1768–1834) was to call them, the God that Kant endorsed as a postulate of the moral life was similarly easily disposed of as nothing more than an imaginary ideal.

Schleiermacher agreed with them. Religion was not a craving for a mass of metaphysical and moral crumbs. Schleiermacher looked for the essence of religion outside theoretical knowledge and moral action. He found it not in thought or will, but in intuition and feeling

(*Anschauung und Gefühl*). Thus, in his 1799 work *On Religion: Speeches to Its Cultured Despisers*, he declared:

> Religion's essence is neither thinking nor acting but intuition and feeling. It wishes to intuit the universe, wishes devoutly to overhear the universe's own manifestations and actions, longs to be grasped and filled by the universe's immediate influences in childlike passivity. Thus religion was opposed to these two [thinking and acting] in everything that makes up its essence and in everything that characterises its effects.[16]

Schleiermacher's divine was immanent within the world. The infinite was felt and intuited within the finite. Religion lives, he wrote, 'in the infinite nature of totality, the one and all'.[17] It is 'the sensibility and taste for the infinite'.[18] This was mysticism with the eyes open – an experience of the ultimate unity of the world beyond its multiplicity and of the ultimate unity between the self and the world. It was an intuition (*Anschauung*) of the noumenal realm – of the universe as it really is. It was a 'knowing' beyond knowing.

For Schleiermacher, religion was there in that mysterious moment when the self and the world flowed one into the other and became one:

> It is as fleeting and transparent as the first scent with which the dew gently caresses the waking flowers, as modest and delicate as a maiden's kiss, as holy and fruitful as a nuptial embrace; indeed not *like* these, but is itself all of these. A manifestation, an event develops quickly and magically into an image of the universe. Even as the beloved and ever-sought-for form fashions itself, my soul flees towards it; I embrace it, not as a shadow, but as the holy essence itself. I lie on the bosom of the infinite world. At this moment I am its soul, for I feel all its powers and its infinite life as my own.[19]

Here, the religion of the heart, derived by Schleiermacher from his upbringing in the traditions of Moravian Pietism, met the religion of nature. To those familiar with the English Romantics, Schleiermacher would not have felt at all alien. His 'feeling and intuition' is a German version of (for example) William Wordsworth's (1770–1850) sentiment in 'Tintern Abbey' in 1798, a year before Schleiermacher's *On Religion* (see Plate 29). 'I have felt,' wrote Wordsworth,

> a sense sublime
> Of something far more deeply interfused,
> Whose dwelling is the light of setting suns,
> And the round ocean, and the living air,
> And the blue sky, and in the mind of man:
> A motion and a spirit that impels
> All thinking things, all objects of all thought,
> And rolls through all things.[20]

Both Schleiermacher and Wordsworth remind the reader of Spinoza – although this time with feeling. And Schleiermacher *was* a devotee of Spinoza. 'The high world permeated him,' wrote Schleiermacher, 'the infinite was his beginning and end, the universe his only and eternal love; in holy innocence and deep humility he was reflected in the eternal world and saw how he too was its most lovable mirror.'[21]

Did Schleiermacher, in the manner of Spinoza, divinise nature and naturalise God? As far as the 1799 first edition of *On Religion* went, the answer is probably yes. It was the ultimate nature of the universe and the relation between it and the individual that was at the heart of Schleiermacher's religious experience. That said, for Schleiermacher, *both theism and pantheism* were secondary considerations, products of the imagination working upon our immediate sense of the universe. As Van Harvey puts it:

> The radicality of Schleiermacher's early position does not consist in his pantheism or, indeed, in any view he articulated regarding the relationship of God to the universe. It consists, rather, in his view that the entire dispute – pantheism versus theism – is irrelevant for religion as he conceives it because religion neither posits nor requires any such relations.[22]

Thus, it was possible to have a religion without a concept of God, whether a transcendent one or one that was both transcendent and immanent. Indeed, for Schleiermacher, a religion without God could be better than one with God.[23]

Just as God was unnecessary to religion, so was immortality. Immortality resided not in a future life but in the present one. Eternal life was the yielding up of one's life in the here and now out of love for the universe. 'Strive here already,' declared Schleiermacher, 'to annihilate your individuality and to live in the one and all; strive to be more than yourselves so that you lose little if you lose yourselves.'[24] As for miracles, these were not fortuitous interventions into the world by a transcendent deity that disrupted the order of nature. 'To me,' declared Schleiermacher, 'everything is a miracle, and for me what alone is a miracle in your mind, namely, something inexplicable and strange, is no miracle in mine.'[25]

As for Schleiermacher, so also for Georg Wilhelm Friedrich Hegel (1770–1831), the central focus of whose philosophy was the relationship of the infinite to the finite and the One to the many. And unlike Kant, for whom knowledge of God was impossible in principle, for Hegel, to know God was the ultimate aim of philosophy. 'The aim of philosophy,' declared Hegel, 'is to know the truth, to know God, for He is the absolute truth, inasmuch as nothing else is worth troubling about save God and the unfolding of God's nature.'[26] However, unlike Spinoza and Schleiermacher, Hegel was no pantheist. God or 'Absolute Spirit' (Geist) transcended the world and was not identical with it. Yet he was no theist who believed that God or Absolute Spirit was totally separate from it. Hegel is best described as a 'panentheist', who held the belief that 'the Being of God includes and penetrates the whole universe, so that every part of it exists in Him, but (as against pantheism) that His Being is more than and not exhausted by, the universe.'[27]

That philosophy could apprehend Absolute Spirit was, simply put, because God was present in finite minds. Absolute Spirit had gone out of itself into finite minds. Thus, the laws of reason (by which minds operated) reflected the nature of ultimate reality. But Absolute Spirit had gone out of itself not only into finite minds but into the world of nature. Thus, it was immanent both in minds and in the world. Because both mind and nature manifested ultimate reality, reality and rationality coincide:

> What is rational is real;
> And what is real is rational [...]

> From it also proceeds the view now under contemplation that the spiritual universe is the natural [...] Against the doctrine that idea is a mere idea, figment or opinion, philosophy preserves the profound view that *nothing is real except the idea.* Hence arises the effort to recognise in the temporal and transient the substance, which is immanent, and the eternal, which is present.[28]

To phrase Hegel in Kantian terms, the noumenal is the phenomenal and vice versa.

Hegel's philosophy of the unity-in-difference between God and the world reminds us of the tradition of Neoplatonism that flowed through the writings of Pseudo-Dionysius into the intellectual German mysticism of Meister Eckhart and his followers (see Chapter 3). Hegel rationalised mysticism, taking what the intellectual mystic said about the identity yet difference between God and the soul and making it a truth about reality overall.

Hegel, too, was excited by what he saw as the relationship between his philosophy and the intellectual mysticism of Eckhart. Thus, in his *Lectures on the Philosophy of Religion,* he quoted Eckhart to the effect that 'the eye with which God sees me is the eye with which I see Him; my eye and his eye are one [...] if I were not, then He were not.'[29] Hegel would make essentially the same point. 'Finite consciousness,' he declared, 'knows God only in so far as God knows himself in it.'[30] Absolute Spirit, having gone out of itself into finite minds, comes to know itself through the activity of human minds. This is a significant moment in the history of God. No longer an immutable deity, God is now incessantly in a process of change in time and in history. As Keith Ward neatly puts it:

Spirit essentially realises or objectifies itself in the material universe [...] [F]or Hegel, Spirit is incomplete and unknown to itself until it does realise itself in an objective universe. So the universe becomes a necessary manifestation of Spirit, and Spirit is essentially changing and developing in and through the history of the universe.[31]

In thus changing and evolving, Absolute Spirit also returns to itself through the processes of time and history. In Neoplatonism, there was, as it were, a 'vertical' relation between the infinite and the finite. The One emanated 'downwards' into the world and the path of return to the One was by ascending 'upwards' to God in the present moment. By contrast, in Hegel, the vertical has become the horizontal. The alienation of Absolute Spirit from itself and its return to itself have occurred not in an 'eternal present' but through the historical process. Thus, the progressive path of history was the way God (or Absolute Spirit) took to achieve a perfect consciousness of himself (itself). When will Absolute Spirit return to itself? Well, for Hegel, it has now done so through his philosophy – when, in the historical development of human consciousness, finite minds have now come to understand that the ultimately real is the rational and that all reality is spiritual (*geistlich*).

It is important to remember that Hegel wrote as a Christian in the tradition of Lutheran Protestantism. And for Hegel, it was Christianity that was the highest form of religion and the closest approximation to philosophical truth. 'It is the Christian religion,' he wrote,

which is the perfect religion, the religion which represents the Being of Spirit in a realized form, or for itself, the religion in which religion has itself become objective in relation to itself. In it the universal Spirit and the particular spirit, the infinite Spirit and the finite spirit, are inseparably connected.[32]

In essence, the philosophy of Absolute Spirit is esoteric Christianity and Christianity is exoteric Hegelianism. That said, Hegel was not mirroring orthodox Christianity. His philosophical reading of the Christian tradition would not have sat easily with his Lutheran

colleagues. His was a salvation through thought, not grace. His was
an academic 'church'. And they would not, for obvious reasons, have
warmed to the implications of Hegel's philosophy – that theology was
really Hegelianism for tiny tots.

In Christianity, God created the world. In Hegel's thought, this
represents God's 'othering' of himself into both physical nature and
finite spirit. As such, man as finite spirit has fallen and is alienated
from God. Redemption consists in man's realisation of his ultimate
unity with God. This ultimate unity has manifested itself to us in
Jesus Christ:

> in one particular man, in a definite individual who is at the same time
> known to be the Divine Idea, not merely a Being of higher kind in
> general, but rather the highest, the absolute Idea, the Son of God.[33]

However, the significance of the life and death of Jesus does not lie
in its historical particularity but in its symbolising a truth that is
universal, namely, that all men are (and have always been) ultimately
both human and divine, both finite *and* infinite. The incarnate God
symbolises religiously what has been realised conceptually in the philosophy of Absolute Spirit – that *all men are God incarnate* and that
all finite nature partakes of the infinite.[34]

Thus, redemption consisted, for Hegel, in the realisation of the
universal philosophical truth that lay beneath the *particular* story of
God's becoming man in Jesus Christ:

> In the Church Christ has been called the God–Man [...] This
> is the extraordinary combination which directly contradicts the
> Understanding [...] It involves the truth that the divine and human
> natures are not implicitly different. God in human form. The truth
> is that there is only one reason, one Spirit, that Spirit as finite has
> no true existence.[35]

In short, Christ was merely a sublime symbol of an intellectual operation performed by every human mind.[36]

God and world topsy-turvy

Hegel had set out to solve the question of the relationship between thinking and being or, we might say, between mind and matter. He had resolved it in favour of the former. Reality was ultimately spiritual and not material. The real was the rational. For Hegel, thought and the world operated dialectically – a thesis generated an antithesis that resolved itself into a synthesis, and so on. Thus, it was perhaps inevitable that the thesis that 'the real is the rational' (Idealism) would generate its antithesis that the 'real is the material' (Materialism). Where in Hegel the material was ultimately spiritual, in his 'left-wing' followers like Ludwig Feuerbach (1804–72), the spiritual was essentially merely material. It was within this materialist framework that, in his *The Essence of Christianity* (1841), Feuerbach's work was an instant success. 'With one blow,' declared Friedrich Engels (1820–95), co-author with Karl Marx (1818–83) of *The Communist Manifesto*, 'it placed materialism on the throne again […] The spell was broken; the "system" [of Hegelianism] was exploded and cast aside […] Enthusiasm was general; we all became at once Feuerbachians.'[37]

It was in *The Essence of Christianity* that Feuerbach mounted the first systematic argument for atheism in the history of Western thought. The key argument can be simply expressed. For Hegel, man was a real projection into the world of God. For Feuerbach, God was an imaginary projection into the heavens of man. God did not so much make man in his own image as man created God in his. Thus, apparent knowledge of God was, in reality, man's true knowledge of himself:

> By his God thou knowest the man, and by the man his God; the two are identical. Whatever is God to a man, that is his heart and soul; and conversely, God is the manifested inward nature, the expressed self of a man – religion the solemn unveiling of a man's hidden treasures, the revelation of his intimate thoughts, the open confession of his love-secrets.[38]

For Feuerbach, as for Hegel, religion was really a childlike phase in human development. Superseded by Hegel in his philosophy of Absolute Spirit, religion was fulfilled by Feuerbach in his celebration of the finite spirit when it was recognised that 'what was formerly contemplated and worshipped as God is now perceived to be something *human*'.[39] Atheism, then, was actually the secret of religion and the essence of Christianity. Religion and Christianity in particular were nothing but the truth of the 'divinity' of human nature. The doctrine that God became man meant that man was 'divine'. God's love, as expressed in the Incarnation, was really about the redemptive power of human love.

Thus, the personal attributes of God were, in actuality, the ideal attributes of man projected onto an imaginary God. 'Thou believest in love as a divine attribute,' wrote Feuerbach,

> because thou thyself lovest; thou believest that God is a wise, benevolent being, because thou knowest nothing better in thyself than benevolence and wisdom [...] Thou knowest no higher human good, than to love, than to be good and wise.[40]

In other words, it was not so much that God was (literally) wise and loving as that wisdom and love were (metaphorically) divine.

For Feuerbach, this projection of the best in humanity onto an imaginary other-worldly being was destructive and alienating. For the human had become defined not in terms of its best features but in terms of its worst, over against a perfect Being before whom humans could only debase themselves as sinful creatures:

> as what is positive in the conception of the divine being can only be human, the conception of man, as an object of consciousness can only be negative. To enrich God, man must become poor; that God may be all in all, man must be nothing.[41]

Karl Marx agreed. But he believed that Feuerbach had failed to go far enough. Feuerbach's critique of heaven needed to become a critique of earth, of its material practices and social relations. For Marx, religion was the opiate of the masses, serving only to reconcile the oppressed classes to their condition. It reinforced the social and economic status quo. As the well-known Anglican hymn 'All Things Bright and Beautiful' put it in 1848 (in a verse now usually omitted):

> The rich man in his castle,
> The poor man at his gate,
> God made them high and lowly,
> And ordered their estate.

Only social and political revolution would bring about the conditions in which it would no longer be necessary to project God. Then, religion would wither away. '[A]fter the earthly family is discovered to be the secret of the holy family,' declared Marx, 'the former must then itself be criticised in theory and revolutionised in practice.'[42]

As for Feuerbach and Marx, so also for Sigmund Freud (1856–1939), the critique of God arose from his commitment to a materialist philosophy. But unlike them, Freud moved the critique of religion from issues of social inequity to matters of psychological inadequacy. For Freud, the history of religion was a history of spiritual illusion that fulfilled the oldest, strongest and most urgent dreams of mankind. This was wish-fulfilment gone cosmic. At the individual level, religious belief was the unhealthy persistence of the desires and wishes of childhood into maturity. Thus, religion, whether in the evolution of humankind or in the development of each individual, was a neurosis 'which the civilised individual must pass through on his way from childhood to maturity.'[43]

Thus, Feuerbach's critique of God significantly influenced the philosophy underpinning the social and psychological sciences. But it was also a key element in the developing philosophy of the physical sciences. We recall that Thomas Huxley's agnosticism was premised on his belief that ultimate reality – whether spiritual or material – was simply unknowable. British natural science had remained neutral between spirit and matter as the ultimate 'stuff' of the universe. That said, in its method, if not in its philosophy, it ruled out the possibility of anything beyond the 'natural' (read the 'material') since it excluded the spiritual or supernatural from any explanatory role in the natural realm. The unknown God of Huxley could no longer be part of knowledge now construed scientifically.

German science, on the other hand, particularly under the influence of Feuerbach, moved decisively towards a materialist philosophy with its attendant atheism.[44] The non-existent God of Feuerbach was now banished from the realm of knowledge. In either case – the methodological naturalism of British science or the philosophical naturalism of German science – the consequence was the same. God had become irrelevant to any 'scientific' account of the world – at worst non-existent, at best redundant. In sum, by the end of the nineteenth century, in a post-Darwinian world, the transcendent designer God of the natural theologians no longer formed a part of any explanation of the natural realm or, one might add, of the social or psychological realms. In a post-Feuerbachian world, the transcendent and immanent God of Hegel had become completely naturalised and thus completely explicable as an illusory by-product of what was ultimately material.

The delusions of Dawkins

In the seventeenth and eighteenth centuries, God and science collaborated with each other. Natural theology was the offspring of this and the argument from design its crowning achievement. But this was to change with the rise of philosophical materialism or naturalism in the nineteenth century. By the end of that century, the philosophical naturalism embedded in science and seemingly verified by the successes of science and technology ruled out theism. It did so in principle. To be a believer in science *and* a believer in God was no longer an option. The history of God from then to the present is the history of the thinking through of this relation between God and science or (more broadly)

God and modernity in four quite different ways – through conflict, capitulation, separation and adaptation.

We can begin with the conflict between God and modernity in the present with Richard Dawkins (1941–) and his work *The God Delusion* (2006). Dawkins's position is a pretty simple, indeed a simplistic one, which shows no awareness of the biography of God as we have been working through it systematically thus far in this book. As Terry Eagleton put it: 'Imagine someone holding forth on biology whose only knowledge of the subject is the *Book of British Birds*, and you have a rough idea of what it feels like to read Richard Dawkins on theology.'[45] Unkind but true (although perhaps unfair to the *Book of British Birds*). Those who have read this far in this work will be a little astounded to read in Dawkins's book that 'theology [...] has not moved on in eighteen centuries'.[46]

That said, *The God Delusion* has nonetheless become the most popular manifesto for atheism in the early twenty-first century. In part, this was because it gave its readers only one choice – irrational religion or rational science. But it also had a more general appeal. In part, this was the consequence of its critique of God including a more general critique of institutional religion. In part too, it was the result of the failure of modern liberal Christian theology, unlike its more conservative counterparts, to have any impact on public discourse. And it undoubtedly appealed to those who were passionately opposed to any fundamentalist understanding of religion, whether Jewish, Christian or Muslim. Whether *The God Delusion* has significantly increased the number of those who formally declare themselves 'atheist' is arguable. But it has undoubtedly resonated with those whose spirituality, focused on the cultivation of the self as sacred and the world as re-enchanted, necessitates neither belief in a transcendent God nor any commitment to the formal structures of religion.

Be all that as it may, Dawkins is one of the so-called 'new' atheists.[47] But it is really all pretty 'old hat'. He is in essence the direct heir of nineteenth-century philosophical naturalism and of the view that science and religion are therefore, of their very nature, in conflict with each other. The atheist as philosophical naturalist, he declared, is somebody who believes that there is nothing beyond the natural, physical world, no *super*natural creative intelligence lurking behind the observable universe, no soul that outlasts the body and no miracles – except in the sense of natural phenomena that we do not yet understand.[48]

In short, the only stuff in the universe is physical or material. This is a war between the natural and the supernatural in which the former excludes the latter *on principle*. 'I am not attacking,' Dawkins wrote, 'any particular version of God or gods. I am attacking God, all gods, anything and everything supernatural, wherever and whenever they have been or will be invented.'[49]

For Dawkins, science is grounded in philosophical naturalism. Thus, scientists cannot be believers and believers cannot be scientists. Moreover, it is science that determines what can and cannot be said to exist. On this account, agnosticism is not an intellectual option: 'God's existence or non-existence is a scientific fact about the universe, discoverable in principle if not in practice.'[50] Thus, the rational is virtuous science and the irrational vicious religion. Reason and faith are irrevocably opposed to each other. And God cannot *in principle* exist. To this, readers of this book will give the short answer: 'Since God by his nature is not, like a planet in the solar system, an observable object within the universe, his existence or otherwise is *not* a scientific fact about the universe.' 'Which,' Dawkins would say, 'rather proves my point.' Stalemate!

One target of Dawkins's critique is the Old Testament God, 'a fiercely unpleasant God, morbidly obsessed with sexual restrictions, with the smell of charred flesh, with his own superiority over rival gods and with the exclusiveness of his chosen desert tribe.'[51] But his principal target is the designer God of the eighteenth century and his principal argument against the designer God is Darwinian natural selection. 'The illusion of design in the living world,' he declares, 'is explained with far greater economy and with devastating elegance by Darwinian natural selection.'[52] Thus, Dawkins's arguments are a revisiting of the nineteenth century's debates about creation and evolution.

But he also has some more contemporary opponents in mind, those who, as (primarily American) supporters of 'creation science' or its more recent incarnation 'intelligent design', mine the natural realm for arguments against natural selection and for evidence that supports purpose and design and therefore an intelligent designer. On the face of it, Intelligent Design is an attempt to move the conflict between religion and science into a different rhetorical register – that of a debate between one form of science and another.[53] But although it presents itself as 'science', there is little doubt about its theological motivations. Its clear intention is to oppose what it sees as Darwinian atheism with the designer God that Darwinism displaced. Intelligent design is very much forward to the past.

The death of God

Capitulation is one way to avoid conflict. So it is not surprising that a number of twentieth-century theologians gave up the battle, declared that science had won the day and proclaimed, literally or metaphorically, the death of God. In so saying, they drew inspiration from the German philosopher Friedrich Nietzsche (1844–1900). It was in his work *The Gay Science* (1882) that Nietzsche first declared that God had been murdered. There the madman cried in the marketplace: 'Where is God [...] I'll tell you! *We have killed him* – you and I.' That was not news to the madman's audience of amused unbelievers. But it was the meaning of God's death that, the madman believed, his audience had failed to grasp. For the death of God meant that meaning itself had died:

> But how did we do this? How were we able to drink up the sea? Who gave us the sponge to wipe away the entire horizon? What were we doing when we unchained this earth from its sun? Where is it moving to now? Where are we moving to? [...] Aren't we straying as though through an infinite nothing? Isn't empty space breathing at us? Hasn't it got colder? [...] Do we still hear nothing of the noise

of the grave-diggers who are burying God? Do we still smell nothing
of the divine decomposition? – Gods too decompose! God is dead!
God remains dead! And we have killed him![54]

Nietzsche was thus proclaiming the end of the Platonic dream – of
grounding both being and goodness in a transcendent realm. There
was, for Nietzsche, nothing beyond the shadows on the wall of the
cave.

Above all, the death of God meant the death of morality. European
morality, built on the foundation of the Christian faith, could not be
genuinely sustained in the absence of God. 'The greatest recent event,'
declared Nietzsche, that

> 'God is dead'; that the belief in the Christian God has become
> unbelievable – is already starting to cast its first shadow over Europe.
> To those few at least whose eyes – or the *suspicion* in whose eyes is
> strong and subtle enough for this spectacle, some kind of sun seems
> to have set; some old deep trust turned into doubt [...] Even less may
> one suppose many to know at all *what* this event really means – and,
> now that this faith has been undermined, how much must collapse
> because it was built on this faith, leaned on it, had grown into it –
> for example, our entire European morality.[55]

That said, the death of God and of the ethical values dependent upon
him opened up the possibility of new values for a godless world, of going
beyond the nihilism that the death of God entailed, of transcending
even the atheism that nihilism provoked. The consequences of this
for ourselves, he wrote,

> are the opposite of what one might expect – not at all sad and gloomy,
> but much more like a new and barely describable type of light,
> happiness, relief, amusement, encouragement, dawn [...] Indeed,
> at hearing the news that 'the old god is dead', we philosophers and
> 'free spirits' feel illuminated by a new dawn; our heart overflows
> with gratitude, amazement, forebodings, expectation.[56]

After all, the madman *did* come into the marketplace crying 'I seek God', thus foreshadowing the quest for new meanings and new values.

But for Nietzsche, these new meanings and values were not for all. They were for the Superman (*Übermensch*), who, with the will-to-power, denied God, transcended both good and evil and discovered thereby true freedom. Both the religious and the ethical were transcended in a Dionysian libertine exuberance. This was a vision of humanity in which self-will was free to run riot, directly opposed to the Platonic ideal of 'a will that rests in something higher than itself, by a will to the Good and the Beautiful'.[57] The choice with which Nietzsche ultimately confronted us was not between theism and atheism but between cosmic meaning and cosmic nihilism.

How to reframe Christianity in the light of Nietzschean nihilism? One way was to construct a Christian atheism according to which God, once alive, had literally died. This was the path that the American theologian Thomas J. J. Altizer (1927–) took in his groundbreaking work *The Gospel of Christian Atheism* (1966). Hegel's view of Absolute Spirit becoming immanent in the world was Altizer's motivation. But Nietzsche was his inspiration:

> If there is one clear portal to the twentieth century, it is a passage through the death of God, the collapse of any meaning or reality beyond the newly discovered radical immanence of modern man, an immanence dissolving even the memory or the shadow of transcendence. With that collapse has come a new chaos, a new meaninglessness brought on by the disappearance of an absolute or transcendent ground, the very nihilism foreseen by Nietzsche as the next stage of history.[58]

For Altizer, the death of God was a historical and a cosmic event. When God became man in Jesus Christ, God laid aside his transcendence, emptying himself into the world of immanence. God's becoming man in Jesus Christ was, *literally*, the death of the transcendent God. The good news of the Christian gospel, according to Altizer, was our liberation from a transcendent beyond, emptied and darkened by God's self-alienation in Christ. But it also marked the beginning of a historical process in which God's original negation of himself in Christ came to be gradually and progressively realised in history in the total range of human experience. The sacred was literally transformed historically into the profane. 'The death of God in Christ,' declared Altizer,

> is an inevitable consequence of the movement of God into the world, of Spirit into flesh, and the actualization of the death of God in the totality of experience is a decisive sign of the continuing and forward movement of the divine process, as it continues to negate its particular and given expressions, by moving ever more fully into the depths of the profane.[59]

Ironically, therefore, a true atheism could only be understood from within the Christian faith (and perhaps only someone determined to remain Christian at any cost would buy all this). Only Christianity (appropriately nuanced by Hegel) provided the intellectual resources truly to understand the death of the transcendent God. Atheism? Well, yes and no. For Altizer was able to find meaning in the universe's ultimate meaninglessness and it had to do with the story of God's emptying of himself into humanity. In short, there remained for Altizer a grand, over-arching historical narrative (grounded in Hegel) in which even the death of God could find a place.

If for Altizer, the death of God was literal, for the Anglican priest and atheist Don Cupitt (1934–) it could only be a metaphorical death because God had never been literally 'alive'. Only now, in the age of modernity, has this been realised. As 'an actually-existing, independent individual being', God 'belongs entirely to traditional culture and must vanish with the changeover to the modern outlook'.[60] Thus, against the tradition of theological realism, Cupitt promoted theological non-realism – the construction of a Christian theology that no longer required an objectively existing God and created a new way of being religious. The old Christian culture, declared Cupitt, was highly realistic in being centered around objective, eternal, necessary, intelligible, and perfect Being [...] Now consider how completely we have reversed the traditional outlook of Christian Platonism. The world above and all the absolutes are gone. The whole of our life and all our standards are now inside language and culture. For good or ill, we make our own history, we shape our own world, we together evolve all norms to which our life is subject. Religion for us must inevitably be very different from what it was in the heyday of Platonic realism. Indeed, it is plain that if I am right, then Christianity must be revolutionized to survive.[61]

Thus, religion is, for Cupitt, human, historical and cultural all the way up and all the way down. It comprises only a set of stories and symbols, values and practices out of which individuals must create their own religious life. Christian non-realism, he wrote, 'is thoroughly naturalistic in outlook, seeing the whole system of supernatural doctrine as poetry to live by – or, as Wittgenstein put it, "rules of life dressed up in pictures"'.[62] Religious believers, like artists, produce their own lives like works of religious art.

Within this Christian non-realism, God becomes a guiding spiritual ideal rather than an objectively existing being. God is, Cupitt declared,

an ideal standard of perfection by which I judge myself and am judged. God is the divinity of Love, which above all else makes our lives worth living. Commitment to God becomes resolved into commitment to and belief in life.[63]

Thus, Nietzsche's cosmic nihilism is here replaced by a radical Christian humanism in which human freedom and happiness mean being given over completely to the world, in spite of its randomness, indeterminateness and apparent evils:

Since commitment to God is commitment to the values of justice and love, belief in God may and should inspire people to try to make

the world a better place, but it does not – and it never did – offer
any kind of magical protection against life's sheer contingency.[64]

In choosing the Christian values of love and justice, Cupitt transcended
the ethical nihilism of Nietzsche. But he remained sufficient of a nihilist
to recognise that this choosing had no final justification. 'We have to
reach a point,' he declared, 'where nothing remains except a pure creative choice ex nihilo (i.e. precisely to get ourselves out of the Nihil),
and that choice [...] is faith.'[65] If, for Cupitt, there was ultimately no
meaning of life, there remained for him the choice of creating meaning
in life through ethical commitment and moral action.

Separating God and nature

The story of the relationship between God and science over the past
three centuries has been one about the meaning of the natural world –
whether to fight for God's place within that meaning or whether to
capitulate or adapt to the increasingly dominant scientific reading of
the natural world. However, much of twentieth-century thought about
God proceeded on the assumption that science and religion occupy
such radically different spaces that an amicable (or not so amicable)
separation was the best outcome for both. Theologians decided to
take it personally. Science, they determined, dealt with the natural
(the meaning of the world), religion with the existential (the meaning
of human existence).

Thus, as natural scientists in the twentieth century lost interest
in natural theology, drifting between methodological and philosophical naturalism in an indifferent cosmos, it was inevitable that
theologians would seek new territories to conquer. They did so
by reframing the distinction between the human and the natural
'embodied' in the idea of the 'image of God' into a distinction
between being and becoming. This, they declared, was the essential distinction between the natural and the human respectively. As
Frederick Gregory remarks,

With newly found confidence in the intellectual autonomy of a personalistic interpretation of the world, [German theologians] tended to devote their energies more and more to the investigation of meaning as determined by personal value, paying less and less attention to the cognitive dimensions of human experience.[66]

Thus, the truth that mattered was not to be found in the objective but in the subjective world, not in the natural but in the personal realm. As the father of existentialism, the Danish philosopher Søren Kierkegaard (1813–55), put it: 'Subjectivity is truth.' His was a critique of the claims to ultimate truth not only in philosophical naturalism but Hegelian idealism also. Thus, according to Kierkegaard, the existence of God was objectively uncertain. This mattered little for truth had to do, not with objective truth, but with the passion with which God was grasped subjectively: '*An objective uncertainty held fast in an appropriation-process of the most passionate inwardness is the truth*, the highest truth attainable for an *existing* individual.'[67] This was Tertullian revisited – an endorsement of subjective faith over objective reason, of Jerusalem over Athens. Thus, 'faith is precisely the contradiction between the infinite passion of the individual's inwardness and the objective uncertainty.'[68]

Out of this Kierkegaardian emphasis on the subjective rather than the objective arose the three most significant Protestant theologies of the twentieth century – those of Paul Tillich (1886–1965), Rudolf Bultmann (1884–1976) and Karl Barth (1886–1968). For Paul Tillich, Christian faith provided the answers to the questions raised by an analysis of human existence. 'These answers,' declared Tillich,

are contained in the revelatory events on which Christianity is based [...] Their content cannot be derived from questions that would come from an analysis of human existence. They are 'spoken' to human existence from beyond it, in a sense. Otherwise, they would not be answers, for the question is human existence itself.[69]

Similarly, for Rudolf Bultmann, the mythological world view of the Bible, now replaced by modern science, needed to be rethought in terms relevant to modern human existence. For Bultmann this meant the existentialist philosophy of Martin Heidegger (1889–1976). Thus, Heidegger's philosophy, like the New Testament, presented us with an analysis of who we are:

> beings existing historically in care for ourselves on the basis of anxiety, ever in the moment of decision between the past and the future whether we will lose ourselves in the world of what is available [...] or whether we will attain our authenticity by surrendering all our securities and being unreservedly free for the future.[70]

The message of Christianity was that God in Christ had simultaneously revealed to us our alienation and provided us with the means to liberate us from our inauthentic existence.

As the limiting twentieth-century instance of the privileging of faith over reason we can take the Swiss theologian Karl Barth. For Barth, there was an impassable chasm between revelation and the results of any form of human enquiry – whether of the natural, the social or the human sciences (including existentialism). Thus did Barth, taking a leaf out of Kierkegaard's book, proclaim the infinite qualitative difference between God and man (caused by the latter's sinful nature) that rendered the path from man to God impassable. And, taking a leaf out of Feuerbach's book, he declared that any theology that began with the world or with man would end up exactly where it began. 'We saw,' he wrote,

> that its [theology's] whole problem had become how to make religion, revelation and the relationship with God something which could also be understood as a necessary predicate of man [...] To Feuerbach at all events, the meaning of the question is whether the theologian, when he thus formulates his problem, is not after all affirming the thing in which the assent of humanity seems to culminate, namely, man's apotheosis.[71]

In the judgement of Barth, eighteenth- and nineteenth-century theology had asked the wrong question. Instead of inquiring about the reality of revelation, it had begun by asking after its possibility. Hence, religion had come to be understood as a datum independently of revelation. The result was that religion was not understood from revelation, but revelation from religion. In Barth's view, the consequence was that religion was a human phenomenon which, as such, found its source not in God but in man: 'In religion man both bolts and bars himself against revelation by providing a substitute, by taking away in advance the very thing which has to be given by God.'[72]

For Barth, on the other hand, God could never be the 'object' of knowledge. He was not at the disposal of human knowledge in its ordinary operations, or amenable to criteria of truth that took no account of the unique nature of this object, namely, that it was always Subject. Rather, for Barth, we are the object of the divine Subject's saving grace in Jesus Christ, in whom God objectified himself for our salvation: 'That God gives himself to be known by man in the revelation of his Word by means of the Holy Spirit means this: He comes before man as Subject in the relation of Object.'[73] But even when an individual leapt across the ravine between unbelief and belief, this was still not a judgement of his own making. Rather, God himself, as Holy Spirit, created the reality and possibility of his being personally appropriated by the leap of faith.[74] Thus was the circle of faith closed against philosophy, the territory of revelation secured against the domain of reason. Matthew Arnold's sea of faith, retreating from modernity like an ebbing tide, had now become an island of faith, reachable only by those willing to abandon the lands of reason.[75]

It is perhaps ironic that twentieth-century Protestant theology's turn to the personal should have been significantly influenced by the Jewish philosopher Martin Buber (1878–1965). Or perhaps not so ironic, for Buber's philosophy, and particularly his 1923 work *Ich und Du* (*I and Thou*) bore the marks not only of Feuerbach and Kierkegaard but of Schleiermacher's immanent God at the depths of self and world, along with Christian and Jewish mysticism.

According to Buber, there are two basic modes of existence: 'I–Thou' relations and 'I–It' relations. The latter has to do with the treating of other things (including people) as objects, collecting, analysing, classifying and theorising. The former has to do with encountering the other (including objects) and entering into a personal loving relation with it:

> When I confront a human being as my You and speak the basic word I–You to him, then he is no thing among things nor does he consist of things [...] I stand in relation to him, in the basic sacred word.[76]

Every encounter with the other as a Thou is also a glimpse of the Eternal Thou, one that is at the depth of all I–You encounters:

> For entering into the pure relationship does not involve ignoring everything but seeing everything in the You, not renouncing the world but placing it upon its proper ground [...] Whoever goes forth to his You with his whole being and carries to it all the being of the world, finds him whom one cannot seek. Of course God is 'the wholly other'; but he is also the wholly same: the wholly present. Of course, he is the *mysterium tremendum* [of Rudolf Otto] that appears and overwhelms; but he is also the mystery of the obvious that is closer to me than my own I.[77]

The deity who adapts

Barth's radical distinction between God and the world, or faith and philosophy more generally, had the hallmarks more of an ugly divorce than an amicable separation. It was the virtue of Buber's understanding of the personal that it could embrace not only persons but also the world more generally. I–Thou relations extended beyond the personal realm to the natural world. It demonstrated that the argument that religion and science inhabited different domains could be made without the former's lapsing into *only* the personal or the existential. If the story of God tells us anything, it is that it has encompassed not only the personal but also the natural – both the existential and the cosmic.

Immutable God may have been, but he was very adaptable to the intellectual currents that swirled around him. Ironically, the biography of the unchangeable God is the story of his seemingly infinite capacity to change. The God of the Old Testament adapted to the New Testament and to the Qur'ān. God absorbed, although not without difficulty, the Neoplatonism of late antiquity and the Aristotelianised Platonism of the high Middle Ages. He survived the rethinking of an earth-centred biblical world view necessitated by Nicolaus Copernicus's (1473–1543) sun-centred cosmology. He adjusted to his loss of immanence in the shift from a spiritualised Platonism to the 'new science' in the seventeenth century. He was well served by natural theology in the eighteenth.

When, in the early nineteenth century, the biblical view of the age of the earth (roughly estimated from around 4000 BCE) was replaced by the millions of years suggested to the geological scientists by the fossil record, it served more to enhance the reputation of the designer God than to depreciate it. Even Darwin could be put to divine use. That God not only created the world but was actively involved in the processes of evolution elevated his status rather than diminished it. The distant, inactive creator God of the eighteenth century became the active providential Deity of the nineteenth, 'working his purpose out as year succeeds to year'.[78] In the twentieth century, the Big Bang account of the origins of the universe comforted those who believed that God preceded its beginnings more than it distressed them. Uncertainties about the nature of reality in the new quantum physics gave pause to those who believed the ultimate stuff of the real to be material, encouragement to idealists and hope to those who sought for certainty in a God who was the spiritual ground of all being.[79]

An Agnostic Spirituality

> But now you will ask me, 'How am I to think of God himself, and
> what is he?' And I cannot answer you except to say 'I do not know!'
> For with this question you have brought me into the same darkness,
> the same cloud of unknowing where I want you to be!
>
> *The Cloud of Unknowing*[1]

God's capacity to survive through adaptation is his greatest asset. In
modernity, it is also his greatest liability. In continually ceding territory
to science, his sphere of relevance and influence became progressively
less. He was a divine emperor still, yet without clothes, a ruler who,
to all intents and purposes, had abdicated his office while maintaining
a real if ghostly and indefinable presence in a world becoming re-enchanted and reinvested with the sacred.

There is, however, another possibility – one that recognises that,
while God and science share the same territory, they do so within
different but totally overlapping provinces. We might say that, while
the province of science was *the how*, that of religion was *the why*. As
Ludwig Wittgenstein (1889–1951) put it rather poetically in his
Tractatus Logico-philosophicus: 'Not how the world is, is the mystical,
but that it is.'[2] This, we recall, was the virtue of the arguments for the
existence of God. They demanded that we confront the mystery of
there being something rather than nothing at all and why the something there is the way it is.

Moreover, the mystery of why there is something rather than
nothing at all includes the mystery not only of life generally but of all
individual lives. Ultimate meaning has existential bearing, both general
and particular. As Pascal eloquently put it:

> When I consider the brief span of my life, absorbed in the eternity
> of time that went before and will come after it, the tiny space that
> I occupy and even that I see, plunged in the infinite immensity of
> the spaces which I do not know and which do not know me, I am
> terrified and astonished to find myself here rather than there [...]
> why now rather than then. Who put me here? By whose order and
> design were this place and time allotted to me? [...] The eternal
> silence of these infinite spaces terrifies me.[3]

Pascal was pointing to the deep agnosticism more characteristic of the
modern world than of his. Pascal, as we know, took the pragmatic way
and took a bet on God. But since the time of Hume and Kant, believers
and unbelievers alike have agreed that we cannot *intellectually know*
whether God exists or not, whether he be conceived as transcendent
or immanent, as beyond yet identical with the world, as personal
or impersonal, as the source of being and of value. Faith *is* because
knowledge *is not*. Jerusalem and Athens have gone their separate ways.

At a deeper level still, beyond both theism and atheism, we cannot
know whether the world has any deeper meaning that may or may not
include a God – the mystics' 'God' beyond God, the unknown God of
Unknowing that is beyond both being and not being, that incomprehensible 'whereof we cannot speak', as Wittgenstein would put it.[4] The
world does not point to ultimate meaning and purpose either within
or beyond itself. The world neither clearly reveals its ultimate meaning
and purpose to us nor loudly proclaims its absence.

Thus, within modernity, there is an epistemic distance between the
world and its meaning. This is why Huxley was right: we are all agnos-
tics – believers and non-believers alike – since none of us has solved
the problem of existence. But it is this very epistemic ambiguity that
allows the world to be experienced religiously or non-religiously – as a
garden or a wilderness, as purposeful or purposeless, as benevolent or
malevolent, as spirit or matter, as a theatre of divine love or of cosmic
indifference on a grand scale, as the best or worst of all possible worlds.
This is the epistemic uncertainty that makes possible belief or unbelief,
hope or despair – the one just as reasonable and defensible as the other

or, in those cases where reason is eschewed, just as unreasonable and indefensible.

That we can ask the question of ultimate meaning is our greatest triumph. It is what separates us from all other species. Is our cognitive capacity to ask this question a sign itself of deeper meaning – 'image of God' yet again – or is it merely evolutionary serendipity? We cannot know. This question, like the question of ultimate meaning more generally, is unanswerable. We are forever poised between, on the one hand, our ability to wonder at the mystery of it all and to search for what all of it might mean and, on the other, our inability ever to find out. This is our greatest tragedy.

The story of God is the story of a search for ultimate meaning. Whatever it means, it means at least this – that ultimate meaning cannot be read off the surface of things. Only thus is the quest for meaning possible. It is dependent upon uncertainty and unknowing. Do the depth of selves and the truth of things become more certain and more known the more we seek them? Probably not. In fact, the contrary may well be the case. The more we seek, the less certain we become that we shall reach the end of the quest.

I am now far less certain of ultimate meaning than I was when I embarked upon the quest as an idealistic theological student of 17 years of age some 50 years ago. Then, there was certainty. For then, the search for meaning was embedded within the certainty of faith in God. In my theological studies, we were encouraged to think critically about our faith. I engaged in this critical thinking sufficiently to think myself right out of my faith. Then, the quest for meaning became just as embedded in loss of belief and in the absence of God. Eventually, that certainty too evaporated. Life since then has been lived through uncertainty, beyond the certainties of belief or unbelief, beyond both theism and atheism.

The story of God is that of a search for ultimate meaning, yet forever elusive. But knowing, in some sense of the word 'knowing', has been found. Uncertainty has become grounded in a feeling of wonder that there is something at all rather than nothing. Unknowing has been established in a sense of awe at the way the world is. There is an awareness of the mystery of it all, not least in the existence of selves that think about all this. Along with this there often goes an intuition that the accidental and the fortuitous have an inevitability about them – a kind of serendipitous providentialism or an accidental fatalism. In either case, for believers there is a sense that all that happens is in accord with the will of God, for unbelievers a Stoic acceptance of the way things are and have been.

Perhaps Rudolf Otto had it right after all. Our experience of life and the world is that of a *mysterium tremendum et fascinans*, a mystery that is both awe-inspiring and fascinating. This is a spirituality grounded in agnosticism and only possible on the basis of it. It is a spirituality that lives in the certainty that we will never really know. For that very reason, it is also a spirituality that finds genuine meaning in the search for the depths of the self and the truth of things, even if without any expectation of success. In spite of that, it is a spirituality that lives in the hope that there might just be an ultimate source of being and goodness, one in whom 'we live and move and have our being' (Acts 17.28). It is a spirituality that tries to live in accord with that hope.

Notes

Prologue

1 Unless otherwise indicated, all biblical quotations come from the New Revised Standard Version.
2 Albert Camus, *The Plague* (1947; London: Penguin, 2002), p. 14.
3 Ibid., pp. 74–5.
4 Ibid., pp. 96–7.
5 Ibid., p. 98.
6 I use the term 'Old Testament' solely for its familiarity for many readers, not implying thereby any superseding of it by the 'New Testament'.

1. The Transcendent God

1 On the call of Isaiah, see Hans Wildberger, *Isaiah 1–12: A Commentary*, trans. Thomas H. Trapp (Minneapolis, MN: Fortress, 1991), pp. 246–78.
2 See Rudolf Otto, *The Idea of the Holy* (Oxford: Oxford University Press, 1958). See also Philip C. Almond, *Rudolf Otto: An Introduction to His Philosophical Theology* (Chapel Hill, NC, and London: University of North Carolina Press, 1984).
3 See 'Akkadian myths and epics', trans. E. A. Speiser, in James B. Pritchard (ed.), *Ancient Near Eastern Texts Relating to the Old Testament* (1950; Princeton: Princeton University Press, 1969), pp. 60–119.
4 Theophilus, *To Autolycus* 3.28, trans. Marcus Dods, in *ANF*, ii, p. 120.
5 Henri-Charles Puech, 'Gnosis and time', in Joseph Campbell (ed.), *Man and Time: Papers from the Eranos Yearbooks* (London: Routledge & Kegan Paul, 1958), p. 40.
6 Lactantius, *The Divine Institutes* 7.14, trans. William Fletcher, in *ANF*, vii, p. 211. Hence the excitement within certain Christian circles that dated the creation around 4000 BCE as we approached the year 2000.

7   'Medieval sourcebook: twelfth ecumenical council: Lateran IV 1215', in H. J. Schroeder (ed.), *Disciplinary Decrees of the General Councils: Text, Translation and Commentary* (St Louis, MO: B. Herder, 1937), pp. 236–96 (my italics). Available at http://www.fordham.edu/halsall/basis/lateran4.asp.

8   Middle Platonism is the modern name given to the Platonism of the period from about 90 BCE until the third century CE, when it was succeeded by the development of Neoplatonism under Plotinus.

9   Justin Martyr, *The First Apology of Justin* 59, trans. A. Cleveland Coxe, in *ANF*, i, p. 182.

10 Quoted in Jaroslav Pelikan, *The Christian Tradition: A History of the Development of Doctrine*, i: *The Emergence of the Catholic Tradition (100–600)* (Chicago and London: University of Chicago Press, 1971), p. 36.

11 Theophilus, *To Autolycus* 2.4 [p. 95].

12 Irenaeus, *Against Heresies* 2.10.4, trans. A. Cleveland Coxe, in *ANF*, i, p. 370.

13 Oscar Cullmann, *Christ and Time: The Primitive Christian Conception of Time and History* (London: SCM Press, 1951), p. 65.

14 Plutarch, *The E at Delphi* 393b, in *Plutarch's Moralia in Sixteen Volumes*, v, trans. Frank Cole Babbitt (London and Cambridge, MA: William Heinemann and Harvard University Press, 1969), p. 245. For this discussion of God's eternity, I am especially indebted to Alan G. Padgett, *God, Eternity and the Nature of Time* (Eugene, OR: Wipf & Stock, 2000). See also Gerhard May, *Creation ex nihilo: The Doctrine of 'Creation out of Nothing' in Early Christian Thought* (Edinburgh: T&T Clark, 1994).

15 Origen, *On First Principles*, trans. G. W. Butterworth (Gloucester, MA: Peter Smith, 1973), 4.4.1 [p. 316].

16 Neoplatonism is a modern name that designates a tradition of philosophy that arose in the third century CE and lasted until early in the sixth century, when the Platonic Academy in Athens was closed.

17 Plotinus, *The Enneads*, trans. Stephen MacKenna (London: Faber, 1956), 3.7.3 [p. 225].

18 Augustine, *The City of God* 11.6, trans. Marcus Dods, in *NPNFI*, ii, p. 208.

19 Augustine, *The Confessions of St Augustine* 11.13, trans. J. G. Pilkington, in *NPNFI*, i, p. 168.

20 'Akkadian myths and epics', p. 68.

21 See Mark S. Smith, 'The three bodies of God in the Hebrew Bible', *Journal of Biblical Literature* 134 (2015), pp. 471–88.

22 Quoted in Epiphanius of Salamis, *The Panarion of Epiphanius of Salamis Books II and III*, trans. Frank Williams (Leiden: Brill, 1994), p. 404.

23 Theodoret, *The Ecclesiastical History of Theodoret* 4.9, trans. Blomfield Jackson, in *NPNFII*, iii, p. 114. We leave aside for the moment the issue of God's becoming man in Jesus Christ and thus having a physical body.

24 See José Costa, 'Le corps de Dieu dans le judaïsme rabbinique ancien: problèmes d'interprétation', *Revue de l'histoire des religions* 227 (2010), pp. 283–316.

25 Origen, *On First Principles* 1.1.1 [p. 7].

26 Ibid., 1.1.6 [p. 10].

27 Ibid., 4.2.4 [p. 276]. See Gedaliahu Stroumsa, 'The incorporeality of God: context and implications of Origen's position', *Religion* 13 (1983), pp. 345–58.

28 Cyril of Alexandria, Letter 83, trans. John McEnerney, in *FC*, lxxvii, p. 109.

29 Except where 'technically' required, I have stayed with the custom and tradition of Judaism, Christianity and Islam and used the masculine personal pronoun (and where appropriate the impersonal pronoun).

30 Athenagoras, *The Resurrection of the Dead* 15, trans. B. P. Pratten, in *ANF*, iii, p. 157.

31 Ambrose, *The Six Days of Creation* 1.6.43, trans. John J. Savage, in *FC*, xlii, p. 256.

32 Athanasius, *On the Incarnation of the Word* 3, trans. Archibald Robertson, in *NPNFII*, iv, p. 37.

33 Augustine, *Two Books on Genesis against the Manichees* 1.18.28, trans. Roland J. Teske, in *FC*, lxxxiv, p. 76.

34 The story of Noah and the flood (Gen. 6.5–9.17) weaves together two separate literary traditions. Distinguishing between them in detail is not necessary for the purposes of this book.

35 Immanuel Kant, *The Conflict of the Faculties (Der Streit der Fakultäten)*, trans. Mary J. Gregor (Lincoln, NE, and London: University of Nebraska Press, 1979), p. 115.

36 On the Abraham stories, see Joseph Blenkinsopp, *Abraham: The Story of a Life* (Grand Rapids, MI: Eerdmans, 2015).

37 See Karen Armstrong, *Fields of Blood: Religion and the History of Violence* (New York: Knopf, 2014).

38 That God was the God of the oppressed and not of the oppressor is the theme of twentieth-century 'liberation theologies'. See Christopher

Rowland (ed.), *The Cambridge Companion to Liberation Theology* (Cambridge: Cambridge University Press, 2007).

39 Plato, *Euthyphro* 10a, in *The Collected Dialogues of Plato*, ed. Edith Hamilton and Huntington Cairns, trans. Lane Cooper (Princeton: Princeton University Press, 1961), p. 178.

40 Augustine, *The City of God* 1.21 [p. 15].

41 Quoted in Philip L. Quinn, 'Divine command theory', in Hugh LaFollette and Ingmar Persson (eds), *The Blackwell Guide to Ethical Theory* (Chichester: Blackwell, 2013), p. 90.

42 Andrew Davies, *Double Standards in Isaiah: Re-evaluating Prophetic Ethics and Divine Justice* (Leiden: Brill, 2000), p. 133.

43 John Barton, *Ethics in Ancient Israel* (Oxford: Oxford University Press, 2014), p. 249.

44 Historical criticism has recognised three separate collections in the book of Isaiah. The earliest, Proto-Isaiah, is contained in chapters 1–39; Deutero-Isaiah (chapters 40–55) is the work of an anonymous sixth-century BCE author writing during the exile of the Jews in Babylon, and Trito-Isaiah (chapters 56–66) was composed after the return from exile.

45 On Jesus and Satan, see Philip C. Almond, *The Devil: A New Biography* (London and Ithaca, NY: I.B.Tauris and Cornell University Press, 2014), pp. 22–7.

46 On the historical Jesus, see especially N. T. Wright, *Jesus and the Victory of God* (London: SPCK, 1996). For the much-neglected topic of the nature of the God of Jesus, see the quite moving work by Alexander J. M. Wedderburn, *The God of Jesus – Our God?* (Eugene, OR: Cascade, 2014), in which the author wrestles with the ambiguities in the God of Jesus.

47 All quotations from the Qur'ān come from *The Qur'ān: A New Annotated Translation*, trans. A. J. Droge (Sheffield: Equinox, 2014).

48 Although not unanimous on this, Islamic tradition, perhaps exalting the transcendence of God, came to understand this as a vision of the angel Gabriel. There is nothing in the text, however, to suggest that it is anything but a vision of God.

49 In spite of the Quranic view that the text was sent down once and for all, Islamic tradition has tended to view the Qur'ān as a gradual revelation that took place over some 20 years. This position has the virtue of enabling inconsistencies in the text to be ironed out by prioritising some texts at the expense of others or contextualising them. See A. J. Droge, 'A book "from heaven"', in *The Qur'ān*, trans. Droge, pp. xxi–xxv.

50 The historicity of the tradition was eventually rejected by Islam.

See Shahab Ahmed, 'Satanic verses', in Jane Dammen McAuliffe (ed.), *Encyclopedia of the Qur'ān* (Leiden: Brill, 2015). Available at http://dx.doi.org/10.1163/1875-3922_q3_EQSIM_00372.

2. The God–Man

1 Irenaeus, *Against Heresies* 3.12.12, trans. A. Cleveland Coxe, in *ANF*, i, p. 435. It needs to be noted that we only know the views of Marcion from his many theological enemies and there are, consequently, many 'Marcions'. See Judith M. Lieu, *Marcion and the Making of a Heretic* (Cambridge: Cambridge University Press, 2015).

2 Irenaeus, *Against Heresies* 1.27.2 [p. 352].

3 Tertullian, *The Five Books against Marcion* 1.6, trans. Peter Holmes, in *ANF*, iii, p. 275.

4 Homer, *The Iliad*, trans. A. T. Murray (Cambridge, MA, and London: Harvard University Press and Heinemann, 1924), 8.1–15. Available at http://www.perseus.tufts.edu/hopper/text?doc=Perseus%3A text%3A1999.01.0134&redirect=true.

5 'Akkadian myths and epics', trans. E. A. Speiser, in James B. Pritchard (ed.), *Ancient Near Eastern Texts Relating to the Old Testament* (1950; Princeton: Princeton University Press, 1969), pp. 69–72.

6 Jan Assmann, *Of God and Gods: Egypt, Israel, and the Rise of Monotheism* (Madison, WI: University of Wisconsin Press, 2008), p. 107. I have profited from this book very much.

7 On religious pluralism in Corinth, see Bruce W. Winter, 'Pluralism – 1 Corinthians 8–10', *Tyndale Bulletin* 41 (1990), pp. 209–26.

8 Larry Hurtado, *One God, One Lord: Early Christian Devotion and Ancient Jewish Monotheism* (London: Bloomsbury, 2015), p. 53. I am indebted to Hurtado for his discussion of post-exilic Judaism.

9 There is some ambiguity in Islam about whether the prophets are with God before or only after the end of the world. In one later tradition of Muhammad's ascent during his lifetime from Jerusalem to God in heaven, he journeyed through seven levels of heaven, where he met at each level seven former prophets: Adam, Jesus, Joseph, Enoch, Aaron, Moses and Abraham. Another tradition has only two prophets in heaven before the end, namely, Jesus and Idris.

10 Philo, *Questions and Answers on Genesis II 62*, in *The Works of Philo: Complete and Unabridged*, trans. C. D. Yonge (Peabody, MA: Hendrickson, 1993), p. 834 (my italics).

11 Philo, *On the Confusion of Tongues* 28.146, in *The Works of Philo*, trans. Yonge, p. 247.

12 The translations from Acts and 1 Corinthians in the preceding passage are my own. Existing English translations write the Trinitarian doctrine of the Holy Spirit back into the New Testament. For an excellent account of 'holy spirit' in early Christianity, see Rick Strelan, 'What might a pagan have understood by "Holy Spirit"?', *Colloquium* 42 (2010), pp. 151–72.

13 *The Pastor of Hermas* 5.6, trans. F. Crombie, in *ANF*, ii, pp. 35–6.

14 Justin Martyr, *The First Apology of Justin* 13, trans. A. Cleveland Coxe, in *ANF*, i, pp. 166–7 (my italics).

15 Ibid., 60 [p. 183].

16 Ibid., 33 [p. 174].

17 Theophilus, *To Autolycus* 2.15, trans. Marcus Dods, in *ANF*, ii, p. 101.

18 Ibid., 1.3 [p. 90].

19 Athenagoras, *A Plea for the Christians* 12, trans. B. P. Pratten, in *ANF*, ii, p. 134 (my italics).

20 Tertullian, *Against Praxeas* 2, trans. Peter Holmes, in *ANF*, iii, p. 598.

21 Origen, *On First Principles*, trans. G. W. Butterworth (Gloucester, MA: Peter Smith, 1973), 1.1.6 [p. 10].

22 Origen, *Contra Celsum*, trans. Henry Chadwick (Cambridge: Cambridge University Press, 1953), 8.12 [p. 460].

23 Origen, *Dialogue of Origen with Heraclides* 2.5–8, in Origen, *Treatise on the Passover and Dialogue of Origen with Heraclides and His Fellow Bishops on the Father, the Son, and the Soul*, trans. Robert J. Daly (Mahwah, NJ: Paulist Press, 1992), p. 58.

24 Origen, *Contra Celsum* 5.39 [p. 296].

25 Gregory of Nazianzus, Oration 45.4, trans. Charles Gordon Browne, in *NPNFII*, vii, p. 424.

26 Gregory of Nazianzus, Oration 40.41, trans. Charles Gordon Browne, in *NPNFII*, vii, p. 375.

27 Origen, *On First Principles* 4.4.1 [pp. 314–15] (my italics).

28 Ibid., 1.1.3 [p. 9].

29 Origen, *On First Principles* 1.3.4 [p. 33].

30 Quoted in Timothy Ware, *The Orthodox Church* (Harmondsworth: Penguin, 1980), pp. 43–4. The Greek text may be found in *PG* 94.1384d.

31 Athanasius, *Councils of Ariminum and Seleucia* 16, trans. John Henry Newman and Archibald Robertson, in *NPNFII*, iv, p. 458.

32 Theodoret, *The Ecclesiastical History of Theodoret* 1.4, trans. Blomfield Jackson, in *NPNFII*, iii, p. 41.

33 Eusebius, *Life of Constantine* 3.10, trans. Ernest Cushing Richardson, in *NPNFII*, i, p. 522.

34 Ibid., 3.12 [p. 523].

35 Quoted in J. N. D. Kelly, *Early Christian Doctrines* (New York: HarperCollins, 1978), p. 232.

36 Basil of Caesarea, *The Treatise De Spiritu Sancto* 30.76, trans. Blomfield Jackson, in *NPNFII*, viii, p. 48.

37 Athanasius, *Councils of Ariminum and Seleucia* 41 [p. 472].

38 Athanasius, *Tome or Synodal Letter to the People of Antioch* 5–6, trans. A. Robertson, in *NPNFII*, iv, pp. 484–5.

39 See Gregory of Nazianzus, *The Fifth Theological Oration: On the Holy Spirit* 5, trans. Charles Gordon Browne and James Edward Swallow, in *NPNFII*, vii, p. 319.

40 I here follow the translation offered of *The Fifth Theological Oration: On the Holy Spirit* 10 in Kelly, *Early Christian Doctrines*, p. 261.

41 Gregory of Nyssa, *On the Holy Spirit against the Followers of Macedonius*, trans. M. Day, in *NPNFII*, v, pp. 315, 319.

42 Gregory of Nyssa, *On 'Not Three Gods': To Ablabius*, trans. H. C. Ogle, in *NPNFII*, v, p. 336.

43 Augustine, *Answer to Maximinus the Arian*, trans. Roland Teske, in Augustine, *Arianism and Other Heresies*, ed. Boniface Ramsey (Hyde Park, NY: New City Press, 1995), p. 280.

44 Augustine, *On the Trinity* 15.17.27, trans. Arthur West, in *NPNFI*, iii, p. 215.

45 See A. Edward Siecienski, *The Filioque: History of a Doctrinal Controversy* (Oxford: Oxford University Press, 2010), ch. 6.

46 Norman P. Tanner (ed.), *Decrees of the Ecumenical Councils*, i: *Nicaea I to Lateran V* (London and Washington, DC: Sheed & Ward and Georgetown University Press, 1990), p. 28.

47 There is an ambiguity in Apollinarius, which need not concern us, as to whether he believed human nature to consist of body and soul or body, soul and spirit.

48 Apollinarius, *Letter to the Bishops at Diocaesarea* 2, in James Stevenson (ed.), *Creeds, Councils and Controversies: Documents Illustrating the History of the Church AD 337–461* (London: SPCK, 1989), p. 88.

49 The four major terms, the meaning of each of which was at any one time uncertain and ambiguous and over time was shifting, were *ousia*, *physis*, *hypostasis* and *prosopon*. For as lucid an account of these as you can get, see especially John McGuckin, *Saint Cyril of Alexandria and the Christological Controversy* (Crestwood, NY: St Vladimir's Seminary Press, 2004), pp. 138–45.

50 Theodoret, Epistle 180, in Stevenson (ed.), *Creeds, Councils and Controversies*, p. 320.

51 Gregory of Nazianzus, *To Cledonius the Priest against Apollinarius*, trans. Charles Gordon Browne and James Edward Swallow, in *NPNFII*, vii, p. 440.

52 Quoted in McGuckin, *Saint Cyril of Alexandria and the Christological Controversy*, p. 160.

53 *Second Letter of Cyril to Succensus* 3, in McGuckin, *Saint Cyril of Alexandria and the Christological Controversy*, p. 361.

54 *First Letter of Cyril to Succensus* 6, in McGuckin, *Saint Cyril of Alexandria and the Christological Controversy*, p. 355.

55 *Second Letter of Cyril to Nestorius* 5, in McGuckin, *Saint Cyril of Alexandria and the Christological Controversy*, p. 264.

56 Tanner (ed.), *Decrees of the Ecumenical Councils*, i, p. 86.

57 See for example *The Tome of St Leo*, trans. Henry R. Percival, in *NPNFII*, xiv, pp. 255, 256.

58 The division between dyophysites and miaphysites has remained a key issue within the Eastern Church. In the present day, the miaphysite churches are known as the Oriental Orthodox communion, as distinct from those known as Eastern Orthodox, who stayed with the Chalcedonian definition.

59 Irenaeus, *Against Heresies* 3.23.1 [p. 456]. See Philip C. Almond, *The Devil: A New Biography* (London and Ithaca, NY: I.B.Tauris and Cornell University Press, 2014), ch. 3.

60 Gregory of Nazianzus, *The Fourth Theological Oration* 20, trans. Charles Gordon Browne and James Edward Swallow, in *NPNFII*, vii, p. 317.

61 Athanasius, *On the Incarnation of the Word* 54.3, trans. Archibald Robertson, in *NPNFII*, iv, p. 65.

62 Quoted in Gerald Bonner, 'Deification, divinization', in Alan D. Fitzgerald (ed.), *Augustine through the Ages: An Encyclopedia* (Grand Rapids, MI: Eerdmans, 1999), p. 265.

3. *The God Within*

1 Plato, *Symposium* 211a–b, in *The Collected Dialogues of Plato*, ed. Edith Hamilton and Huntington Cairns, trans. Lane Cooper (Princeton: Princeton University Press, 1961), p. 562.

2 Plato, *Republic* 516b, in *The Collected Dialogues of Plato*, ed. Hamilton and Cairns, trans. Cooper, p. 748.

3 William Ralph Inge, *The Platonic Tradition in English Religious Thought* (New York: Longmans, Green, 1926), p. 9.

4 Plato, *Republic* 518c [pp. 750–1].

5 Ibid., 517c [p. 750].

6 Plato, *Timaeus* 29d–30a, in *The Collected Dialogues of Plato*, ed. Hamilton and Cairns, trans. Cooper, p. 1162.

7 Ibid., 92c [p. 1211].

8 Tertullian, *The Prescription against Heretics* 7, trans. Peter Holmes, in *ANF*, iii, p. 246.

9 Philo, *The Special Laws*, III 34.185, in *The Works of Philo: Complete and Unabridged*, trans. C. D. Yonge (Peabody, MA: Hendrickson, 1993), p. 613. See also Harry Austryn Wolfson, *Philo: Foundations of Religious Philosophy in Judaism, Christianity, and Islam*, i: *Structure and Growth of Philosophical Systems from Plato to Spinoza* (Cambridge, MA: Harvard University Press, 1968), pp. 138–43.

10 Philo, *The Special Laws*, III 34.189 [p. 613].

11 Justin Martyr, *The Second Apology of Justin* 12, trans. A. Cleveland Coxe, in *ANF*, i, p. 191.

12 Augustine, *The City of God* 7.9, trans. Marcus Dods, in *NPNFI*, ii, p. 150.

13 Augustine, *Concerning the Nature of Good* 1, trans. Richard Stothert and Albert H. Newman, in *NPNFI*, iv, p. 351.

14 Ibid.

15 E. R. Dodds, *The Ancient Concept of Progress* (Oxford: Clarendon, 1973), p. 126.

16 Plotinus, *The Enneads*, trans. Stephen MacKenna (London: Faber, 1956), 6.9.3 [p. 617]. For this discussion of Plotinus, I am indebted to Andrew Louth, *The Origins of the Christian Mystical Tradition* (Oxford: Oxford University Press, 2009).

17 Quoted in Arthur O. Lovejoy, *The Great Chain of Being* (New York: Harper & Row, 1960), p. 62.

18 Plotinus, *The Enneads* 1.8.7 [p. 72].

19 Ibid., 3.8.10 [p. 249].

20 Ibid., 5.1.1 [p. 369].

21 Ibid., 1.8.13 [p. 76].

22 Louth, *Origins of the Christian Mystical Tradition*, p. 39.

23 The limiting case of the mystical path occurs in Mādhyamaka Buddhism, according to which all reality is ultimately empty (*śūnya*) and there is neither world nor self.

24 Plotinus, *The Enneads* 6.9.11 [pp. 624–5].

25 Augustine, *The Confessions of St Augustine* 1.1.1, trans. J. G. Pilkington, in *NPNFI*, i, p. 45.

26 Ibid., 9.10.24 [p. 137].

27 Ibid., 9.10.25 [p. 138].

28 Even with ultimately 'atheistic' mystical traditions like Buddhism, there remains a sense of 'enlightenment' breaking in from 'outside' only when the individual gives up the pursuit of it.

29 Ibid., 10.27.38 [pp. 152–3].

30 Augustine, *The City of God* 22.24 [p. 502].

31 Augustine, *On the Holy Trinity* 14.12.15, 20, trans. Arthur West Haddan, in *NPNFI*, iii, p. 191, 194.

32 See Paul L. Gavrilyuk, *The Sufferings of the Impassible God: The Dialectics of Patristic Thought* (Oxford: Oxford University Press, 2004).

33 Julian, Emperor of Rome, *The Arguments of the Emperor Julian against the Christians*, ed. Willis Nevins (London: Williams & Norgate, 1873), p. 31.

34 *Recognitions of Clement* 10.48, trans. Thomas Smith, in *ANF*, viii, p. 205.

35 Augustine, *Patience* 1, trans. Mary Sarah Muldowney, in *FC*, xvi, p. 237.

36 Cyril of Alexandria, *Scholia on the Incarnation* 33, in John McGuckin, *Saint Cyril of Alexandria and the Christological Controversy* (Crestwood, NY: St Vladimir's Seminary Press, 2004), p. 327. In twentieth-century theology, the problem was resolved by giving up on the notion of the impassible God, a solution which, while it avoided the conflict between the impassible God of the philosophers and the passible God of the Bible, did so at the expense of the necessity of the Incarnation. For 'in this case the flesh would merely duplicate in its imperfect way the suffering that the Word had already undergone in its own nature' (Gavrilyuk, *Sufferings of the Impassible God*, p. 175). In more radical circles, it could be resolved by the denial of Christ's divinity and the belief that his suffering on behalf of others was only that of the exemplary ideal human.

37 I place 'beyond' and 'within' in inverted commas to indicate that these are only metaphors, since God, being a wholly spiritual being, cannot be said to be here rather than there. As such they refer to theological emphases. Technically, because God is omnipresent, he is both everywhere and nowhere in particular.

38 Although doubts about the attribution of authorship to the Dionysius of Acts of the Apostles had been raised as early as the sixteenth century, it was only in 1895 that parts of Dionysius's *The Divine Names* (specifically the discussion on evil in the fourth chapter) were definitively shown to have been dependent on Proclus and thus were linked to a period around the late fifth or early sixth century.

39 Dionysius the Areopagite, *The Divine Names* 4.13, in Dionysius the Areopagite, *On the Divine Names and the Mystical Theology*, trans. C. E. Rolt (London: SPCK, 1920), p. 106. For an excellent commentary on the writings of Pseudo-Dionysius, see Paul Rorem, *Pseudo-Dionysius: A Commentary on the Texts and an Introduction to their Influence* (New York: Oxford University Press, 1993).

40 Dionysius the Areopagite, *The Divine Names* 4.17 [p. 109].

41 Dionysius the Areopagite, *The Mystical Theology* 3, in Dionysius the Areopagite, *On the Divine Names and the Mystical Theology*, trans. Rolt, p. 196. Pseudo-Dionysius is here referring to the content of another (now lost, perhaps fictitious) work entitled *The Theological Representations*. See also *The Divine Names* 1.

42 These are the five major themes in chapters 4–8 of *The Divine Names*.

43 Again, Pseudo-Dionysius is here referring to the content of another (now lost, perhaps fictitious) work, entitled *Symbolic Theology*.

44 Dionysius the Areopagite, *The Mystical Theology* 3 [p. 198].

45 Ibid., 4 [p. 199].

46 Dionysius the Areopagite, *The Divine Names* 7.3 [p. 152].

47 Ibid., 13.3 [p. 189].

48 Dionysius the Areopagite, *The Mystical Theology* 5 [p. 201].

49 Ibid., 1 [p. 194].

50 Dionysius the Areopagite, *The Divine Names* 4.13 [p. 106].

51 *Denis's Hidden Theology*, in *The Pursuit of Wisdom and Other Works*, by the Author of *The Cloud of Unknowing*, trans. James A. Walsh (Mahwah, NJ: Paulist Press, 1988), p. 77 (my italics).

52 Ibid., p. 75 (my italics).

53 *The Cloud of Unknowing*, trans. Clifton Wolters (Harmondsworth: Penguin, 1961), § 6 [p. 60].

54 Quoted in H. P. Owen, 'Christian mysticism: a study in Walter Hilton's *The Ladder of Perfection*', *Religious Studies* 7 (1971), pp. 31–2.

55 Quoted in Grace M. Jantzen, *Power, Gender and Christian Mysticism* (Cambridge: Cambridge University Press, 1995), p. 135.

56 On the theology of Albert the Great and its relation to Pseudo-Dionysius, see Albert the Great and Thomas Aquinas, *Albert and Thomas: Selected Writings*, ed. Simon Tugwell (Mahwah, NJ: Paulist Press, 1988). On Eckhart, see Bernard McGinn, *The Harvest of Mysticism in Medieval Germany* (New York: Herder & Herder, 2005) and Meister Eckhart, *The Essential Sermons, Commentaries, Treatises, and Defense*, trans. Edmund Colledge and Bernard McGinn (New York: Paulist Press, 1981).

57 Meister Eckhart, Sermon 15, in Eckhart, *Essential Sermons*, trans. Colledge and McGinn, p. 192. See also Sermon 5b [p. 183].

58 Quoted in McGinn, *Harvest of Mysticism*, p. 127. There was an ambiguity in Eckhart about whether this 'boiling' occurred in the Godhead itself or the Father.

59 Meister Eckhart, Sermon 53, in Eckhart, *Essential Sermons*, trans. Colledge and McGinn, p. 205.

60 Ibid.

61 Meister Eckhart, *On Detachment*, in Eckhart, *Essential Sermons*, trans. Colledge and McGinn, p. 288.

62 Meister Eckhart, Sermon 6, in Eckhart, *Essential Sermons*, trans. Colledge and McGinn, p. 187.

63 Meister Eckhart, Sermon 48, in Eckhart, *Essential Sermons*, trans. Colledge and McGinn, p. 198.

64 Quoted in McGinn, *Harvest of Mysticism*, p. 182.

65 *The Bull 'In agro dominico'* (March 27, 1329), in Eckhart, *Essential Sermons*, trans. Colledge and McGinn, p. 77. On the trial of Eckhart, see Kurt Flasch, *Meister Eckhart: Philosopher of Christianity*, trans. Anne Schindel and Aaron Vanides (New Haven, CT: Yale University Press, 2015).

66 Thomas Aquinas, *Summa theologiae, prima pars*, 1–49, trans. Laurence Shapcote (Lander, WY: Aquinas Institute for the Study of Sacred Doctrine, 2012), 2.112.1 [p. 473]. See also Luke Davis Townsend, 'Deification in Aquinas: a supplementum to *The Ground of Union*', *Journal of Theological Studies* 66 (2015), pp. 204–34.

67 For an excellent account of 'deification' in the West from Aquinas onwards, see Paul Collins, *Partaking in Divine Nature: Deification and Communion* (London: Bloomsbury, 2012), ch. 5.

68 Pseudo-Dionysius, *The Ecclesiastical Hierarchy* 1.3, in Pseudo-Dionysius, *The Complete Works*, trans. Colm Luibheid (New York and Mahwah, NJ: Paulist Press, 1987), p. 198.

69 See Norman Russell, *The Doctrine of Deification in the Greek Patristic Tradition* (Oxford: Oxford University Press, 2006), pp. 262–95.

70 Maximus the Confessor, *Commentary on the Our Father* 5, in Maximus the Confessor, *Selected Writings*, trans. George C. Berthold (London: SPCK, 1985), p. 118.

71 Maximus the Confessor, *The Church's Mystagogy* 21, in Maximus the Confessor, *Selected Writings*, trans. Berthold, p. 203.

72 Quoted in Andrew Louth, *Maximus the Confessor* (London: Routledge, 2005), p. 43.

73 On the political complexities, see ibid., pp. 12–18.

74 Norman P. Tanner (ed.), *Decrees of the Ecumenical Councils*, i: *Nicaea I to Lateran V* (London and Washington, DC: Sheed & Ward and Georgetown University Press, 1990), pp. 129–30.

75 Quoted in A. J. Arberry, *Sufism: An Account of the Mystics of Islam* (London: George Allen & Unwin, 1950), p. 55.

76 Ibid.

77 Quoted in Alexander Knysh, *Islamic Mysticism: A Short History* (Leiden: Brill, 2000), p. 79. For excellent brief accounts of the lives of al-Bistami and al-Hallaj, see pp. 69–82.

78 Al-Ghāzali, *The Niche of Lights*, trans. David Buchman (Provo, UT: Brigham Young University Press, 1998), 1.45–8 [pp. 17–18].

79 Ibid., 1.45–8 [p. 18].

80 Ibid., 1.42 [p. 16].

81 Quoted in William C. Chittick, *The Sufi Path of Love: The Spiritual Teachings of Rumi* (Albany, NY: State University of New York, 1983), p. 180.

82 Ibid., p. 192.

83 Quoted in R. A. Nicholson, *The Mystics of Islam* (New York: Schocken, 1975), p. 119.

84 *The Zohar: The Book of Splendor*, trans. Gershom Scholem (New York: Schocken, 1949), 1.15a [p. 27].

85 Gershom Scholem, *Major Trends in Jewish Mysticism* (New York: Schocken, 1995), p. 180.

86 Arthur Green, 'Introduction', in *The Zohar*, i, trans. Daniel C. Matt (Stanford, CA: Stanford University Press, 2004), pp. 70–1. I am particularly indebted to Green for his discussion of the *Zohar*.

87 Quoted in Scholem, *Major Trends*, p. 177.

4. *The God of Reason and Revelation*

1 See Daniel Jeremy Silver, *Maimonidean Criticism and the Maimonidean Controversy 1180–1240* (Leiden: Brill, 1965).

2 Moses Maimonides, *A Guide for the Perplexed*, trans. M. Friedlaender (New York: E. P. Dutton, 1904), intro. [p. 2]. Available at http://oll.libertyfund.org/titles/maimonides-a-guide-for-the-perplexed.

3 Ibid., 1.52 [pp. 69–72].

4 Ibid., 1.50 [pp. 67–8].

5 Ibid., 2.25 [pp. 199–200].

6 What Maimonides might have meant by 'creation' is a matter of much scholarly dispute. There is plenty of ambiguity in Maimonides, so much so that the limiting case among critics is those who say that, whatever Maimonides overtly wrote about anything, he covertly believed the exact opposite.

7 Joseph A. Buijs, 'Religion and philosophy in Maimonides, Averroes, and Aquinas', *Medieval Encounters* 8 (2002), p. 181. This is a particularly helpful and succinct account of this issue.

8 On various versions of Maimonides's 13 principles, see Arthur Hyman, 'Maimonides' "thirteen principles"', in Alexander Altmann (ed.), *Jewish Medieval and Renaissance Studies* (Cambridge, MA: Harvard University Press, 1967), pp. 119–44.

9 Averroes, *The Decisive Treatise, Determining the Nature of the Connection between Religion and Philosophy* 2. Available at http://people.uvawise.edu/philosophy/phil205/Averroes.html.

10 Ibid., 1.

11 Ibid., 2.

12 Buijs, 'Religion and philosophy', p. 166.

13 Averroes, *An Exposition of the Methods of Arguments Concerning the Beliefs of the Faith, and a Determination of Uncertain Doubts and Misleading Innovations in Interpretations*, in Averroes (Ibn Rushd), *The Philosophy and Theology of Averroes: Tractacta*, trans. Mohammad Jamil-Ub-Behman Barod ([1160]; Baroda: Manibhai Mathurbhal Gupta, 1921). Available at http://oll.libertyfund.org/titles/rushd-the-philosophy-and-theology-of-averroes. See also Majid Fakhry, *A History of Islamic Philosophy* (3rd edn, New York: Columbia University Press, 2004), pp. 291–2.

14 Averroes, *Decisive Treatise* 2.

15 Quoted in Buijs, 'Religion and philosophy', pp. 168–9.

16 Thomas Aquinas, *Summa theologiae, prima pars*, 1–49, trans. Laurence Shapcote (Lander, WY: Aquinas Institute for the Study of Sacred Doctrine, 2012), 1.1.1 [p. 4].

17 Ibid., 1.2.1 [p. 17].

18 Ibid., 1.2.3 [p. 21].

19 Aristotle, *Metaphysics* 12.7–9, in *The Philosophy of Aristotle*, trans. A. E. Wardman and J. L. Creed (New York: Mentor, 1963), pp. 128, 129, 127.

20 I leave the fifth way, the argument from or to design (or purpose) until a later chapter.

21 See Herbert A. Davidson, 'John Philoponus as a source of medieval Islamic and Jewish proofs of creation', *Journal of the American Oriental Society* 89 (1969), pp. 375–91.

22 Quoted in William Lane Craig, *The Kalām Cosmological Argument*
    (London: Macmillan, 1979), p. 45.
23 On Saadia, see Eliezer Schweid, *The Classic Jewish Philosophers: From
    Saadia through the Renaissance* (Leiden: Brill, 2008), ch. 1.
24 Aquinas, *Summa theologiae*, 1.46.2 [p. 478].
25 Blaise Pascal, *Pensées*, trans. A. J. Krailsheimer (Harmondsworth:
    Penguin, 1966), p. 150.
26 Ibid.
27 Ibid., p. 151.
28 Anselm, *Proslogion* 1.34, in Ian Logan, *Reading Anselm's Proslogion:
    The History of Anselm's Argument and Its Significance Today* (Farnham:
    Ashgate, 2009), p. 32.
29 Ibid., 4.4 [p. 35].
30 Gaunilo, *Pro insipiente* 6.1, in Logan, *Reading Anselm's Proslogion*, p. 64.
31 Ibid., 6.3 [p. 65].
32 Anselm, *Proslogion* 3.5 [p. 34].
33 See especially Logan, *Reading Anselm's Proslogion*, chs 7–8.
34 Anselm, *Proslogion* 5.3 [p. 36].
35 Ibid., 18.9 [p. 49].
36 Augustine, *The City of God* 5.9, trans. Marcus Dods, in *NPNFI*, ii, pp. 90,
    92.
37 See John Moorhead, 'Boethius' life and the world of late antique
    philosophy', in John Marenbon (ed.), *The Cambridge Companion to
    Boethius* (Cambridge: Cambridge University Press, 2009), pp. 13–33.
38 Boethius, *The Consolation of Philosophy*, trans. H. R. James (London:
    Elliot Stock, 1897), 5.3. Available at https://www.gutenberg.org/
    files/14328/14328-h/14328-h.htm#Page_233.
39 Ibid.
40 Ibid.
41 Ibid., 5.6.
42 Ibid.
43 Augustine, *The City of God* 5.10 [p. 92].
44 Anselm, *Proslogion* 7.3 [p. 37].
45 Saadia Gaon [Saadia ben Joseph], *The Book of Beliefs and Opinions*, trans.
    Samuel Rosenblatt (New Haven, CT: Yale University Press, 1948), 7.1
    [p. 412].
46 Maimonides, *A Guide for the Perplexed* 1.15.
47 Thomas Aquinas, *Summa contra Gentiles*, ii: *Creation*, trans. James F.
    Anderson (Notre Dame, IN: Notre Dame University Press, 1975), 2.25
    [pp. 73–6].

48 Aquinas, *Summa theologiae* 1.25.3 [p. 277].

49 See Brian Leftow, 'Omnipotence', in Thomas P. Flint and Michael C. Rea
    (eds), *The Oxford Handbook of Philosophical Theology* (Oxford: Oxford
    University Press, 2011), pp. 167–99.

50 Anselm, *Monologion* 22, in Anselm, *Complete Philosophical and Theological
    Treatises of Anselm of Canterbury*, trans. Jasper Hopkins and Herbert
    Richardson (Minneapolis, MN: Arthur J. Banning Press, 2000), p. 39.

51 Anselm, *Proslogion* 19.4 [p. 50].

52 Anselm, *Monologion* 22 [p. 39].

53 Aquinas, *Summa theologiae* 1.8.3 [p. 71].

54 Nicholas Everitt, 'The divine attributes', *Philosophy Compass* 5 (2010),
    p. 89. The modern debate on omnipresence is generally conducted in
    the terms that Aquinas set. See, for example, Richard Swinburne, *The
    Coherence of Theism* (Oxford: Clarendon, 1993), p. 230.

55 Aquinas, *Summa theologiae* 1.2.3 [p. 20].

56 Lactantius, *A Treatise on the Anger of God* 13, trans. William Fletcher,
    in *ANF*, vii, p. 271.

57 Plotinus, *The Enneads*, trans. Stephen MacKenna (London: Faber, 1956),
    1.8.7 [p. 72].

58 See John Hick, *Evil and the God of Love* (Basingstoke: Palgrave
    Macmillan, 2010). I am indebted to this work.

59 Origen, *On First Principles*, trans. G. W. Butterworth (Gloucester, MA:
    Peter Smith, 1973), 1.8.1 [p. 67].

60 Ibid., 2.9.2 [p. 130].

61 See Philip C. Almond, *The Devil: A New Biography* (London and Ithaca,
    NY: I.B.Tauris and Cornell University Press, 2014), ch. 2.

62 Origen, *On First Principles* 1.pref.5 [p. 4].

63 Keats used the phrase in a letter of 21 April 1819 to George and
    Georgiana Keats (respectively the poet's brother and sister-in-law).
    John Hick attributes this solution of the problem of evil to the early
    Church Father Irenaeus some 100 years before Origen. As a result, it has
    become known as the 'Irenaean solution'. Mark S. M. Scott has made a
    better case for it to be attributed to Origen. See especially Mark S. M.
    Scott, *Journey Back to God: Origen on the Problem of Evil* (Oxford: Oxford
    University Press, 2012) and 'Suffering and soul-making: rethinking John
    Hick's theodicy', *Journal of Religion* 90 (2010), pp. 313–34.

64 Origen, *On First Principles* 2.10.6 [p. 143].

65 Quoted in Scott, *Journey Back to God*, p. 133.

66 It may of course have been the case that God did not create beings that
    he could not control but rather, although he could control them, always

refrained from doing so. But this would maintain his omnipotence at the expense of his goodness, since there are times when, granting God could have intervened to restrain evil humans in their misuse of freedom of choice, a truly good God would have done so.

67 Augustine, *Against the Epistle of Manichaeus Called Fundamental* 24.26, trans. Richard Stothert, in *NPNFI*, iv, p. 140.

68 Hick, *Evil and the God of Love*, p. 75.

69 Augustine, *The City of God* 12.6 [p. 229].

70 See Almond, *The Devil*.

71 Augustine, *The City of God* 13.14 [p. 251].

72 For an excellent overview of Augustine, omnipotence and evil, see John M. Rist, *Augustine: Ancient Thought Baptized* (Cambridge: Cambridge University Press, 1994), ch. 7.

73 Augustine, *The Confessions of St Augustine* 7.13.19, trans. J. G. Pilkington, in *NPNFI*, i, p. 110.

74 Augustine, *The City of God* 11.18 [pp. 214–5].

75 John Calvin, *Institutes of the Christian Religion*, i, ed. John T. McNeill (Louisville, KT: Westminster John Knox Press, 2006), 2.1.6 [p. 248].

76 John Calvin, *Commentaries on the First Book of Moses Called Genesis*, trans. John King (Grand Rapids, MI: Christian Classics Ethereal Library, n.d.), 1.62–3 (my italics). Available at http://www.ccel.org/ccel/calvin/calcom01.html.

77 Gottfried Wilhelm Leibniz, 'Essays on the justice of God and the freedom of man in the origin of evil: part one', in Gottfried Wilhelm Leibniz, *Theodicy: Essays on the Goodness of God, the Freedom of Man and the Origin of Evil*, trans. E. M. Huggard (Peru, IL: Open Court, 1985), §§ 9–10 [pp. 128–9].

78 Voltaire, *Candide or Optimism*, ed. Nicholas Cronk (New York: Norton, 2016), p. 4.

79 Ibid.

80 Voltaire, *Philosophical Dictionary*, ed. and trans. Theodore Besterman (London: Penguin, 2004), p. 70.

81 Ibid., pp. 73–4.

5. *The God of Wrath, Mercy and Justice*

1 Quoted in Peter Harrison, *The Bible, Protestantism, and the Rise of Natural Science* (Cambridge: Cambridge University Press, 1998), p. 108.

2   Thomas Aquinas, *Summa theologiae, prima pars,* 1–49, trans. Laurence
    Shapcote (Lander, WY: Aquinas Institute for the Study of Sacred
    Doctrine, 2012), 1.1.10 [p. 15].

3   The one exception in mainstream Protestantism was the late seventeenth-
    century movement of Anglican Cambridge Platonism.

4   John Calvin, *Institutes of the Christian Religion,* i, ed. John T. McNeill
    (Louisville, KT: Westminster John Knox Press, 2006), 2.16.17 [p. 525].

5   Augustine, *On Grace and Free Will* 8.20, trans. Peter Holmes and Robert
    Ernest Wallis, in *NPNFI,* v, p. 452.

6   Quoted in Alister E. McGrath, *Luther's Theology of the Cross* (Chichester:
    Wiley–Blackwell, 2011), p. 129.

7   Ibid., p. 130.

8   See Philip C. Almond, *Afterlife: A History of Life after Death* (London
    and Ithaca, NY: I.B.Tauris and Cornell University Press, 2016), ch. 4.
    A significant amount of the material in this chapter is drawn from ch.
    6 of this work.

9   Calvin, *Institutes of the Christian Religion* 3.21.7 [p. 931].

10 Ibid., 3.23.2 [p. 949].

11 Ibid.

12 Ibid., 3.23.3 [p. 950].

13 Robert Burton, *The Anatomy of Melancholy,* i, ed. Thomas C. Faulkner et al.
    (Oxford: Clarendon, 1989), p. 110. See also Angus Gowland, 'The problem
    of early modern melancholy', *Past and Present* 191 (2006), pp. 77–120.

14 John Yates, *Gods Arraignment of Hypocrites* (London, 1615), pp. 357–8.

15 Ibid., p. 356.

16 Ibid., p. 357.

17 Ibid.

18 Ibid., p. 358. See also Leif Dixon, *Practical Predestinarians in England,
    c.1590–1640* (Farnham: Ashgate, 2014).

19 Stephen Denison, *A Compendious Catechisme* [...] (London, 1621),
    pp. 2–3. On Denison, see Peter Lake, *The Boxmaker's Revenge:
    'Orthodoxy', 'Heterodoxy' and the Politics of the Parish in Early Stuart
    London* (Stanford, CA: Stanford University Press, 2001).

20 Stephen Denison, *The Doctrine of Both the Sacraments: To Witte,
    Baptisme, and the Supper of the Lord* [...] (London, 1621), pp. 145–6.

21 Max Weber, *The Protestant Ethic and the Spirit of Capitalism,* trans.
    Talcott Parsons (New York and London: Charles Scribner's Sons and
    George Allen & Unwin, 1950), p. 115.

22 Augustine, Letter 190, quoted in Alan D. Fitzgerald (ed.), *Augustine through
    the Ages: An Encyclopedia* (Grand Rapids, MI: Eerdmans, 1999), p. 44.

23 Hieremy Drexelius, *A Pleasant and Profitable Treatise of Hell* (n.p., 1668), p. 148.

24 Tobias Swinden, *An Enquiry into the Nature and Place of Hell* (London, 1727), p. 92.

25 Ibid.

26 Ibid., p. 87.

27 Christopher Love, *Hells Terror: Or, A Treatise of the Torments of the Damned, as a Preservative against Security* (London, 1653), p. 66. By the time this was published, he had already met his destiny, having been executed for treason in 1651.

28 Gottfried Wilhelm Leibniz, 'Essays on the justice of God and the freedom of man in the origin of evil: part one', in Gottfried Wilhelm Leibniz, *Theodicy: Essays on the Goodness of God, the Freedom of Man and the Origin of Evil*, trans. E. M. Huggard (Peru, IL: Open Court, 1985), § 5 [pp. 126].

29 Thomas Aquinas, *Compendium of Theology*, trans. Cyril Vollert (St Louis, MO, and London: Herder, 1947), 174. Available at http://dhspriory.org/thomas/Compendium.htm.

30 Augustine, *On the Soul and Its Origin*, 2.8, trans. Peter Holmes and Robert Ernest Wallis, in *NPNFI*, v, p. 334.

31 See Almond, *Afterlife*, ch. 4.

32 [Henry Hallywell], *A Private Letter of Satisfaction to a Friend* (n.p., 1667), p. 35.

33 Ibid., p. 36.

34 Ibid., pp. 38–9.

35 Immanuel Kant, *Critique of Practical Reason*, trans. Lewis White Beck (Indianapolis: Bobbs-Merrill Co., 1956), p. 128.

36 Immanuel Kant, *On History*, ed. Lewis White Beck (Indianapolis: Bobbs-Merrill Co., 1957), p. 70.

37 Matthew Horbery, *An Enquiry into the Scripture-doctrine Concerning the Duration of Future Punishments* [...] (London, 1744), p. 305.

38 Thomas Burnet, *A Treatise Concerning the State of Departed Souls before, and at, and after the Resurection* [*sic*] (London, 1733), p. 357.

39 Thomas Goodwin, *A Discourse of the Punishment of Sin in Hell; Demonstrating the Wrath of God to Be the Cause Thereof* (London, 1680), p. 79.

40 Jonathan Edwards, 'Sermon II: sinners in the hands of an angry God', in *The Works of Jonathan Edwards*, ii, ed. Edward Hickman (Edinburgh: Banner of Truth, 1974), 2.27. Available at http://www.ccel.org/ccel/edwards/works2.

41 Ibid., 2.18.

42 Matthew Tindal, *Christianity as Old as the Creation: Or the Gospel, a Republication of the Religion of Nature* (London, 1730), p. 67.

43 Francis Blyth, *Eternal Misery the Necessary Consequence of Infinite Mercy Abused: A Sermon [...]* (London, 1740), p. 26.

44 D. P. Walker, *The Decline of Hell: Seventeenth-century Discussions of Eternal Torment* (London: Routledge & Kegan Paul, 1964), p. 63.

45 William Whiston, *The Eternity of Hell Torments Considered [...]* (London, 1740), pp. 18–19.

46 William Whiston, *Sermons and Essays [...]* (London, 1709), p. 220.

47 William Whiston, *Astronomical Principles of Religion Natural and Reveal'd in Nine Parts [...]* (London, 1717), p. 156.

48 Hence, the alternative name for annihilationism, namely, conditionalism.

49 Henry Constable, *The Duration and Nature of Future Punishment* (London: Kellaway, 1876), p. 211. This work ran to six editions between 1868 and 1886. For Victorian views on annihilationism, see Geoffrey Rowell, *Hell and the Victorians* (Oxford: Clarendon, 1974). I am indebted to Rowell for his discussion of the Victorian period.

50 See Walker, *Decline of Hell*, pp. 59ff.; Philip C. Almond, *Heaven and Hell in Enlightenment England* (Cambridge: Cambridge University Press, 2008); and especially Richard Bauckham, 'Universalism: a historical survey', *Themelios* 4 (1978), pp. 47–54. For a list of seventeenth- and eighteenth-century universalists, see Ezra Abbott's bibliography appended to William R. Alger, *A Critical History of the Doctrine of a Future Life* (New York: W. J. Widdleton, 1878).

51 Friedrich Schleiermacher, *The Christian Faith* (Edinburgh: T&T Clark, 1928), p. 722.

52 Broad Church Anglicans attempted to steer a middle path between the extremes of Anglo-Catholic (High Church) Anglicans and evangelical (Low Church) Anglicans.

53 F. W. Farrar, *Eternal Hope* (New York: E. P. Dutton, 1878), pp. 64–5.

54 Ibid., pp. 70, 72.

55 Ibid., p. 75.

56 Ibid., p. 86 (my italics).

57 Ibid.

58 Ibid., p. 88.

59 Samuel Taylor Coleridge, *Aids to Reflection and the Confessions of an Inquiring Spirit* (London: George Bell, 1884), p. 102.

60 Don Cupitt, *Crisis of Moral Authority* (London: SCM Press, 1985), p. 22.

61 Quoted in Rowell, *Hell and the Victorians*, p. 212.

6. The Designer God

1   Quoted in Roy Porter, *Enlightenment* (London: Penguin, 2000), p. 105.

2   Quoted in Peter Harrison, *The Territories of Science and Religion* (Chicago: University of Chicago Press, 2015), p. 88. On Bacon, see James A. T. Lancaster, 'Francis Bacon on the moral and political character of the universe', in Guido Giglioni, James A. T. Lancaster et al. (eds), *Francis Bacon on Motion and Power* (Dordrecht: Springer, 2016), pp. 231–48.

3   Robert Hooke, *Micrographia* (London, 1665), preface.

4   John Passmore, *Man's Responsibility for Nature: Ecological Problems and Western Traditions* (New York: Scribner, 1974), p. 19. See also Philip C. Almond, *Adam and Eve in Seventeenth-Century Thought* (Cambridge: University of Cambridge Press, 2008).

5   William Whiston, *A New Theory of the Earth* (London, 1696), p. 3.

6   See Frank E. Manuel, *The Religion of Isaac Newton* (Oxford: Clarendon, 1974).

7   Francis Bacon, *The Advancement of Learning* (London: Cassell & Co., 1893), 1.1.3. Available at http://www.gutenberg.org/files/5500/5500-h/5500-h.htm.

8   Manuel, *Religion of Isaac Newton*, p. 33.

9   See Peter Harrison, *'Religion' and the Religions in the English Enlightenment* (Cambridge: Cambridge University Press, 1990).

10 Steven Nadler, 'Baruch Spinoza and the naturalization of Judaism', in Michael L. Morgan and Peter Eli Gordon (eds), *The Cambridge Companion to Modern Jewish Philosophy* (Cambridge: Cambridge University Press, 2007), p. 15. This is a particularly helpful overview of Spinoza, to which I am indebted.

11 Baruch Spinoza, *Ethics* 1.app., in Baruch de Spinoza, *Complete Works*, ed. Michael L. Morgan, trans. Samuel Shirley (Indianapolis: Hackett, 2002), p. 239.

12 Ibid., 1.15 [p. 224].

13 Ibid., 1.app. [p. 241].

14 Ibid., 5.24 [p. 374].

15 Spinoza himself would have rejected this on the grounds that the non-existence of God or Nature was a logical impossibility. See ibid., 1.11 [p. 222].

16 Edward Herbert of Cherbury, *De veritate*, trans. Meyrick H. Carré (Bristol: University of Bristol, 1937), p. 150.

17 Ibid., p. 291.

18 Ibid., p. 295.

19 See ibid., p. 299.

20 Ibid., p. 302.

21 John Locke, *The Reasonableness of Christianity, as Delivered in the Scriptures* 1.3, in John Locke, *Writings on Religion*, ed. Victor Nuovo (Oxford: Clarendon, 2002), p. 91.

22 Ibid., 11.199 [p. 169].

23 Ibid., 13.252–3 [p. 190].

24 Ibid., 14.265 [p. 195].

25 Ibid., 14.281 [p. 201].

26 I forbear calling Tindal a 'deist'. Although he has traditionally been so called (and perhaps the foremost of them), the term is currently so contested as to mean little.

27 Matthew Tindal, *Christianity as Old as the Creation: Or the Gospel, a Republication of the Religion of Nature* (London, 1730), pp. 7–8.

28 Ibid., p. 18.

29 Ibid., p. 51.

30 Ibid., p. 158.

31 Ibid., p. 307.

32 Ibid., p. 310.

33 Ibid., p. 239.

34 On the cessation of miracles and miracles in the seventeenth and eighteenth centuries generally, see Jane Shaw, *Miracles in Enlightenment England* (New Haven, CT, and London: Yale University Press, 2006). See also Diego Lucci and Jeffrey R. Wigelsworth, '"God does not act arbitrarily, or interpose unnecessarily": providential deism and the denial of miracles in Wollaston, Tindal, Chubb, and Morgan', *Intellectual History Review* 25 (2015), pp. 167–89.

35 John Hooper, 'A brief and clear confession of the Christian faith', in *Later Writings of Bishop Hooper*, ed. Charles Nevinson (Cambridge: Cambridge University Press, 1852), pp. 44–5.

36 See D. P. Walker, 'The cessation of miracles', in Ingrid Merkel and Allen G. Debus (eds), *Hermeticism and the Renaissance: Intellectual History and the Occult in Early Modern Europe* (Washington, DC: Folger Shakespeare Library, 1988), pp. 111–12.

37 John Calvin, *Commentary on a Harmony of the Evangelists, Matthew, Mark, and Luke*, iii, trans. William Pringle (Grand Rapids, MI: Baker Book House, 1984), p. 140.

38 See John Calvin, *Institutes of the Christian Religion*, i, ed. John T. McNeill (Louisville, KT: Westminster John Knox Press, 2006), pref.3 [p. 16].

39 Ibid., pref.3 [p. 17].

40 Calvin, *Commentary on a Harmony of the Evangelists*, p. 389.

41 Quoted in William J. Bouwsma, *John Calvin: A Sixteenth-Century Portrait* (Oxford: Oxford University Press, 1988), p. 167.

42 Calvin, *Institutes of the Christian Religion* 1.16.8 [p. 207].

43 Ibid., 1.16.9 [p. 208].

44 Quoted in Bouwsma, *John Calvin*, p. 172.

45 John Pelling, *A Sermon of the Providence of God* (London, 1607), pp. 29–30.

46 See J. Waterworth (ed. and trans.), *The Canons and Decrees of the Sacred and Oecumenical Council of Trent* (London: Burns & Oates, 1838), p. 236. It is an interesting correlation of science and religion that modern Catholicism requires two medically accredited miracles as one of its criteria for sanctification.

47 William Ames, *The Marrow of Sacred Divinity Drawne out of the Holy Scriptures [...]* (London, 1642), pp. 40–1.

48 Alexandra Walsham, *Providence in Early Modern England* (Oxford: Oxford University Press, 1999), p. 230.

49 Quoted in Shaw, *Miracles in Enlightenment England*, p. 170.

50 Ibid., pp. 170–1.

51 It was also held by William Wollaston, Thomas Chubb and Thomas Morgan, along with Matthew Tindal traditionally called 'deists'. See Lucci and Wigelsworth, "'God does not act arbitrarily'".

52 Tindal, *Christianity as Old as the Creation*, p. 51.

53 Ibid., p. 100.

54 Included among those who argued for the impossibility of miracles, we can include Charles Blount, John Toland, Anthony Collins and Thomas Woolston. See Lucci and Wigelsworth, "'God does not act arbitrarily'". For these, William Wollaston, Thomas Chubb and Thomas Morgan, as well as Tindal and Annet, see also Wayne Hudson, *Enlightenment and Modernity: The English Deists and Reform* (London: Pickering & Chatto, 2009).

55 [Peter Annet], *Supernaturals Examined in Four Dissertations on Three Treatises* (London, 1747), p. 44.

56 Ibid., p. 40.

57 David Hume, *An Enquiry Concerning Human Understanding* 10.1, in *Hume on Religion*, ed. Richard Wollheim (London: Collins, 1963), p. 206.

58 Ibid., 10.1 [pp. 210, 211].

59 Ibid., 10.1 [p. 211].

60 Ibid., 10.2 [p. 215].

61 Ibid., 10.2 [p. 225].

62 Ibid., 10.2 [p. 226].

63 Calvin, *Institutes of the Christian Religion* 1.16.1 [p. 197].

64 Quoted in Walsham, *Providence in Early Modern England*, p. 124.

65 For an excellent account of the relation between providential interpretation and natural explanation, see Peter Jordan, 'Providence and natural causation in early modern England', PhD dissertation, University of Queensland, 2016.

66 Thomas Sprat, *The History of the Royal Society of London for the Improving of Natural Knowledge* (London, 1667), p. 359.

67 Ibid., pp. 361–2.

68 Lorraine Daston and Katharine Park, *Wonders and the Order of Nature* (New York: Zone, 2001), p. 337.

69 It was Immanuel Kant who first coined the terms 'ontological', 'cosmological' and 'teleological' for the three families of proofs for the existence of God.

70 Cicero, *The Nature of the Gods* 2.5, in *The Treatises of M. T. Cicero*, trans. C. D. Yonge (London: Henry G. Bohn, 1853), p. 50.

71 It has been revived in the twenty-first century among proponents of 'intelligent design' opposed to the doctrine of evolution (although it resists asserting that the designer is God). See Chapter 7.

72 William Paley, *Natural Theology: Or Evidences of the Existence and Attributes of the Deity, Collected from the Appearances of Nature* (Oxford: Oxford University Press, 1802), pp. 1–2.

73 Ibid., p. 19.

74 Ibid., p. 473.

75 Ibid., p. 490.

76 Quoted in J. Vernon Jensen, 'Return to the Wilberforce–Huxley debate', *British Journal for the History of Science* 21 (1988), p. 168. For a full account of the debate and its background, see Ian Hesketh, *Of Apes and Ancestors: Evolution, Christianity, and the Oxford Debate* (Toronto: University of Toronto Press, 2009).

77 Charles Darwin, *On the Origin of Species by Means of Natural Selection* (London: John Murray, 1860), p. 490 (my italics).

78 See Peter Harrison, 'Evolution, providence, and the problem of chance', in Karl W. Giberson (ed.), *Abraham's Dice: Chance and Providence in the Monotheistic Traditions* (Oxford: Oxford University Press, 2016), pp. 260–90.

79 Darwin, *On the Origin of Species*, p. 490.

80 Charles Darwin, *The Autobiography of Charles Darwin, 1809–1882*, ed. Nora Barlow (London: Collins, 1958), p. 87.

81 Darwin, *On the Origin of Species*, p. 488.

82 Charles Darwin, *The Descent of Man, and Selection in Relation to Sex*, i (London: John Murray, 1871), p. 205.

83 Darwin, *Descent of Man*, ii, pp. 404–5.

84 Ibid.

85 Quoted in John Hedley Brooke, *Science and Religion: Some Historical Perspectives* (Cambridge: Cambridge University Press, 2014), p. 314.

86 Thomas Henry Huxley, *Darwiniana: Essays* (New York: D. Appleton, 1896), pp. 22–3.

87 Samuel Wilberforce, 'On the Origin of Species' [review], *Quarterly Review* 108 (1860), p. 258.

7. *The Known and Unknown God*

1 Thomas Henry Huxley, 'Agnosticism', in Henry Wace, Thomas Henry Huxley et al., *Christianity and Agnosticism: A Controversy* (New York: D. Appleton, 1889), p. 37.

2 Ibid., p. 38.

3 Thomas Henry Huxley, *Life and Letters of Thomas Henry Huxley*, i, ed. Leonard Huxley (London: Macmillan, 1908), p. 347.

4 Thomas Henry Huxley, *On the Physical Basis of Life* (New Haven, CT: College Courant, 1869), p. 21.

5 Ibid., pp. 18, 24.

6 See ibid., p. 22.

7 David Hume, *Dialogues Concerning Natural Religion* 5, in *Hume on Religion*, ed. Richard Wollheim (London: Collins, 1963), p. 142.

8 Ibid., 12 [p. 189].

9 Ibid., 12 [pp. 203, 204].

10 David Hume, *The Natural History of Religion* 15, in *Hume on Religion*, ed. Wollheim, p. 98.

11 Basil of Caesarea, Letter 134, trans. Blomfield Jackson, in *NPNFII*, viii, p. 274.

12 See Don Cupitt, 'Kant and the negative theology', in Stewart Sutherland and Brian Hebblethwaite (eds), *The Philosophical Frontiers of Christian Theology* (Cambridge: Cambridge University Press, 1982), pp. 55–67.

13 Immanuel Kant, *Critique of Practical Reason*, trans. Lewis White Beck (Indianapolis: Bobbs-Merrill Co., 1956), p. 127.

14 Ibid., p. 130.

15 Immanuel Kant, *Critique of Pure Reason*, trans. Norman Kemp Smith
    (London: Macmillan, 1933), p. 29. Available at https://web.archive.
    org/web/20090505020636/http://hermes.arts.cuhk.edu.hk/cgi-bin/
    cprframe.pl?query=02pref-b.htm,017.

16 Friedrich Schleiermacher, *On Religion: Speeches to Its Cultured Despisers*,
    ed. and trans. Richard Crouter (Cambridge: Cambridge University Press,
    1988), p. 102.

17 Ibid.

18 Ibid., p. 103.

19 Ibid., pp. 112–13.

20 William Wordsworth, 'Lines composed a few miles above Tintern
    Abbey, on revisiting the banks of the Wye during a tour. July 13, 1798'.
    Available at https://www.poetryfoundation.org/poems-and-poets/
    poems/detail/45527.

21 Schleiermacher, *On Religion*, ed. and trans. Crouter, p. 104.

22 Van A. Harvey, 'On the new edition of Schleiermacher's *Addresses on
    Religion*', *Journal of the American Academy of Religion* 39 (1971), p. 504.

23 There is a significant debate within Schleiermacher scholarship over
    the extent to which Schleiermacher brought God back into the
    later editions of *On Religion*, in 1806 and 1821. See Schleiermacher,
    On Religion, ed. and trans. Crouter, pp. 55–73, and Harvey, 'On
    the new edition'. The English version with which many readers of
    Schleiermacher are most familiar is the translation of the 1806 second
    edition by John Oman, a version more sympathetic to 'God' than
    the first edition. See Friedrich Schleiermacher, *On Religion: Speeches
    to Its Cultured Despisers*, trans. John Oman (New York: Harper &
    Row, 1958).

24 Schleiermacher, *On Religion*, ed. and trans. Crouter, p. 139.

25 Ibid., p. 133.

26 Quoted in Robert C. Whittemore, 'Hegel as panentheist', *Tulane Studies
    in Philosophy* 9 (1960), p. 135. I am especially indebted to Whittemore
    for this discussion.

27 'Panentheism', in F. L. Cross, *The Oxford Dictionary of the Christian
    Church* (London: Oxford University Press, 1966), p. 1010.

28 Georg Wilhelm Friedrich Hegel, *Hegel's Philosophy of Right*, trans.
    S. W. Dyde (London: George Bell & Sons, 1896), p. xxvii (my
    italics).

29 Georg Wilhelm Friedrich Hegel, *Lectures on the Philosophy of Religion*,
    i, trans. E. B. Speirs and J. Burdon Sanderson (London: Kegan Paul,
    Trench, Trübner, & Co., 1895), p. 218.

30 Quoted in Frederick C. Copleston, 'Hegel and the rationalisation of mysticism', in N. H. G. Robinson et al. (eds), *Talk of God* (London: Macmillan, 1969), p. 126.

31 Keith Ward, *God and the Philosophers* (Minneapolis, MN: Fortress, 2009), p. 94.

32 Hegel, *Lectures on the Philosophy of Religion*, ii, p. 330.

33 Ibid., iii, p. 73.

34 Hegel is 'theologised' in twentieth-century 'process theology'. See Charles Hartshorne, *A Natural Theology for Our Time* (La Salle, IL: Open Court, 1967).

35 Hegel, *Lectures on the Philosophy of Religion*, iii, p. 77.

36 I am grateful to my colleague Professor Ian Hunter, who graciously provided helpful comments on this section.

37 Frederick Engels, 'Hegel', in Frederick Engels, *Ludwig Feuerbach and the End of Classical German Philosophy* (1886). Available at https://www.marxists.org/archive/marx/works/1886/ludwig-feuerbach/ch01.htm. As did the author of this book, who read Feuerbach when he was 20. The follies of youth? Perhaps. For the material on atheism in this chapter, I am especially indebted to Gavin Hyman, *A Short History of Atheism* (London: I.B.Tauris, 2010).

38 Ludwig Feuerbach, *The Essence of Christianity*, trans. George Eliot [Marian Evans] (London: John Chapman, 1854), p. 12.

39 Ibid.

40 Ibid., p. 18.

41 Ibid., p. 25.

42 Karl Marx, 'Theses on Feuerbach', in Karl Marx and Friedrich Engels, *The Marx–Engels Reader*, ed. Robert C. Tucker (New York: Norton, 1978), p. 144.

43 Sigmund Freud, 'Lecture xxxv: a philosophy of life', in Sigmund Freud, *New Introductory Lectures on Psycho-analysis* (London: Hogarth Press, 1933), p. 206.

44 See especially Frederick Gregory, *Scientific Materialism in Nineteenth Century Germany* (Dordrecht: D. Reidel, 1977).

45 Terry Eagleton, 'Lunging, flailing, mispunching' [review of *The God Delusion* by Richard Dawkins], *London Review of Books* 28/20 (October 2006), pp. 32–4.

46 Richard Dawkins, *The God Delusion* (London: Bantam Press, 2006), p. 34.

47 Along with Christopher Hitchens, Sam Harris and Daniel Dennett.

48 Dawkins, *God Delusion*, p. 14.

49 Ibid., p. 4.

50 Ibid., p. 50.

51 Ibid., p. 37.

52 Ibid., p. 2.

53 For a good summary of intelligent design and arguments against it, see H. Allen Orr, 'Devolution: why intelligent design isn't', *New Yorker* (30 May 2005). Available at http://www.newyorker.com/magazine/2005/05/30/devolution-2.

54 Friedrich Nietzsche, *The Gay Science*, ed. Bernard Williams (Cambridge: Cambridge University Press, 2017), 125 [pp. 119–20].

55 Ibid., 343 [p. 199].

56 Ibid.

57 Ward, *God and the Philosophers*, p. 129.

58 Thomas J. J. Altizer, *The Gospel of Christian Atheism* (Philadelphia: Westminster Press, 1966), p. 22.

59 Ibid., p. 110.

60 Quoted in Hyman, *Short History of Atheism*, p. 163.

61 Don Cupitt, *Is Nothing Sacred?: The Non-Realist Philosophy of Religion: Selected Essays* (Ashland, OH: Fordham University Press, 2002), pp. 37–8.

62 Ibid., p. 48.

63 Ibid., p. 101.

64 Ibid., p. 107.

65 Ibid., p. 147.

66 Frederick Gregory, *Nature Lost? Natural Science and German Theological Traditions of the Nineteenth Century* (Cambridge, MA: Harvard University Press, 1992), p. 261.

67 Søren Kierkegaard, *Concluding Unscientific Postscript*, trans. David F. Swenson (Princeton: Princeton University Press, 1941), p. 182.

68 Ibid.

69 Paul Tillich, *Systematic Theology*, i (Chicago: University of Chicago Press, 1951), p. 64.

70 Rudolf Bultmann, *New Testament and Mythology and Other Basic Writings* (Philadelphia: Fortress Press, 1984), p. 23.

71 Karl Barth, *The Word of God and the Word of Man* (London: Hodder & Stoughton, 1928), p. 24.

72 Karl Barth, *Church Dogmatics: Selections by H. Gollwitzer* (Edinburgh: T&T Clark, 1961), p. 54.

73 Quoted in James Brown, *Subject and Object in Modern Theology* (London: SCM Press, 1955), p. 150.

74 See Philip C. Almond, 'Karl Barth and anthropocentric theology', *Scottish Journal of Theology* 31 (1978), pp. 435–47.
75 For a very sophisticated separatist account, coming out of intellectual history rather than conservative Protestant theology, see Peter Harrison, *The Territories of Science and Religion* (Chicago: University of Chicago Press, 2015).
76 Martin Buber, *I and Thou*, trans. Walter Kaufmann (Edinburgh: T&T Clark, 1970), pp. 59–60.
77 Ibid., p. 127.
78 A. C. Ainger, 'God is working his purpose out', in *The New English Hymnal* (Norwich: Canterbury Press, 1986), pp. 495–6 [hymn 495].
79 See John Hedley Brooke, *Science and Religion: Some Historical Perspectives* (Cambridge: Cambridge University Press, 2014) and Keith Ward, *The Big Questions in Science and Religion* (West Conshohocken, PA: Templeton, 2008).

Epilogue

1 *The Cloud of Unknowing*, trans. Clifton Wolters (Harmondsworth: Penguin, 1961), § 6 [p. 59].
2 Ludwig Wittgenstein, *Tractatus Logico-philosophicus* (London: Kegan Paul, Trench, Trübner, & Co., 1922), 6.44.
3 Blaise Pascal, *Pensées*, trans. Martin Turnell (London: Harvill, 1962), pp. 142, 221.
4 Wittgenstein, *Tractatus Logico-philosophicus*, 7.

Bibliography

Abbreviations

ANF   Alexander Roberts, James Donaldson and A. Cleveland Coxe (eds), *Ante-Nicene Fathers*, 10 vols (Buffalo, NY: Christian Literature, 1885–97).

FC   Hermigild Dressler et al. (eds), *The Fathers of the Church: A New Translation*, 127 vols (Washington, DC: Catholic University Press of America, 1947–2013).

NPNFI   Philip Schaff (ed.), *Nicene and Post-Nicene Fathers: First Series*, 14 vols (Buffalo, NY: Christian Literature, 1886–90).

NPNFII   Philip Schaff and Henry Wace (eds), *Nicene and Post-Nicene Fathers: Second Series*, 14 vols (Buffalo, NY: Christian Literature, 1890–1900).

PG   J.-P. Migne (ed.), *Patrologia Graeca*, 161 vols (Paris: Imprimerie Catholique, 1857–86). Available at http://patristica.net/graeca/.

Works consulted

Ahmed, Shahab, 'Satanic verses', in Jane Dammen McAuliffe (ed.), *Encyclopedia of the Qur'ān* (Leiden: Brill, 2015). Available at http://dx.doi.org/10.1163/1875-3922_q3_EQSIM_00372.

'Akkadian myths and epics', trans. E. A. Speiser, in James B. Pritchard (ed.), *Ancient Near Eastern Texts Relating to the Old Testament* (1950; Princeton: Princeton University Press, 1969), pp. 60–119.

Al-Ghāzali, *The Niche of Lights*, trans. David Buchman (Provo, UT: Brigham Young University Press, 1998).

Albert the Great and Thomas Aquinas, *Albert and Thomas: Selected Writings*, ed. Simon Tugwell (Mahwah, NJ: Paulist Press, 1988).

Alger, William R., *A Critical History of the Doctrine of a Future Life* (New York: W. J. Widdleton, 1878).

Almond, Philip C., 'Karl Barth and anthropocentric theology', *Scottish Journal of Theology* 31 (1978), pp. 435–47.

—— *Rudolf Otto: An Introduction to His Philosophical Theology* (Chapel Hill, NC, and London: University of North Carolina Press, 1984).

—— *Adam and Eve in Seventeenth-Century Thought* (Cambridge: University of Cambridge Press, 2008).

—— *Heaven and Hell in Enlightenment England* (Cambridge: Cambridge University Press, 2008).

—— *The Devil: A New Biography* (London and Ithaca, NY: I.B.Tauris and Cornell University Press, 2014).

—— *Afterlife: A History of Life after Death* (London and Ithaca, NY: I.B.Tauris and Cornell University Press, 2016).

Altizer, Thomas J. J., *The Gospel of Christian Atheism* (Philadelphia: Westminster Press, 1966).

Ames, William, *The Marrow of Sacred Divinity Drawne out of the Holy Scriptures [...]* (London, 1642).

[Annet, Peter], *Supernaturals Examined in Four Dissertations on Three Treatises* (London, 1747).

Anselm, *Complete Philosophical and Theological Treatises of Anselm of Canterbury*, trans. Jasper Hopkins and Herbert Richardson (Minneapolis, MN: Arthur J. Banning Press, 2000).

Aquinas, Thomas, *Compendium of Theology*, trans. Cyril Vollert (St Louis, MO, and London: Herder, 1947). Available at http://dhspriory.org/thomas/Compendium.htm.

—— *Summa contra Gentiles*, ii: *Creation*, trans. James F. Anderson (Notre Dame, IN: Notre Dame University Press, 1975).

—— *Summa theologiae, prima pars*, 1–49, trans. Laurence Shapcote (Lander, WY: Aquinas Institute for the Study of Sacred Doctrine, 2012).

—— *Summa theologiae, prima secundae*, 71–114, trans. Laurence Shapcote (Lander, WY: Aquinas Institute for the Study of Sacred Doctrine, 2012).

Arberry, A. J., *Sufism: An Account of the Mystics of Islam* (London: George Allen & Unwin, 1950).

Aristotle, *The Philosophy of Aristotle*, trans. A. E. Wardman and J. L. Creed (New York: Mentor, 1963).

Armstrong, Karen, *A History of God: The 4,000-Year Quest of Judaism, Christianity and Islam* (New York: Ballantine, 1993).

—— *Fields of Blood: Religion and the History of Violence* (New York: Knopf, 2014).

Assmann, Jan, *Of God and Gods: Egypt, Israel, and the Rise of Monotheism* (Madison, WI: University of Wisconsin Press, 2008).

Augustine, *Answer to Maximinus the Arian*, trans. Roland Teske, in Augustine, *Arianism and Other Heresies*, ed. Boniface Ramsey (Hyde Park, NY: New City Press, 1995).

Averroes (Ibn Rushd), *The Philosophy and Theology of Averroes: Tractacta*, trans. Mohammad Jamil-Ub-Behman Barod ([1160]; Baroda: Manibhai Mathurbhal Gupta, 1921). Available at http://oll.libertyfund.org/titles/rushd-the-philosophy-and-theology-of-averroes.

—— *The Decisive Treatise, Determining the Nature of the Connection between Religion and Philosophy*. Available at http://people.uvawise.edu/philosophy/phil205/Averroes.html.

Bacon, Francis, *The Advancement of Learning* (London: Cassell & Co., 1893). Available at http://www.gutenberg.org/files/5500/5500-h/5500-h.htm.

Barth, Karl, *The Word of God and the Word of Man* (London: Hodder & Stoughton, 1928).

—— *Church Dogmatics: Selections by H. Gollwitzer* (Edinburgh: T&T Clark, 1961).

Barton, John, *The Theology of the Book of Amos* (Cambridge: Cambridge University Press, 2012).

—— *Ethics in Ancient Israel* (Oxford: Oxford University Press, 2014).

Bauckham, Richard, 'Universalism: a historical survey', *Themelios* 4 (1978), pp. 47–54.

The Bhagavad-Gītā: With a Commentary Based on the Original Sources, trans. R. C. Zaehner (Oxford: Oxford University Press, 1969).

Blenkinsopp, Joseph, *Abraham: The Story of a Life* (Grand Rapids, MI: Eerdmans, 2015).

Blyth, Francis, *Eternal Misery the Necessary Consequence of Infinite Mercy Abused: A Sermon [...]* (London, 1740).

Boethius, *The Consolation of Philosophy*, trans. H. R. James (London: Elliot Stock, 1897). Available at https://www.gutenberg.org/files/14328/14328-h/14328-h.htm#Page_233.

Bouwsma, William J., *John Calvin: A Sixteenth-Century Portrait* (Oxford: Oxford University Press, 1988).

Brooke, John Hedley, *Science and Religion: Some Historical Perspectives* (Cambridge: Cambridge University Press, 2014).

Brown, James, *Subject and Object in Modern Theology* (London: SCM Press, 1955).

Buber, Martin, *I and Thou*, trans. Walter Kaufmann (Edinburgh: T&T Clark, 1970).

Buijs, Joseph A., 'Religion and philosophy in Maimonides, Averroes, and Aquinas', *Medieval Encounters* 8 (2002), pp. 160–83.

Bultmann, Rudolf, *New Testament and Mythology and Other Basic Writings* (Philadelphia: Fortress Press, 1984).

Burnet, Thomas, *A Treatise Concerning the State of Departed Souls before, and at, and after the Resurection* [*sic*] (London, 1733).

Burton, Robert, *The Anatomy of Melancholy*, i, ed. Thomas C. Faulkner et al. (Oxford: Clarendon, 1989).

Calvin, John, *Commentaries on the First Book of Moses Called Genesis*, trans. John King (Grand Rapids, MI: Christian Classics Ethereal Library, n.d.). Available at http://www.ccel.org/ccel/calvin/calcom01.html.

————*Commentary on a Harmony of the Evangelists, Matthew, Mark, and Luke*, iii, trans. William Pringle (Grand Rapids, MI: Baker Book House, 1984).

————*Institutes of the Christian Religion*, i, ed. John T. McNeill (Louisville, KT: Westminster John Knox Press, 2006).

Camus, Albert, *The Plague* (1947; London: Penguin, 2002).

Chittick, William C., *The Sufi Path of Love: The Spiritual Teachings of Rumi* (Albany, NY: State University of New York, 1983).

Cicero, *The Treatises of M. T. Cicero*, trans. C. D. Yonge (London: Henry G. Bohn, 1853).

The Cloud of Unknowing, trans. Clifton Wolters (Harmondsworth: Penguin, 1961).

Coleridge, Samuel Taylor, *Aids to Reflection and the Confessions of an Inquiring Spirit* (London: George Bell, 1884).

Collins, Paul, *Partaking in Divine Nature: Deification and Communion* (London: Bloomsbury, 2012).

Constable, Henry, *The Duration and Nature of Future Punishment* (London: Kellaway, 1876).

Copleston, Frederick C., 'Hegel and the rationalisation of mysticism', in N. H. G. Robinson et al. (eds), *Talk of God* (London: Macmillan, 1969), pp. 118–32.

Costa, José, 'Le corps de Dieu dans le judaïsme rabbinique ancien: problèmes d'interprétation', *Revue de l'histoire des religions* 227 (2010), pp. 283–316.

Craig, William Lane, *The Kalām Cosmological Argument* (London: Macmillan, 1979).

Cross, F. L., *The Oxford Dictionary of the Christian Church* (London: Oxford University Press, 1966).

Cullmann, Oscar, *Christ and Time: The Primitive Christian Conception of Time and History* (London: SCM Press, 1951).

Cupitt, Don, 'Kant and the negative theology', in Stewart Sutherland and Brian Hebblethwaite (eds), *The Philosophical Frontiers of Christian Theology* (Cambridge: Cambridge University Press, 1982), pp. 55–67.

————*Crisis of Moral Authority* (London: SCM Press, 1985).

———— *Is Nothing Sacred?: The Non-Realist Philosophy of Religion: Selected Essays* (Ashland, OH: Fordham University Press, 2002).

Darwin, Charles, *On the Origin of Species by Means of Natural Selection* (London: John Murray, 1860).

———— *The Descent of Man, and Selection in Relation to Sex*, 2 vols (London: John Murray, 1871).

———— *The Autobiography of Charles Darwin, 1809–1882*, ed. Nora Barlow (London: Collins, 1958).

Daston, Lorraine, and Katharine Park, *Wonders and the Order of Nature* (New York: Zone, 2001).

Davidson, Herbert A., 'John Philoponus as a source of medieval Islamic and Jewish proofs of creation', *Journal of the American Oriental Society* 89 (1969), pp. 375–91.

Davies, Andrew, *Double Standards in Isaiah: Re-evaluating Prophetic Ethics and Divine Justice* (Leiden: Brill, 2000).

Dawkins, Richard, *The God Delusion* (London: Bantam Press, 2006).

Denis's Hidden Theology, in *The Pursuit of Wisdom and Other Works, by the Author of The Cloud of Unknowing*, trans. James A. Walsh (Mahwah, NJ: Paulist Press, 1988), pp. 49–98.

Denison, Stephen, *A Compendious Catechisme [...]* (London, 1621).

———— *The Doctrine of Both the Sacraments: To Witte, Baptisme, and the Supper of the Lord [...]* (London, 1621).

Dionysius the Areopagite, *On the Divine Names and the Mystical Theology*, trans. C. E. Rolt (London: SPCK, 1920).

Dixon, Leif, *Practical Predestinarians in England, c.1590–1640* (Farnham: Ashgate, 2014).

Dodds, E. R., *The Ancient Concept of Progress* (Oxford: Clarendon, 1973).

Drexelius, Hieremy, *A Pleasant and Profitable Treatise of Hell* (n.p., 1668).

Eagleton, Terry, 'Lunging, flailing, mispunching' [review of *The God Delusion* by Richard Dawkins], *London Review of Books* 28/20 (October 2006), pp. 32–4.

Eckhart, Meister, *The Essential Sermons, Commentaries, Treatises, and Defense*, trans. Edmund Colledge and Bernard McGinn (New York: Paulist Press, 1981).

Edwards, Jonathan, 'Sermon II: sinners in the hands of an angry God', in *The Works of Jonathan Edwards*, ii, ed. Edward Hickman (Edinburgh: Banner of Truth, 1974). Available at http://www.ccel.org/ccel/edwards/works2.

Engels, Frederick, 'Hegel', in Frederick Engels, *Ludwig Feuerbach and the End of Classical German Philosophy* (1886). Available at https://www.marxists.org/archive/marx/works/1886/ludwig-feuerbach/ch01.htm.

Epiphanius of Salamis, *The Panarion of Epiphanius of Salamis Books II and III*, trans. Frank Williams (Leiden: Brill, 1994).

Everitt, Nicholas, 'The divine attributes', *Philosophy Compass* 5 (2010), pp. 78–90.

Fakhry, Majid, *A History of Islamic Philosophy* (3rd edn, New York: Columbia University Press, 2004).

Farrar, F. W., *Eternal Hope* (New York: E. P. Dutton, 1878).

Feuerbach, Ludwig, *The Essence of Christianity*, trans. George Eliot [Marian Evans] (London: John Chapman, 1854).

Fitzgerald, Alan D. (ed.), *Augustine through the Ages: An Encyclopedia* (Grand Rapids, MI: Eerdmans, 1999).

Flasch, Kurt, *Meister Eckhart: Philosopher of Christianity*, trans. Anne Schindel and Aaron Vanides (New Haven, CT: Yale University Press, 2015).

Freud, Sigmund, 'Lecture xxxv: a philosophy of life', in Sigmund Freud, *New Introductory Lectures on Psycho-analysis* (London: Hogarth Press, 1933).

Gaon, Saadia, *The Book of Beliefs and Opinions*, trans. Samuel Rosenblatt (New Haven, CT: Yale University Press, 1948).

Gavrilyuk, Paul L., *The Sufferings of the Impassible God: The Dialectics of Patristic Thought* (Oxford: Oxford University Press, 2004).

Goodwin, Thomas, *A Discourse of the Punishment of Sin in Hell; Demonstrating the Wrath of God to Be the Cause Thereof* (London, 1680).

Gowland, Angus, 'The problem of early modern melancholy', *Past and Present* 191 (2006), pp. 77–120.

Green, Arthur, 'Introduction', in *The Zohar*, i, trans. Daniel C. Matt (Stanford, CA: Stanford University Press, 2004).

Gregory, Frederick, *Scientific Materialism in Nineteenth Century Germany* (Dordrecht: D. Reidel, 1977).

——— *Nature Lost? Natural Science and German Theological Traditions of the Nineteenth Century* (Cambridge, MA: Harvard University Press, 1992).

[Hallywell, Henry], *A Private Letter of Satisfaction to a Friend* (n.p., 1667).

Harrison, Peter, *'Religion' and the Religions in the English Enlightenment* (Cambridge: Cambridge University Press, 1990).

——— *The Bible, Protestantism, and the Rise of Natural Science* (Cambridge: Cambridge University Press, 1998).

——— *The Territories of Science and Religion* (Chicago: University of Chicago Press, 2015).

——— 'Evolution, providence, and the problem of chance', in Karl W. Giberson (ed.), *Abraham's Dice: Chance and Providence in the Monotheistic Traditions* (Oxford: Oxford University Press, 2016), pp. 260–90.

Hartshorne, Charles, *A Natural Theology for Our Time* (La Salle, IL: Open Court, 1967).

Harvey, Van A., 'On the new edition of Schleiermacher's *Addresses on Religion*', *Journal of the American Academy of Religion* 39 (1971), pp. 488–512.

Hegel, Georg Wilhelm Friedrich, *Lectures on the Philosophy of Religion*, trans. E. B. Speirs and J. Burdon Sanderson, 3 vols (London: Kegan Paul, Trench, Trübner, & Co., 1895).

—— *Hegel's Philosophy of Right*, trans. S. W. Dyde (London: George Bell & Sons, 1896).

Herbert of Cherbury, Edward, *De veritate*, trans. Meyrick H. Carré (Bristol: University of Bristol, 1937).

Hesketh, Ian, *Of Apes and Ancestors: Evolution, Christianity, and the Oxford Debate* (Toronto: University of Toronto Press, 2009).

Hick, John, *Evil and the God of Love* (Basingstoke: Palgrave Macmillan, 2010).

Homer, *The Iliad*, trans. A. T. Murray (Cambridge, MA, and London: Harvard University Press and Heinemann, 1924). Available at http://www.perseus.tufts.edu/hopper/text?doc=Perseus%3Atext%3A1999.01.0134&redirect=true.

Hooke, Robert, *Micrographia* (London, 1665).

Hooper, John, 'A brief and clear confession of the Christian faith', in *Later Writings of Bishop Hooper*, ed. Charles Nevinson (Cambridge: Cambridge University Press, 1852).

Horbery, Matthew, *An Enquiry into the Scripture-doctrine Concerning the Duration of Future Punishments [...]* (London, 1744).

Hudson, Wayne, *Enlightenment and Modernity: The English Deists and Reform* (London: Pickering & Chatto, 2009).

Hume, David, *Hume on Religion*, ed. Richard Wollheim (London: Collins, 1963).

Hurtado, Larry, *One God, One Lord: Early Christian Devotion and Ancient Jewish Monotheism* (London: Bloomsbury, 2015).

Huxley, Thomas Henry, *On the Physical Basis of Life* (New Haven, CT: College Courant, 1869).

—— 'Agnosticism', in Henry Wace, Thomas Henry Huxley et al., *Christianity and Agnosticism: A Controversy* (New York: D. Appleton, 1889).

—— *Darwiniana: Essays* (New York: D. Appleton, 1896).

—— *Life and Letters of Thomas Henry Huxley*, i, ed. Leonard Huxley (London: Macmillan, 1908).

Hyman, Arthur, 'Maimonides' "thirteen principles"', in Alexander Altmann (ed.), *Jewish Medieval and Renaissance Studies* (Cambridge, MA: Harvard University Press, 1967), pp. 119–44.

Hyman, Gavin, *A Short History of Atheism* (London: I.B.Tauris, 2010).

Inge, William Ralph, *The Platonic Tradition in English Religious Thought* (New York: Longmans, Green, 1926).

Jantzen, Grace M., *Power, Gender and Christian Mysticism* (Cambridge: Cambridge University Press, 1995).

Jensen, J. Vernon, 'Return to the Wilberforce–Huxley debate', *British Journal for the History of Science* 21 (1988), pp. 161–79.

Jordan, Peter, 'Providence and natural causation in early modern England', PhD dissertation, University of Queensland, 2016.

Julian, Emperor of Rome, *The Arguments of the Emperor Julian against the Christians*, ed. Willis Nevins (London: Williams & Norgate, 1873).

Kant, Immanuel, *Critique of Pure Reason*, trans. Norman Kemp Smith (London: Macmillan, 1933). Available at https://web.archive.org/web/20090505020636/http://hermes.arts.cuhk.edu.hk/cgi-bin/cprframe.pl?query=02pref-b.htm,017.

——— *Critique of Practical Reason*, trans. Lewis White Beck (Indianapolis: Bobbs-Merrill Co., 1956).

——— *On History*, ed. Lewis White Beck (Indianapolis: Bobbs-Merrill Co., 1957).

——— *The Conflict of the Faculties (Der Streit der Fakultäten)*, trans. Mary J. Gregor (Lincoln, NE, and London: University of Nebraska Press, 1979).

Kelly, J. N. D., *Early Christian Doctrines* (New York: HarperCollins, 1978).

Kierkegaard, Søren, *Concluding Unscientific Postscript*, trans. David F. Swenson (Princeton: Princeton University Press, 1941).

Knysh, Alexander, *Islamic Mysticism: A Short History* (Leiden: Brill, 2000).

Lake, Peter, *The Boxmaker's Revenge: 'Orthodoxy', 'Heterodoxy' and the Politics of the Parish in Early Stuart London* (Stanford, CA: Stanford University Press, 2001).

Lancaster, James A. T., 'Francis Bacon on the moral and political character of the universe', in Guido Giglioni, James A. T. Lancaster et al. (eds), *Francis Bacon on Motion and Power* (Dordrecht: Springer, 2016), pp. 231–48.

Leftow, Brian, 'Omnipotence', in Thomas P. Flint and Michael C. Rea (eds), *The Oxford Handbook of Philosophical Theology* (Oxford: Oxford University Press, 2011), pp. 167–99.

Leibniz, Gottfried Wilhelm, *Theodicy: Essays on the Goodness of God, the Freedom of Man and the Origin of Evil*, trans. E. M. Huggard (Peru, IL: Open Court, 1985).

Lieu, Judith M., *Marcion and the Making of a Heretic* (Cambridge: Cambridge University Press, 2015).

Locke, John, *Writings on Religion*, ed. Victor Nuovo (Oxford: Clarendon, 2002).

Logan, Ian, *Reading Anselm's Proslogion: The History of Anselm's Argument and Its Significance Today* (Farnham: Ashgate, 2009).

Louth, Andrew, *Maximus the Confessor* (London: Routledge, 2005).

—— *The Origins of the Christian Mystical Tradition* (Oxford: Oxford University Press, 2009).

Love, Christopher, *Hells Terror: Or, A Treatise of the Torments of the Damned, as a Preservative against Security* (London, 1653).

Lovejoy, Arthur O., *The Great Chain of Being* (New York: Harper & Row, 1960).

Lucci, Diego, and Jeffrey R. Wigelsworth, "'God does not act arbitrarily, or interpose unnecessarily': providential deism and the denial of miracles in Wollaston, Tindal, Chubb, and Morgan', *Intellectual History Review* 25 (2015), pp. 167–89.

McGinn, Bernard, *The Harvest of Mysticism in Medieval Germany* (New York: Herder & Herder, 2005).

McGrath, Alister E., *Luther's Theology of the Cross* (Chichester: Wiley–Blackwell, 2011).

McGuckin, John, *Saint Cyril of Alexandria and the Christological Controversy* (Crestwood, NY: St Vladimir's Seminary Press, 2004).

Maimonides, Moses, *A Guide for the Perplexed*, trans. M. Friedlaender (New York: E. P. Dutton, 1904). Available at http://oll.libertyfund.org/titles/maimonides-a-guide-for-the-perplexed.

Malinar, Angelika, *The Bhagavadgītā: Doctrines and Contexts* (Cambridge: Cambridge University Press, 2007).

Manuel, Frank E., *The Religion of Isaac Newton* (Oxford: Clarendon, 1974).

Marx, Karl, 'Theses on Feuerbach', in Karl Marx and Friedrich Engels, *The Marx–Engels Reader*, ed. Robert C. Tucker (New York: Norton, 1978).

Maximus the Confessor, *Selected Writings*, trans. George C. Berthold (London: SPCK, 1985).

May, Gerhard, *Creation ex nihilo: The Doctrine of 'Creation out of Nothing' in Early Christian Thought* (Edinburgh: T&T Clark, 1994).

'Medieval sourcebook: twelfth ecumenical council: Lateran IV 1215', in H. J. Schroeder (ed.), *Disciplinary Decrees of the General Councils: Text, Translation and Commentary* (St Louis, MO: B. Herder, 1937), pp. 236–96. Available at http://www.fordham.edu/halsall/basis/lateran4.asp.

Miles, Jack, *God: A Biography* (New York: Vintage, 1996).

Moorhead, John, 'Boethius' life and the world of late antique philosophy', in John Marenbon (ed.), *The Cambridge Companion to Boethius* (Cambridge: Cambridge University Press, 2009), pp. 13–33.

Nadler, Steven, 'Baruch Spinoza and the naturalization of Judaism', in Michael L. Morgan and Peter Eli Gordon (eds), *The Cambridge Companion to Modern Jewish Philosophy* (Cambridge: Cambridge University Press, 2007), pp. 14–34.

The New English Hymnal (Norwich: Canterbury Press, 1986).

Nicholson, R. A., *The Mystics of Islam* (New York: Schocken, 1975).

Nietzsche, Friedrich, *The Gay Science*, ed. Bernard Williams (Cambridge: Cambridge University Press, 2017).

Origen, *Contra Celsum*, trans. Henry Chadwick (Cambridge: Cambridge University Press, 1953).

—— *On First Principles*, trans. G. W. Butterworth (Gloucester, MA: Peter Smith, 1973).

—— *Treatise on the Passover and Dialogue of Origen with Heraclides and His Fellow Bishops on the Father, the Son, and the Soul*, trans. Robert J. Daly (Mahwah, NJ: Paulist Press, 1992).

Orr, H. Allen, 'Devolution: why intelligent design isn't', *New Yorker* (30 May 2005). Available at http://www.newyorker.com/magazine/2005/05/30/devolution-2.

Otto, Rudolf, *The Idea of the Holy* (Oxford: Oxford University Press, 1958).

Owen, H. P., 'Christian mysticism: a study in Walter Hilton's *The Ladder of Perfection*', *Religious Studies* 7 (1971), pp. 31–42.

Padgett, Alan G., *God, Eternity and the Nature of Time* (Eugene, OR: Wipf & Stock, 2000).

Paley, William, *Natural Theology: Or Evidences of the Existence and Attributes of the Deity, Collected from the Appearances of Nature* (Oxford: Oxford University Press, 1802).

Pascal, Blaise, *Pensées*, trans. Martin Turnell (London: Harvill, 1962).

—— *Pensées*, trans. A. J. Krailsheimer (Harmondsworth: Penguin, 1966).

Passmore, John, *Man's Responsibility for Nature: Ecological Problems and Western Traditions* (New York: Scribner, 1974).

Pelikan, Jaroslav, *The Christian Tradition: A History of the Development of Doctrine, i: The Emergence of the Catholic Tradition (100–600)* (Chicago and London: University of Chicago Press, 1971).

Pelling, John, *A Sermon of the Providence of God* (London, 1607).

Philo, *The Works of Philo: Complete and Unabridged*, trans. C. D. Yonge (Peabody, MA: Hendrickson, 1993).

Plato, *The Collected Dialogues of Plato*, ed. Edith Hamilton and Huntington Cairns, trans. Lane Cooper (Princeton: Princeton University Press, 1961).

Plotinus, *The Enneads*, trans. Stephen MacKenna (London: Faber, 1956).

Plutarch, *Plutarch's Moralia in Sixteen Volumes*, v, trans. Frank Cole Babbitt (London and Cambridge, MA: William Heinemann and Harvard University Press, 1969).

Porter, Roy, *Enlightenment* (London: Penguin, 2000).

Pseudo-Dionysius, *The Complete Works*, trans. Colm Luibheid (New York and Mahwah, NJ: Paulist Press, 1987).

Puech, Henri-Charles, 'Gnosis and time', in Joseph Campbell (ed.), *Man and Time: Papers from the Eranos Yearbooks* (London: Routledge & Kegan Paul, 1958), pp. 38–84.

Quinn, Philip L., 'Divine command theory', in Hugh LaFollette and Ingmar Persson (eds), *The Blackwell Guide to Ethical Theory* (Chichester: Blackwell, 2013), pp. 81–102.

The Qur'ān: A New Annotated Translation, trans. A. J. Droge (Sheffield: Equinox, 2014).

Rist, John M., *Augustine: Ancient Thought Baptized* (Cambridge: Cambridge University Press, 1994).

Rorem, Paul, *Pseudo-Dionysius: A Commentary on the Texts and an Introduction to their Influence* (New York: Oxford University Press, 1993).

Rowell, Geoffrey, *Hell and the Victorians* (Oxford: Clarendon, 1974).

Rowland, Christopher (ed.), *The Cambridge Companion to Liberation Theology* (Cambridge: Cambridge University Press, 2007).

Russell, Norman, *The Doctrine of Deification in the Greek Patristic Tradition* (Oxford: Oxford University Press, 2006).

Schleiermacher, Friedrich, *The Christian Faith* (Edinburgh: T&T Clark, 1928).

——— *On Religion: Speeches to Its Cultured Despisers*, trans. John Oman (New York: Harper & Row, 1958).

——— *On Religion: Speeches to Its Cultured Despisers*, ed. and trans. Richard Crouter (Cambridge: Cambridge University Press, 1988).

Scholem, Gershom, *Major Trends in Jewish Mysticism* (New York: Schocken, 1995).

Schweid, Eliezer, *The Classic Jewish Philosophers: From Saadia through the Renaissance* (Leiden: Brill, 2008).

Scott, Mark S. M., 'Suffering and soul-making: rethinking John Hick's theodicy', *Journal of Religion* 90 (2010), pp. 313–34.

——— *Journey Back to God: Origen on the Problem of Evil* (Oxford: Oxford University Press, 2012).

Shaw, Jane, *Miracles in Enlightenment England* (New Haven, CT, and London: Yale University Press, 2006).

Siecienski, A. Edward, *The Filioque: History of a Doctrinal Controversy* (Oxford: Oxford University Press, 2010).

Silver, Daniel Jeremy, *Maimonidean Criticism and the Maimonidean Controversy 1180–1240* (Leiden: Brill, 1965).

Smith, Mark S., 'The three bodies of God in the Hebrew Bible', *Journal of Biblical Literature* 134 (2015), pp. 471–88.

Spinoza, Baruch de, *Complete Works*, ed. Michael L. Morgan, trans. Samuel Shirley (Indianapolis: Hackett, 2002).

Sprat, Thomas, *The History of the Royal Society of London for the Improving of Natural Knowledge* (London, 1667).

Stevenson, James (ed.), *Creeds, Councils and Controversies: Documents Illustrating the History of the Church AD 337–461* (London: SPCK, 1989).

Strelan, Rick, 'What might a pagan have understood by "Holy Spirit"?', *Colloquium* 42 (2010), pp. 151–72.

Stroumsa, Gedaliahu, 'The incorporeality of God: context and implications of Origen's position', *Religion* 13 (1983), pp. 345–58.

Swinburne, Richard, *The Coherence of Theism* (Oxford: Clarendon, 1993).

Swinden, Tobias, *An Enquiry into the Nature and Place of Hell* (London, 1727).

Tanner, Norman P. (ed.), *Decrees of the Ecumenical Councils, i: Nicaea I to Lateran V* (London and Washington, DC: Sheed & Ward and Georgetown University Press, 1990).

Tillich, Paul, *Systematic Theology*, i (Chicago: University of Chicago Press, 1951).

Tindal, Matthew, *Christianity as Old as the Creation: Or the Gospel, a Republication of the Religion of Nature* (London, 1730).

Townsend, Luke Davis, 'Deification in Aquinas: a supplementum to *The Ground of Union*', *Journal of Theological Studies* 66 (2015), pp. 204–34.

Voltaire, *Philosophical Dictionary*, ed. and trans. Theodore Besterman (London: Penguin, 2004).

——*Candide or Optimism*, ed. Nicholas Cronk (New York: Norton, 2016).

Walker, D. P., *The Decline of Hell: Seventeenth-century Discussions of Eternal Torment* (London: Routledge & Kegan Paul, 1964).

——'The cessation of miracles', in Ingrid Merkel and Allen G. Debus (eds), *Hermeticism and the Renaissance: Intellectual History and the Occult in Early Modern Europe* (Washington, DC: Folger Shakespeare Library, 1988), pp. 110–24.

Walsham, Alexandra, *Providence in Early Modern England* (Oxford: Oxford University Press, 1999).

Ward, Keith, *The Big Questions in Science and Religion* (West Conshohocken, PA: Templeton, 2008).

——— *God and the Philosophers* (Minneapolis, MN: Fortress, 2009).

Ware, Timothy, *The Orthodox Church* (Harmondsworth: Penguin, 1980).

Waterworth, J. (ed. and trans.), *The Canons and Decrees of the Sacred and Oecumenical Council of Trent* (London: Burns & Oates, 1838).

Weber, Max, *The Protestant Ethic and the Spirit of Capitalism*, trans. Talcott Parsons (New York and London: Charles Scribner's Sons and George Allen & Unwin, 1950).

Wedderburn, Alexander J. M., *The God of Jesus – Our God?* (Eugene, OR: Cascade, 2014).

Whiston, William, *A New Theory of the Earth* (London, 1696).

——— *Sermons and Essays [...]* (London, 1709).

——— *Astronomical Principles of Religion Natural and Reveal'd in Nine Parts [...]* (London, 1717).

——— *The Eternity of Hell Torments Considered [...]* (London, 1740).

Whittemore, Robert C., 'Hegel as panentheist', *Tulane Studies in Philosophy* 9 (1960), pp. 134–64.

Wilberforce, Samuel, 'On the Origin of Species' [review], *Quarterly Review* 108 (1860), pp. 225–64.

Wildberger, Hans, *Isaiah 1–12: A Commentary*, trans. Thomas H. Trapp (Minneapolis, MN: Fortress, 1991).

Winter, Bruce W., 'Pluralism – 1 Corinthians 8–10', *Tyndale Bulletin* 41 (1990), pp. 209–26.

Wittgenstein, Ludwig, *Tractatus Logico-philosophicus* (London: Kegan Paul, Trench, Trübner, & Co., 1922).

Wolfson, Harry Austryn, *Philo: Foundations of Religious Philosophy in Judaism, Christianity, and Islam*, i: *Structure and Growth of Philosophical Systems from Plato to Spinoza* (Cambridge, MA: Harvard University Press, 1968).

Wright, N. T., *Jesus and the Victory of God* (London: SPCK, 1996).

Yates, John, *Gods Arraignment of Hypocrites* (London, 1615).

The Zohar: The Book of Splendor, trans. Gershom Scholem (New York: Schocken, 1949).

Index